HISTORY OF THE LOW COUNTRIES
EPISODES AND PROBLEMS

HISTORY OF
THE LOW COUNTRIES

EPISODES AND PROBLEMS

*

The Trevelyan Lectures 1963
with four additional essays

BY

PIETER GEYL

Emeritus Professor of Modern History
in the University of Utrecht

LONDON
MACMILLAN & CO LTD
NEW YORK · ST MARTIN'S PRESS
1964

MACMILLAN AND COMPANY LIMITED
St Martin's Street London WC2
also Bombay Calcutta Madras Melbourne

THE MACMILLAN COMPANY OF CANADA LIMITED
70 Bond Street Toronto 2

ST MARTIN'S PRESS INC
175 Fifth Avenue New York 10 NY

PRINTED IN GREAT BRITAIN

PREFACE

I CANNOT, I feel, publish these lectures without referring, however briefly, to George Macaulay Trevelyan, under the auspices of whose name they were delivered. This made me regard the invitation as even more of an honour, and it was sad news when I learned, last year, that I should not find him among the living any more.

While preparing the six G. M. Trevelyan Lectures for print the idea occurred to me that this volume offered a natural opportunity to bring some earlier studies of mine, also dealing with 'Episodes and Problems of Netherlands History', before the English public. I am grateful to Messrs. Macmillan that they accepted, and indeed welcomed, the suggestion.

These four additional studies, here numbered III, IV, VII and VIII, had been included in the American edition of my *Encounters in History*, published by Meridian Books, New York, in 1961. In the English edition brought out by Messrs. Collins in 1963 I had omitted them, not because I set less store by them myself — it was a painful decision to take — but to make room for two later publications of mine, 'Toynbee's Answer' and 'Huisinga as Accuser of his Age', which seemed to fit in better with the contents of that volume so largely concerned with historiography and theory of history.

Of these four pieces, two (VII, 'Historical Appreciations of the Holland Regent Régime', and VIII, 'The Batavian Revolution') were originally also lectures : the first delivered at the Royal Flemish Academy, Brussels, in 1954, the second in the 'Special Lectures in History' series of the University of London in 1956. The other two (III and IV, 'Frederick Henry of Orange and King Charles I, 1641–1647', and 'William II and the Stuarts, 1647–1650') are the opening sections, published as long ago as 1923 in the *English Historical Review* and the *Scottish Historical Review* respectively, of a monograph planned to cover a much longer period. Interrupted by many other activities in the field of history, this work was not completed until 1939, when it appeared (in Dutch only) under the title of *Oranje en Stuart, 1641–72*; paperback edition 1963. The present sections III and IV form chapter i and ii of that book.

I must apologize for certain repetitions occurring as a result of combining the earlier essays with the lectures of 1963. I am thinking especially of VII compared with V.

I owe thanks to Meridian Books for permitting these articles to be here reproduced.

PIETER GEYL

November 1963

CONTENTS

I

The Sixteenth-Century Split of the Netherlands and Modern Dutch and Belgian Historians

I AM going to speak to you on Netherlands history, to most of you probably an unfamiliar subject. Yet here we are, your near neighbours, partners in our common European civilization, to which we also have through the centuries made contributions at times perhaps more than commensurate to our numeric strength.

When I say 'our common European civilization', I mean that there are ways of thinking and ways of living, convictions and instinctive reactions, rooted in age-long history, through which we belong together — we European nations and the offshoots across the oceans of English society and culture, the dominions and the United States — as against the rest of the world. But we must never forget that this civilization is a composite structure. Its enduring quality, to which it owes much of its inexhaustible fertility, is its diversity. Each of the national component parts has traditions of its own. It is true that it is through these traditions that the common civilization primarily manifests itself, but at the same time practically every form of national self-expression will show signs of some influence received from other members of the group, or will in its turn radiate influence upon them. There is a constant interplay between unity and particularism.

We live in a dynamic age, an age of change. We hear it said and repeated on all sides, and it is true. But I reject the conclusion drawn by some that the state of affairs I have indicated above is a thing of the past, that these national differences are now no more than slight hindrances in the path of progress, be it progress towards a universal world or progress towards a united Europe.

There is Professor Barraclough, for instance, who contemptuously refers to Louis XIV, Napoleon and Bismarck as neolithic figures without any relevance to our present-day problems ; indeed, the loss of status of Western Europe has led him to depreciate the history of its past and to suggest that we should do better to devote our attention to the past of the great powers to the East and to the West of us. We have no lack of universalists on the Continent either, men who are so much impressed by the revolutionary changes we have witnessed of late that they are inclined to discount all that was earlier regarded as worthy of our especial devotion. We have European enthusiasts too, who see the movement for European organization as the preparation of a union in which the national identities are to be merged.

I realize that the shifts and changes caused by the revolutions and wars of our century must to some extent influence our approach to the past. But the historian should not search the past to find only the foreshadowing of his own, or his generation's, hopes and aspirations. He should recognize that the past has an objective existence, and although he is aware that he will never succeed in finally fixing its significance, it is part of his function patiently and lovingly to study it, not only, as Mr. Carr (my distinguished predecessor in this lectureship) seems to think, to place his knowledge and his imagination joyfully at the service of 'achievement, opportunity, progress' — in other words, of the future.

I do not want to impede progress, I do not want us to let ourselves be enslaved by the past ; life is a constant struggle to free ourselves from its control and to move on to fresh ground. But for that very reason, and more than ever when we are in the midst of revolutionary changes, history can warn us where we must walk warily so as to avoid disastrous clashes. I am very far from thinking, however, that the only way in which the past shows its power over us is in delaying and restraining us. If the march forward is well planned, it can lend us positive support; and in any case the acquaintance, the intercourse, with the past provides a preservative force indispensable for the well-being of culture.

This is why we must — as did earlier generations, without having to be so much on the defensive about it, without having to advance such ponderous arguments — we must, we *still* must, pay attention first to our respective national histories. World universalism, and even a united Europe in the sense of the enthusiasts, are a long way off — if they are ever realized! Meanwhile let us, each one of us, cultivate our own domain first. Professor Knowles put this very simply and very strikingly when he said:

> Whether or not it is greatly to our credit, we remain Englishmen, and we are the direct or indirect heirs of the English past. We have a heritage which no one else will fully understand or appreciate if we fail to do so. History, like charity, begins at home.

Now you may turn on me and say: 'All this may justify you in having devoted so much of your life and labours to the study of Netherlands history, but it does not justify you in inflicting the results upon us!' True! But in what I have said above I have not, for one moment, intended to imply that we should shut ourselves up, each within his own particular circle. On the contrary, the more we can get to know about each other the better Europeans we shall be, and to be good Europeans should be as much our concern as to be well grounded in our own particular traditions. And, after all, the Committee who invited me to deliver these lectures suggested that I should speak on Netherlands history! This I remember gratefully, and I feel it as an encouragement now that I am setting out upon my task.

I shall not, of course, try to survey the whole of Netherlands history. Nor shall I deal exhaustively with any one period or question or aspect. I shall select episodes and problems, striding through the centuries until in the last lecture I reach the Second World War and the beginnings of European federation. I hope

3

I shall succeed in showing that there is a connection, a continuity, between the topics I have selected, various as they are and widely separated in time.

Today I shall deal — not for the first time [1] — with one

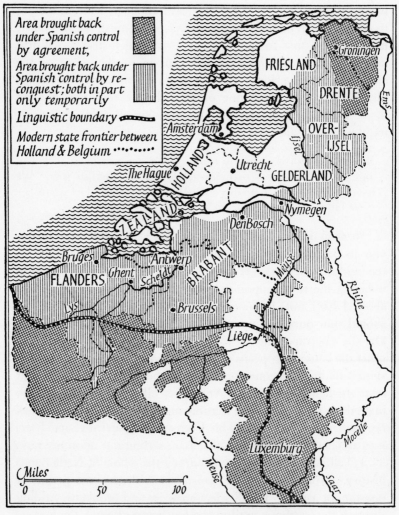

Area brought back under Spanish control by agreement,

Area brought back under Spanish control by reconquest; both in part only temporarily

Linguistic boundary

Modern state frontier between Holland & Belgium

FRIESLAND

Groningen

DRENTE

OVER-IJSEL

Amsterdam

The Hague

HOLLAND

Utrecht

GELDERLAND

ZEALAND

Nymegen

DenBosch

Bruges

Antwerp

BRABANT

FLANDERS

Ghent

Scheldt

Lys

Brussels

Liège

Luxemburg

Miles

0   50   100

THE SEVENTEEN NETHERLANDS
after the split resulting from the war with Spain

problem in connection with the revolt of the Netherlands against their overlord, Philip II of Spain, in the closing decades of the sixteenth century — the problem of why only the Northern provinces succeeded in liberating themselves and in the end came to form the Protestant Republic of the Seven United Provinces, while the Southern provinces failed and were reduced to obedience.

I have brought this map with me in order to help you to visualize the framework of political, geographical and ethnical conditions in which these great events took place. The red line running right across the seventeen Netherlands represents the linguistic boundary which separates the French-speaking from the Dutch-speaking area.[2] I had to draw it on the map with my own hand, a good many years ago, when the linguistic boundary was not thought worth the attention of the makers of historical maps. To me it seems of primary importance.

In the later Middle Ages the seventeen provinces were feudal principalities and bishoprics, most of which nominally owed fealty to the German Emperor, the rest, especially the County of Flanders, to the King of France. Actually, they had become practically independent, but had then, mainly in the fifteenth century, but for the North-Eastern provinces only in the first half of the sixteenth century, been brought under the rule of the Dukes of Burgundy, later to be replaced by the Habsburgs. It was in this way, by the forcible intervention of an alien dynasty, originally French, that the seventeen Netherlands had come to be united.

It was a purely dynastic union, then. Yet soon there grew up something more than a feeling of loyalty to the common ruler. In the assembly of the States-General in Brussels, each province was no doubt inclined to measure everything by its particular interest, and provincial rivalries and animosities were rife. Yet the discussion of common affairs was accustoming the leading classes to regard themselves as participating in a larger union. In the long run this found an outlet, paradoxically enough, in opposition to the central government and administration built up by the ruler and which he kept firmly in his own hands. The French-speaking dynasty had made French the language of that central government organization in Brussels. The nobility was adopting French as the language of polite intercourse and of public affairs. Yet the process of the formation of a common culture, based on the Netherlandish language,[3] which had begun in the area north of the linguistic boundary before ever the Dukes of Burgundy appeared on the scene (that is, before the fifteenth century) was not interrupted. The North-East — Friesland, with a language of its own, Groningen, Overijsel, Gelderland, where dialects were spoken similar to those of the adjoining German area — stood somewhat apart ; but as between Holland, Utrecht, Zeeland, Flanders and Brabant, one can see a distinct Netherlandish culture growing up.

It was Flanders and Brabant that had the lead in this process. They were economically the most advanced and the most active regions (I need only mention Ghent and Bruges in Flanders, Antwerp in Brabant), and their influence radiated northward. The municipal constitutions of certain Brabant towns, for instance, had served, as early as the fourteenth century, as models for those granted by the Counts of Holland to towns in their own province. The literary language, too, as shaped about that time, and earlier, in Flanders and Brabant, was largely adopted in Holland and Zeeland ; the dialects of these Southern provinces were more closely akin to those of the North-West than either group was to those of the North-Eastern provinces. One of the manifestations of this common Netherlands culture can be found in the art of painting that flourished in so striking a fashion in the fifteenth and sixteenth centuries, and that was largely confined to the provinces of Flanders, Brabant, Holland and Utrecht. The remarkable religious movement of the Brethren of the Common Life, on the contrary, had a firm footing in the North-Eastern provinces, spreading from there to the North-West and to the South.

I am not of course suggesting that there was any consciousness of a particular Dutch-speaking Netherlands national destiny, or any desire for the setting-up of a national state together, held

6

in common by Flanders, Brabant and Holland. These were feelings or aspirations that could hardly stir the masses or even the leading classes at that period.

The violent turn events took under Philip II, however, did inspire a new sense of national solidarity which overrode the old provincial particularisms. The centralizing tendencies of the Spanish monarchy and its devoted councillors in the Brussels administration aroused the resentment of the members of the aristocracy, who felt themselves ousted from the royal confidence, of the provincial noblemen generally, and even of the town magistrates, whose cherished old-time 'privileges' were no longer the immutable law. The pitiless persecution of heretics roused widespread indignation. The country had long been riddled with Lutheran and Baptist influences. These were now largely swept aside by the much more uncompromising spirit of Calvinism penetrating from the south. In 1566, the first frankly revolutionary year, came the 'Breaking of the Images' and the 'Hedge-row Sermons'. The outburst was particularly vehement in Flanders and Brabant, in Ghent, Bruges, Antwerp. The example set there led to scattered disturbances in Holland and Zeeland as well.

The following year the Duke of Alva appeared at the head of a Spanish army to re-establish the royal power in all its inexorable severity. The Counts of Egmont and Horne were beheaded in the market-place in Brussels. The Prince of Orange, like them a great figure among the high-ranking noblemen surrounding the Regent Margaret, Philip's half-sister, had taken refuge in his ancestral Nassau, where he waited for the moment when he might invade the country now groaning under Alva's rule.

Thousands, hailing from all the provinces, had likewise fled to Germany. To some of these 'Beggars', as they called themselves, the Prince issued letters of marque, and from then on his corsairs harassed Spanish shipping on the high seas. Even before he had his army ready for the invasion of Brabant, the Sea Beggars captured the Brill, a small seaport in Holland, and from there managed to bring over practically the whole of Holland and Zeeland to the Prince's side.

Although the rebels were for the time being in command of those two provinces only, they were animated by a feeling of being the advanced force of an opposition movement spread over all the Netherlands. They felt themselves to be engaged in a fight for Netherlands liberties and for religion against the alien Spanish enemy. The famous Beggar songs, the warlike poetry that accompanied the rebellion, sounded that note insistently. 'The Netherlands', 'Netherland' — the term recurs again and again. The poets were not thinking of the Dutch-speaking provinces alone; their aspirations were for the seventeen provinces as they had been represented on the States-General — which were not, of course, meeting under Alva's governorship.

Let us try to imagine a present-day historian who has made a close study of these events up to this point, but whose mind is by some magic cleared of all knowledge of what happened in the Netherlands afterwards. Suppose we ask this man to guess at the sequel. He might reflect that the Spanish dominion over the Netherlands had something accidental and artificial about it, and so the establishment of an independent Netherlands nationality on the flank of the German Empire and north of France would not seem to him an unlikely outcome of the crisis. 'You are right in a way,' we tell him, 'Spanish power in that outlying corner of Europe was not, in the long run, to survive; but not all of the Netherlands managed to free themselves in the course of the revolt of which you have seen only the beginning. Indeed, the revolt was to result in a split of the Netherlands.' Would not our imaginary historian point to the linguistic boundary and exclaim : 'I have always felt there was a possible weakness there; I suppose the Walloon provinces gravitated towards France?' — 'No, you are wrong,' we should have to say. 'There *were* to be Northern and Southern Netherlands, the former predominantly Protestant, the latter Catholic, but the definitive frontier between them established by the peace of Münster in

1648, after the so-called Eighty Years War, ran right across the Dutch-speaking area, leaving most of Flanders and Brabant united, not with their co-linguals — Holland, Zeeland and the rest — but with the Walloon provinces.' I am sure that my bewitched historian would be at a loss to explain these results. 'Why Holland Protestant and Flanders and Brabant Catholic?' he would wonder. 'In 1566 it was in Flanders and Brabant that Calvinism seemed most vital and aggressive. And anyhow, were not cultural relations especially close between the south of the Dutch-speaking area and the North-West? If a disruption had to occur in the Dutch-speaking area, I should have expected the North-East to gravitate eastward, leaving Holland and Zeeland still connected with Flanders and Brabant.' — 'Well,' I should reply, 'I am not surprised that you are puzzled. The fact is that what happened had not been slowly prepared in the preceding centuries; it was the sudden, the catastrophic result of military operations conditioned by the geographical configuration of the country.'

Now let me develop — briefly — this thesis.

In 1572 already the descent of the Sea Beggars on Holland and Zeeland is to be explained in this way. Why did this band of desperadoes, exiles of 1566, compromised in the Calvinist outburst of that year, for the most part Flemings, Brabanters and Walloons — why did they select those two provinces for their enterprise? Not because the population there inclined to Calvinism more than in the other provinces, but because Alva had recalled most of the Spanish garrisons to Brabant, the heart of the Netherlands, where he was expecting the invasion that William the Silent had long been preparing; also because the estuaries and seaports of Holland and Zeeland facilitated their attack. Of the heroic popular rising into which legend soon turned the event, little is left when one studies in detail what actually happened.

After the capture of the Brill, town after town in Holland waited until a Beggar force appeared before its walls, then the town government engaged in negotiations with the redoubtable deliverers and a formal capitulation was agreed upon by which always the security of Catholic priests, churches and monasteries was stipulated. Once inside, however, the intruders disregarded their promises. The large majority of the inhabitants had no desire to be unfaithful to the old religion, but the detestation of Spanish rule which they shared with the Beggars laid them open to persuasion, and everywhere, of course, there were small groups of thorough-going sympathizers. With their help the invaders managed to have the town governments purged of definitely pro-Spanish members. Returned exiles were reinstated. In fact, town after town was placed under a regular minority dictatorship. Instead of Holland and Zeeland freeing themselves in a spontaneous popular rising, might we not rather say that Holland and Zeeland were conquered by the Sea Beggars? Later in the summer the States of Holland assembled, unauthorized, at Dort ; but this assembly was no more than the sum of these revolutionized town governments. Not only did they recognize as their Stadholder the outlawed Prince of Orange (then with his invading force in Brabant), but in the following year they forbade the exercise of the Catholic religion in the province. Yet even then, and indeed for a long time to come, the Reformed were no more than a tiny group, making up for their small numbers by fanatical self-assurance, and more especially by their monopoly of political power backed by the only armed force available on the side of the rebellion, the Sea Beggars.

Later in that same summer of 1572 the Prince of Orange's invasion of Brabant was repulsed, and Alva easily reduced and mercilessly punished the towns that had risen to welcome the Prince, there and in Gelderland. But while South and East collapsed so easily, Holland and Zeeland continued to provide a formidable bulwark of the rebellion. Owing to the uninterrupted adherence of Amsterdam to the King's side, a Spanish army led by Alva's son was able to enter Holland from the east, but four years of embittered fighting on Holland and Zeeland soil did not break down resistance there. Again, the explanation of the difference is to be looked for in factors extraneous to what we are inclined to regard as the organic development of history. First there was the presence of the Sea Beggars. Then there was the Prince of Orange himself, who after his failure in Brabant had thrown in his lot with the only provinces where resistance was still being offered. His moral authority was considerable. But above all there were the immense advantages these waterlogged provinces, with their numerous islands and lakes, offered to the defence.

Then, in 1576, the situation underwent a radical change. Alva had been recalled in disgrace the year before. His successor died unexpectedly, the badly-paid Spanish troops mutinied, and now the other provinces too rose in rebellion. It was Brussels which took the initiative. Soon an assembly of the States-General met there, unauthorized, like that of the States of Holland in 1572, and it seemed as if the whole of the Netherlands might be lost to the King of Spain.

But to begin with, this general revolt differed from what had happened in Holland and Zeeland four years earlier in that it was spontaneous and autochthonous. There was no extremist organization here, coming from overseas to set it going. It was the leading classes themselves that controlled the movement, or tried to. And discontented as these noblemen and magistrates were with Spanish rule, they were, like their counterparts in Holland, largely Catholic, or at least disinclined to proscribe Catholicism. Nevertheless, one of the first things these States-General did was to conclude a peace with the two rebel provinces, which were now suddenly freed from the threat of Spanish aggression. This was achieved by the treaty called the Pacification of Ghent. The union of the seventeen Netherlands, originally brought about by force, was now freely confirmed by the several provinces for the purpose of driving the Spanish soldiers out of the country. Soon the Prince of Orange was invited to Brussels to act as adviser to the States-General. But the assembly was far from being of one mind. Against the leanings towards reconciliation of many, especially noblemen, the Prince found his most determined supporters in the Calvinists who were gradually, in most of the important towns of Brabant and Flanders, establishing minority dictatorships after the model of those which had come into being in Holland and Zeeland. Yet the blind zeal of these men was far from agreeing with his moderate and subtle statesmanship.

It was especially the excesses of the Calvinist extremists at Ghent which alienated the neighbouring Walloon provinces, with their numerous nobility, and contributed early in 1579 to their seceding from the Pacification of Ghent and concluding a separate peace with the King, who was already making a determined attempt to crush the rebellion by force of arms. A fresh Spanish army had been sent overland to Luxembourg, the outlying province in the south-east, which had kept outside the movement all along, and from there the Duke of Parma had started upon a systematic campaign of re-conquest. From now on it was the fortune that attended him in his military operations, and the obstacles that the geographical features of the country put in his way, that were to determine the future of the Netherlands for centuries to come.

Parma first captured one town after another along the river Maas. Then was to come the turn of Brabant and Flanders. For these provinces had not followed the example of the Walloons. On the contrary: they had joined the closer union which the Northern provinces, in view of the menace of Parma's army, set up at Utrecht — they joined it, in fact, before some of the North-Eastern provinces did. By this union all the Dutch-speaking provinces of the Netherlands undertook to remain together for ever and always as if they were but one province. And Flanders and Brabant were still represented on the States-General when these, two years later, in 1581, formally renounced their allegiance to Philip II. The Act of Deposition opened with that striking preamble in which it was stated that no allegiance was due to a ruler who oppressed his subjects, robbing them of their old liberties and privileges and treating them as if they were slaves; and that such a ruler was to be considered not as a prince but as a tyrant.

Brave words! But if the Flemings and Brabanters were not able to live up to them, while not only Holland and Zeeland but the whole of the Northern Netherlands in the end carried on under that famous Union of Utrecht, it was due entirely to the fortunes of war, which were in their turn determined by the geographical configuration of the country. The great rivers proved an unsurmountable obstacle in Parma's path of victory, and it was they that proved the salvation of the Northern provinces.

From Limburg, Parma had already, in 1581, penetrated into Brabant ; next, from his basis in the submissive Walloon provinces, he advanced into Flanders. In a few years' time, bit by bit, town by town, the two provinces were subjected, until Antwerp, after a siege lasting for nearly a twelve-month, was compelled to capitulate in 1585. As he advanced, the victor naturally imposed a rigid conformity to Catholicism on every town or district that was forced to submit to him. After every capture a stream of refugees flowed northwards, strengthening the Protestant element in the provinces that were still defying the might of Spain, and leaving their native region even more docile towards the triumphant Church.

Having reduced to obedience all the country south of the great rivers, Parma's troops crossed the Rhine upstream and, making use of allied territory in Germany, overran the entire region east of the river IJsel and the Zuiderzee — only Friesland, behind its lakes and marshes, was less easy to get at. The town of Groningen, as a matter of fact, and the Stadholder of that province, the Walloon nobleman Rennenberg, had made their peace with the King as early as 1580, before a Spanish soldier had set foot on Groningen soil. By the end of the 'eighties, at any rate, it looked as if it were only a question of time before Parma would cross the IJsel and subdue the provinces still carrying on the rebellion — Holland, the mainstay of what was left of the Union, Zeeland, Utrecht, the western part of Gelderland and Friesland protected by its lakes and marshes.

But at that moment the war took an unexpected turn. Philip II decided that intervention in the French civil war was imperatively needed — on the side of the Catholic League, of course — and Parma had to march southward. The rebel provinces used the respite to good effect. The Advocate of Holland, Oldenbarnevelt, was a great organizer; the young Stadholder, Maurice, William the Silent's son, was a great commander. For the first time the rebels were able to take the offensive, and in a series of boldly-conceived raids Maurice succeeded both in firmly securing the river barrier to which the truncated Union owed its survival and in clearing the North-Eastern provinces. It should not be thought that the populations of these North-Eastern provinces were impatiently waiting to be freed. The citizens of Groningen town, for instance, were good Catholics, and assisted the Spanish garrison that was trying to defend them from having the Protestant régime imposed upon them. The decisive factor that led to the incorporation into the Union of the North-Eastern provinces, and consequently to the Protestantization of their inhabitants, while Flanders and Brabant had to be left to Spain and Catholicism, was again a strategic one. The North-Eastern provinces were far removed from the centre of Spanish military power and easily got at by the Union forces. For these to cross the great rivers and face the Spanish forces concentrated south of them would, on the contrary, have been from the military point of view a formidable undertaking. There were probably many more sympathizers in Antwerp, Ghent or Brussels than there were in Groningen, but in practice that made no difference.

In 1609 exhausted Spain consented to a twelve years' truce, by which she agreed to recognize the unconquered provinces as a sovereign Republic, or rather, 'as if they were' a sovereign Republic. The frontier then traced provisionally in the main followed the great rivers. South of them the Republic retained possession only of the district of Breda in North-West Brabant and of a narrow strip of Flanders along the river Scheldt. The war was resumed in 1621, and at the final settlement of 1648 the frontier was pushed a little farther southward. The Stadholder Frederick Henry had, without venturing too far away from the support in the rear afforded by the great rivers, captured some further towns and districts — Maastricht in Limburg on the Maas, 's Hertogenbosch in Brabant and some more territory on the south bank of the Scheldt in Flanders. But the really decisive turn in the development of the Netherlands can already be discerned in the treaty of 1609.

Here then, behind the river barrier, the Republic of the Seven Provinces, Protestant, that is to say under Protestant leadership, with the population in process of being Protestantized ; there, on the wrong side of the rivers, the Southern Netherlands, Catholic, that is to say forcibly re-Catholicized. The Republic an active member of the European community of states, the Spanish Netherlands (the Austrian Netherlands, as they became after further complications of princely marriages and deaths), passive, ruled by foreigners, the leading classes of Flanders and Brabant gradually taking to the use of French for purposes of culture or public affairs. And this in the seventeenth century, at a time when in the North so remarkable a cultural and literary activity was to be found! In the South, which before the separation had led in these respects, there was now nothing comparable, and the difference in religion created an estrangement between the Northerners and the Southerners which prevented the example of the North from having its full effect. The popular language in Flanders and Brabant fared even worse when in 1794 the Southern Netherlands were overrun by the French revolutionary armies and came to form a part, first of the French Republic, then of the Empire. For fully twenty years the strongly-centralized French state subjected the Dutch-speaking population of Flanders and Brabant to its relentless system of gallicization. During most of that same period the Dutch, in their Republic, now transformed into the Batavian Republic, retained full control of their domestic affairs. When, after the downfall of Napoleon in 1814, the two halves of the Netherlands were re-united under King William I of Orange, a dualism had grown up such as had not existed in the sixteenth century, a contrast between a Northern Netherlands, remembering its glorious past and, for all that its numerous Catholics were now in possession of equal rights, still dominated by Protestantism, and a Catholic Southern Netherlands ; a contrast, too, between a country where all affairs were conducted in the national language and one where the leading classes had become accustomed to using French for administration, jurisdiction, culture, polite intercourse, where indeed the standard language had almost fallen into disuse and people spoke only their numerous local dialects. These contrasts were richly productive of misunderstandings and suspicions, and although it may be doubted whether matters would have come to a crisis without the Walloons, once that crisis was under way these contrasts contributed not a little to the second disruption of the Netherlands, that is, to the secession of the South in 1830, to set up house as the kingdom of Belgium.

The point I want to stress now is that all this is to be explained as the protracted effect of the break-up of the Netherlands, and of the *Dutch-speaking* Netherlands, in the course of the revolt against Spain.

As I see it — and the remark I am going to make transcends the parochial interests of Netherlands history — we have here a striking instance of the truth that what one might call a natural development can be interrupted or deflected by factors entirely outside the normal working of social or cultural causes, by catastrophic events, the interference, in this case, by force of arms of a foreign power, helped or impeded by the geographical configuration of the country.

A truth? So it seems to me ; indeed, an obvious truth! But it is a fact that to many historians this view of history is unpalatable — indeed, Mr. Carr rejected it somewhat heatedly in his Trevelyan lectures two years ago. But to him I shall return in my next lecture. For the moment I want to quote some pronouncements by Dutch and Belgian historians on the causes of the sixteenth-century split of the Netherlands, and you will notice how very differently they all appreciated the events from the way in which I have been presenting them.

Let us take Robert Fruin first, by common consent the greatest Dutch historian of the nineteenth century, a master of technique, a man of cool and critical judgement. According to him, writing in 1859 :

> The failure of the union must be imputed not to accidental but to necessary causes. No passing misunderstanding had brought about the separation, but a profound difference between the Northern and the Southern Netherlands, in origin, in national character, in history, in religion, in mode of government, in social conditions.

Every single one of the points he mentions seems to be completely unhistorical. There certainly was nothing like uniformity in the medieval or sixteenth-century Netherlands, but the differences cannot possibly be grouped on the simple pattern of North against South. In mentioning difference of origin, Fruin must have been thinking of the Walloons. But what about Flanders and Brabant? It is the break-up of the Dutch-speaking area that more particularly needs explanation. That the difference of religion was not the cause but the consequence of the separation I have already made clear. But the way in which Protestantism came to be the dominant creed in the North is so important and so fascinating a subject that I shall devote part of my next lecture to a more searching examination of it.

Belgian historians were no less inclined than was Fruin to represent the separation as due to an inherent divergence between North and South. Listen to De Gerlache, a fervent Catholic, who wrote, as early as 1839, under the immediate impression of the Revolution of 1830 :

> The failure of the project of a greater Netherlands union [of the Pacification of Ghent, in other words] was brought about, not by the Catholic provinces, but by the defection of the North, which had gone over to Protestantism.

No doubt De Gerlache was alluding to the Union of Utrecht, which was, however, in its inception not an exclusively Northern association. The fact that Flanders and Brabant began by joining it has often been overlooked by later historians. In any case, to speak of a deliberate defection by the North is absurd.

Some generations later (I can only pick out a very few instances out of the many that present themselves), at the time of the First World War, Kürth, a professional historian of merit, wrote in the same sense, although *he* ascribed the initiative, not to the Protestant North, but to the Catholic South :

> In order to remain faithful to Catholicism we, in the sixteenth century, parted from our Dutch brethren, who had identified love for our national liberties with Protestantism.

'We parted from?' This might be said of the Walloons, who made their peace with the King and seceded from the Pacification in the same year, 1579, in which the other provinces concluded the Union of Utrecht. But again, what of Flanders and Brabant, who did not 'part from' their Dutch brethren, but were forcibly detached from them? — and who had not been so unanimously faithful to Catholicism either!

There is one Belgian historian who must of course be consulted in this connection, a man with unique gifts of imagination and presentation — I mean Pirenne, who between 1900 and 1932 wrote his seven-volume *Histoire de Belgique*. In his account of the revolt and of the separation he does not indulge in those clearly untenable simplifications which strike us in reading so many others, Dutch and Belgian alike. As a matter of fact he did not need to, for the view that the North and the South, Holland and Belgium, were predestined to separate destinies is one that dominates the whole of his brilliant work. In the preface to his first volume he had announced his intention to bring out 'the character of unity' of the history of Belgium, from the earliest times when, properly speaking, Belgium was still far to seek. In that preface the character of the work that was to follow is accurately forecast ; the 'growing together and forming a nationality' of the French-speaking Walloon provinces and the Dutch-speaking provinces of Flanders and Brabant is throughout represented by Pirenne as a perfectly natural process : 'Our destiny has not been the plaything of accident and arbitrariness.' But notice that the Northern provinces, Holland and Zeeland, are never mentioned! This ignoring of the relations between Flanders and Brabant and their 'Dutch brethren' (as we once heard another Belgian historian put it) is the method by which Pirenne obtains his effect of a predestined, a natural, Belgian nation, which is the great message of his book. And in that setting there was no need for him to lay particular stress on the naturalness and inevitability of the break-up of the seventeen Netherlands in the 1580s. These qualities could be taken for granted, for in the light of the earlier volumes such a break-up could not but appear as the culmination of an age-long process.

On looking up that preface, when I was preparing this lecture, in my own copy of the first volume of the *Histoire de Belgique*, I was struck to find, on the last page, a pencil note scribbled by myself in 1909, when I was twenty-one :

> What I object to in this *avant-propos* is that Pirenne speaks too exclusively of *Belgian* where the context would often require *Netherlandish*. How many of his observations apply just as much to North-Netherlandish civilization! The North-South union, too, lasted too long and was too real to be thus completely ignored.

I gave expression there to a view with which I came into the open some ten years later, and which I continued to establish and elaborate for many years after. It is the view which, you will have noticed, underlies my present argument. But in those early years it involved me in endless polemics, not so much with Pirenne, who never deigned to reply, or with his Belgian disciples and admirers, as with the leading Dutch historians, my elders, the men who at that time dominated our little Dutch world of historical scholarship.

These men accepted Pirenne's authority as unreservedly as did their Belgian colleagues. It may seem extraordinary — it did seem so to me — that Dutch intellectuals were so eager to applaud a historical system by which the Flemings were not only politically but culturally separated from their 'Dutch brethren' in order to be incorporated in a Belgium where in those days it was considered perfectly in order and, again, *natural* for the

Flemish well-to-do classes to have adopted French as their language, for the administration and jurisdiction in Flanders to be carried on in French (of which the large majority of Flemish people remained ignorant), and for secondary and university education to use French as their medium. Pirenne, the great apostle of that conception of Belgian nationality, was himself a Walloon teaching history in French to Flemish students in the University of Ghent.

To understand how it was possible for the Dutch public, historians included, to accept Pirenne and his masterly Belgian propaganda, it is enough to remember that the chain of events following upon the forcible disruption of the Netherlands in the sixteenth century had indeed driven the two peoples far apart. While the Flemings were apt to resent the Dutchman's airs, and memories still rankled of the blockade applied to Antwerp for two hundred years in order to enable Amsterdam to become a great European trading town, the Dutch for their part were inclined to look down upon the Flemings, both for their Catholicism (because although the Dutchman's own Protestantism might have been watered down to an extent that would have roused the sixteenth-century Calvinist to fury, he still venerated the tradition of the Protestant nation), and for their dialectical language, without pausing to consider how the decline had come about. So the Dutch were content to shut themselves up within their narrow frontiers and left the Flemings to Pirenne and gallicization without compunction.

Colenbrander, Fruin's last disciple and his second successor in the Chair of National History at Leyden, was inspired by the first volumes of Pirenne's great work to write a little book in which he pretended to trace through the centuries preceding the enforced break-up of the Netherlands the reality and distinctness of the Dutch, *i.e.* of North-Netherlands, civilization, just as the Belgian historian was doing for Belgium. Protestantism he saw as a natural form of belief for the Dutch, while the Flemings could only feel at home in Catholicism. He avoided the error that Fruin and so many others had fallen into, for he knew (as

indeed Fruin too must have known!) that the Southern Netherlands had preceded the Northern in Calvinistic proclivities and
manifestations. This is how he gets round that difficulty :

> It is once more a case of Flemish susceptibility and action as against
> Dutch sturdiness and constancy. The shallow water is moved
> more violently, but the high waves rising there are the first to
> subside.

A Leyden colleague of Colenbrander's, the Professor of
Dutch Literature, Kalff, borrowed this explanation, phrasing it
as follows :

> The South, more easily inflamed, had started the struggle ; the
> North, slower to be moved, persevered.

How pleasant it was for Dutch readers to find themselves
described as stubborn and profound, as surpassing the Flemings
in perseverance! But if Holland and Zeeland persevered, was it
not because their uncommonly advantageous position enabled
them to do so? Kalff speaks of 'the North'. But did not
Gelderland, Overijsel, Groningen, succumb to the Spanish
attack even before Ghent and Antwerp had done so, and had
they not to be brought back on the side of the rebellion by the
army that Holland and Zeeland, firmly based on the sea and
trading with the outside world, could keep in the field and pay
for? An entirely imaginary contrast in national character is here
suggested, very flattering to national self-conceit — but not a
word is said, no more than by Fruin, De Gerlache, Kürth and
countless others, about the Duke of Parma and the great rivers.

I mentioned a little earlier that Mr. Carr somewhat con-
tumeliously rejected the idea that what we might regard as the
normal course of history can be interrupted by unforeseeable
catastrophic events. We have now seen that he is not alone in
that position. We have also seen how disputable are the interpretations by which these kindred spirits attempt to safeguard
history against that indignity. There were, no doubt, very
special circumstances and sentiments at the back of their special
pleadings. Is it fair, some of you may be asking, to place Mr. Carr

in the same category as these Dutch and Belgian 'worshippers of the outcome'? We are confronted here with a very important problem, and I shall begin, next time, by discussing it in a more general fashion, as a problem of the theory of history.

After which, as I have hinted already, I shall examine a little more closely the problem of the spread of Protestantism — in Europe, and particularly in the Northern Netherlands.

II

*Mr. Carr's Theory of History—The Protestantization
of the Northern Netherlands*

In my first lecture I gave you my explanation of how the
break-up of the seventeen Netherlands in the course of the
revolt against Spain came about. I tried to show that there
was nothing in the earlier history of the country, in the history
of the mutual relations between the provinces, that would lead
the unprejudiced observer to expect the North-South cleavage
that actually came about. I also hinted at the unhappy consequences of the estrangement, and often antagonism, which
resulted between the two halves into which the Dutch-speaking
area came to be divided. The situation was made worse by the
partial gallicization of the Flemish leading classes, in itself also
promoted by the loss of contact with the North; a socially
unhealthy state of affairs which entailed a deplorable decadence
of cultural creativeness in Flanders.

The whole of this long concatenation of phenomena I represented as a catastrophic deviation from what would have been
the normal course of Netherlands history; a deviation brought
about initially by the interference of the military power of Spain,
by the campaigns of the Duke of Parma and by the counter-
campaigns of the Stadholder Maurice, the outcome of which was
determined, not by the inclinations of the people or any supposed divergent tendencies as between North and South, but by
the strategic importance of the geographical configuration of
the country, especially of the great rivers.

But I also quoted a number of nineteenth- and twentieth-
century historians, Dutch and Belgian, who had not the slightest
doubt that the separation *was* due to the different temperaments

or cultural traditions of the populations concerned. You will remember that in order to present their case they had to distort, for example, the true significance of the Union of Utrecht, and that they never even mentioned the Duke of Parma or the great rivers.

How was it possible for such an extraordinary misconception of so important an event to gain currency?

It is very simple. After the divergence in religion consequent upon the separation and the ever-deepening estrangement, the prevailing sentiment both in the North and in the South was one of satisfaction with the outcome. The failure in 1830 of the early nineteenth-century re-union was largely due to this dualism which had by now become traditional, and in its turn intensified it; the Belgian revolution roused anti-Dutch passions in Belgium and anti-Belgian passions in Holland.

The Protestant Dutch were not only satisfied with the Protestant character of their state; more than ever they gloried in it, and considered themselves well rid of the Belgian rebels. The Catholics in Holland had been in possession of equal rights ever since the Revolution of 1795, but, numerous as they were, they counted as yet for little in the cultural life of the country. Their real, as distinct from their legal, emancipation was still to be a long and laborious process. One Catholic historian, writing on the revolt in the late 1860s, showed an inkling of the truth, but he had no successors.[1]

Similarly the Belgians were satisfied with their Catholic Belgium and rejoiced in having severed the connection with the Dutch. As far as the language question was concerned, it added intensity to the satisfaction with which Walloons and Fransquillons[2] saw Holland in a position where she could not meddle in their affairs. The dominance of French could never have been imposed upon the Flemish people had they been able to draw upon the support of Dutch society and civilization. The Belgian unity celebrated by Pirenne in his great work was a device to absorb Flanders into a state where only the French language enjoyed respect. For long it was only a small and, in spite of all the noise it made, uninfluential minority which kicked against the humiliations to which the popular language was subjected in Flanders. Very few Dutch intellectuals were interested. To most of them the Flemish movement wore a slightly ridiculous aspect of hollow enthusiasm. The Dutch spoken by these flag-wavers was in any case not up to standard. That this was due to the deplorable neglect of the mother tongue in secondary education and at the universities was a fact that escaped the attention of these supercilious Dutchmen. Even when from among the crowd a highly intelligent writer appeared,[3] a staunch Liberal who, like the Catholic Hollander I mentioned, illuminated the problem of the sixteenth-century separation with a flash of insight, his view made very little impact.

The Dutch accepted Holland ; the Belgians, including most Flemings of the leading and articulate classes (articulate in French, be it understood) accepted Belgium ; both accepted the separation. And so historians in both countries searched history for confirmation of this desirable state of affairs. And now along comes Mr. Carr, and proclaims a philosophy of history which reduces the historian's task to just this — the justification of the present! No doubt his 'present' is something entirely different from that acclaimed by the somewhat narrow-minded Dutch or Belgian nationalism which inspired historians to represent the separation of the Netherlands as an inevitable and natural event. Carr's 'present' is a moment in the continuous movement of history, in its irresistible progress ; it is orientated towards the future.

> It is the sense of direction in history which alone enables us to order and interpret the events of the past.

The current scepticism about general patterns of history, the dis- inclination to arrange the multiplicity of facts and phenomena in a comprehensive scheme, he imputes to the feelings of unease and fear aroused by the rise of Russian Communism as a world power, feelings which he does not share, which indeed he derides. Who are we to judge?

We are born into history. No moment occurs when we are offered a ticket of admission with the option to accept or reject it.

He insists on 'the impossibility of erecting an abstract and super-historical standard by which historical actions can be judged'.

Let me admit that there is a problem here, but the way in which Mr. Carr absolutizes his demand that the historian should abstain from moral judgements, and should unquestioningly accept what is decided by the mysterious world force that he sees as making history without consulting us, is anathema to me.

Carr quotes, and expresses agreement with, Hegel's pronouncement:

> The great man of the age is the one who can put into words the will of his age, tell his age what its will is, and accomplish it.

Has the age a will? Is nothing left to us but to find out what that will is and abjectly bow down to it? And if Mr. Carr tells us, in effect: 'I have found out, and *this* is what it is', can we not reply: 'That is what you say, but you are wrong, and all the interpretations of history that you derive from your certainty are not objective (as, after some deprecatory remarks on the term itself, you suggest they are), but to the highest degree subjective.'

I am reminded of the criticism to which, years ago, I subjected our Dutch Marxist historian Romein, the Amsterdam professor, and his theory of history[4]. According to him:

> Objective is, and certainty gives, *that* history-writing which is in agreement with the spirit of the age.

After making this bold pronouncement, the writer reflects that there may be another spirit of the age, but *that* can only be the false one. To achieve objectivity, therefore, one must begin by making 'the right choice'. How is one to know that one is not in error? One might expect an adherent of his philosophy to feel that only the future can decide this point. But this did not satisfy Romein. He wanted to enjoy certainty *now*. Fortunately, he reflects, it is possible to check one's choice without delay, namely by the inner certainty of the historian who is fortunate enough to have chosen aright. Objectivity is thus obtained by bowing down to the revelation of the true spirit of the age confirmed by something in the nature of a religious experience.

I do not think, however, that blind obedience to that questionable godhead is the attitude that will best ensure a true understanding of the movement of history, which results from action and counter-action, from the struggle between progress and tradition and also between different conceptions of progress. The historian should not abdicate, he should preserve his independence. Mr. Carr has observed with satisfaction how in my *Napoleon: For and Against* I bring out the influence exercised by the circumstances of their own day on the appreciations of Napoleon presented by successive generations of French historians. But in the conclusion to that book I said that 'the eternal postulates of respect for the human personality, of the feeling for spiritual freedom, of lofty idealism, of truthfulness, should be taken into account in the final reckoning'. In Mr. Carr's view this must be a thoroughly unhistorical declaration. I have already admitted that there is a problem here ; nevertheless, when faced by his depreciation of moral judgements and subservience to success, I take my stand on what I have said above.

I have been indulging in a little digression to distinguish the particular inspiration of Mr. Carr's presentment of history from that of the Dutch and Belgian historians about whom I spoke last time. I shall now go on to point out that his method and theirs in using the past in the service of their different aims are none the less identical.

The historian, according to Mr. Carr, should write 'as if what happened was in fact bound to happen, and as if it was his business simply to explain what happened and why'. As for indulging in speculations as to what might have happened if certain apparently fortuitous factors had presented themselves in a somewhat different fashion, Mr. Carr is very contemptuous about this :

> One can always play a parlour game with the might-have-beens of history. But they have nothing to do with history.

Nearly forty years ago, in 1924, when I had just launched the great controversy concerning the causes of the disruption of the Netherlands, Huizinga, addressing a group of American students in Leyden, referred to it ; he called it, by the way, not 'the great controversy', but 'a little controversy'. And it is curious to notice how exactly like Carr he expressed himself on the suggestion I made then that the course of events does not always present itself to contemporaries as being as inevitable as it looks to those living later in the conditions created by the outcome of those events — a suggestion which I felt must stimulate the historical imagination.

> As for me [he said] I am inclined to side with those who regard historical development with the eyes of determinism, rather searching the past to find out why things came about as they did than to prove — what theoretically always *can* be proved — that they might have fallen out otherwise.

I did not fail to reply, and pointed out that the word 'determinism' is one which we should not transfer from the abstract regions of philosophy to apply it to our interpretations of history, subject as these are to our human limitations. Mr. Carr, on the contrary, indirectly defending Hegel and Marx, argues away the distinction, here implied, between determinism as a philosophical tenet applied to the world's movements in general and determinism as a method applicable to historical interpretation. To scholars who attack historical determinism he thinks it necessary to explain that the actions of private persons, of a Robinson or a Jones, or whatever happenings they — the scholars — point to as interrupting the rigid concatenation of cause and effect postulated by the deterministic view also are determined, also have their causes which can be rationally understood. The explanation seems to me quite superfluous. I am sure that Professor Popper and Sir Isaiah Berlin never meant to question this. In a little essay I wrote on Berlin's *Historical Inevitability* I summarized his argument as follows :

> The contention is not that determinism is a fallacy, but that to apply determinism to history is an impossible and necessarily misleading method.

The multiplicity and heterogeneous nature of the factors composing the historical process are such that the historian cannot embrace them all in his mind, still less reduce them to their proper order of importance with unerring exactness. Yet when historians suggest that 'things could not have fallen out otherwise', or when, like Mr. Carr, they deride suggestions of alternative developments and results as being inspired by a merely personal aversion to the 'will of History'[5], or the 'will of the Age', as being mere 'wishful thinking', their implication is that the case for a straightforward line of historical development can be proved by referring to one set of factors only, namely those of a general character, social or cultural, in which we can, all of us, discern direction and a certain regularity or amenability to laws.

Mr. Carr does occasionally refer to the distinction between these factors and those which may to some extent interfere with their (to him 'progressive') working and which escape either the observation or the exact valuation of the historian. But he gives himself away, not only by his constant gibing at the factors of this second category (Cleopatra's nose, Bajazet's gout, Alexander's monkey-bite), but especially by the positive advice he tenders to the working historian. Accidents may have had their momentary importance, but 'in so far as they were accidental, they do not enter into any rational interpretation of history, or into the historian's hierarchy of significant causes'. The historian must, like the scientist [it is a scientist's statement that he quotes here really, but he adopts it for his own purpose without anything but the slightest qualification], 'from the rag-bag of observed "facts", select, piece and pattern together, the *relevant* observed facts, rejecting the *irrelevant*'. In an earlier passage, after recalling Talcott Parson's phrase (with which I do not quarrel) that 'history is a selective system', Carr continues:

> Just as from the infinite ocean of facts the historian selects those which are significant for his purpose, so from the multiplicity of sequences of cause and effect he extracts those, and only those, which are historically significant; and the standard of historical

significance is his ability to fit them into his pattern of rational explanation and interpretation. Other sequences of cause and effect have to be rejected as accidental . . . because such sequences are irrelevant.

These are prescriptions that do indeed amount to a drastic simplification of the historian's procedure. And their dogmatic nature becomes even more startling when we remember that they are ruled by the doctrine that 'the ultimate criterion of historical judgement is found in the future'. Allied to this is, of course, the assumption that Mr. Carr knows what this future will be. Like Professor Romein, he enjoys a complete 'inner certainty' as to that. And so he is content to pick out from the past only those tendencies which led to the great changes that we have lived through and especially to those further ones that he anticipates. Even the objection that history approached in this state of mind becomes 'a success story' does not make him flinch.

History is, by and large, a record of what people did, not of what they failed to do; to this extent it is inevitably a success story.

Let me remind you for one moment of those Dutch and Belgian historians about whom I told you last time and whom I have not really been losing sight of while speaking about Carr. They too turned their histories into success stories, the Dutch glorifying their truncated Union, the prototype of their Protestant Kingdom, the Belgians their obedient and re-Catholicized remnant that was to blossom out into the Belgian Kingdom; and I pointed out how they distorted and mutilated history in order to do so more effectively.

But speaking generally, we see here revealed a temptation to which historians were exposed long before Carr's teachers Hegel and Marx tried to rationalize and systematize the method — the temptation to read history backwards, so to speak, to light up in the past all that seems to forecast the developments to come, and to leave in the dark those tendencies which might have retarded or deflected the movement towards that achievement with which the historian's generation is familiar, but of which the contemporary actors were unaware.

These observations which I am making now have been made before, many times. Mr. Carr himself quotes — only to reject, of course — a warning of Professor Tawney's, which seems to me very telling. But let me quote — and this will surprise you — Huizinga — Huizinga who, as I told you, in 1924 shrugged away my explanation of the separation of the Netherlands into a Northern and a Southern half with a pronouncement on the desirability of a deterministic view of history — a pronouncement that reads like a forecast of Mr. Carr's theorizing, in spite of the latter's doubts about the word determinism. In 1939 that same Huizinga wrote :

> The historian must approach his subject from an indeterministic point of view. Only by keeping an eye open for the unlimited possibilities can he do justice to the fullness of life.

I had felt all along that Huizinga's profession of a deterministic view fifteen years earlier did not fit in with the reality of his outlook on history ; it was nothing more than an unthinking reaction of impatience to my unconventional approach to the history of the revolt. Anyhow, on this second occasion I could agree with him wholeheartedly. 'An eye open for the unlimited possibilities' — this is something very different from the contemptuous saying of 1924 about attempting 'to prove, what theoretically always *can* be proved, that things might have fallen out otherwise' — a saying, moreover, which did less than justice to my intention ; [6] and it is very different, too, from Mr. Carr's sarcasm about 'a parlour game'.

But there is much more to be said about this large question of theory. I shall not try to say all of it, but I must unburden myself of a few remarks on 'the success story' which, according to Mr. Carr, history must inevitably be.

To me this is a lowering of its function and significance. I see history as an unending struggle between forces of which not 'one swallows up the others',[7] but — that is how I should put it — of which even the (momentarily) victorious one has to find itself off with traces of the influence left by the one (sometimes no more than seemingly) defeated. To reduce that struggle to a walkover for the victors may be all right for party purposes, but it is robbing history of most of its instructiveness for the present.

I too consider that instructiveness as eminently valuable. It is not, in my view, merely a matter of generosity when the historian considers it his duty to listen to the losers, those losers of whom Mr. Carr has no more to say than that 'the losers pay'. In resisting the movement that proved victorious, they will probably have contributed something that will outlast their discomfiture. It is wrong to think that they are of no account when one speculates about the future. Besides, the future? The future will soon be replaced by a later future ; and who shall say that principles cast aside in the heat of passion will not come to be honoured again, and their revival may then owe something to sacrifices only seemingly made in vain. In any case, the future, and the next future, are not made simply by the victors, they are the product of the struggle. And history is not merely a story of progress and success, it is, as I said a moment ago, made by action and counter-action. To each of these the historian's attention is due.

I now come to the second point that, as I told you last time, I mean to go into a little more deeply today.

The success of the revolt in the North resulted not only in political independence, but was accompanied by a revolution in religion. And more than anything else this religious aspect contributed to the inclination of Dutch historians to gloss over the factor of force on which I laid so much stress in my exposition of events. The basic principle of my explanation, my thesis that something so intimate as the religious faith unquestioningly accepted in one's environment should have been determined, not by the free choice of one's ancestors, but by the pressure or coercion to which they were exposed from a secular authority ultimately resting on military force, is repugnant to the believer.

So we find historians, faced by this great fact of a predominantly Protestant North, searching the centuries preceding the revolt for its spiritual origins. They point to rationalistic as well as to mystic tendencies, they mention the Brethren of the Common Life and Erasmus. But why were these traditions, which were at one time spread over the whole of the Netherlands, cut off in the South, to culminate only in the North? In fact, of course, the powerful rise of Calvinism which came in time to dominate the Dutch Republic makes a revolutionary appearance rather than one of just continuing these earlier soul-searchings; these can at best be traced in a number of Protestant sects which never attained a position of power.

I do not for a moment deny the importance of these purely spiritual antecedents. The spiritual life has an independence and a continuity of its own. It is there, no doubt, that one has to look for the origins of great religious changes and movements. But a distinction should be kept in view between the rise of the Protestant idea in minds attuned to religious experience and its triumph in political and social reality; between the appeal made to the religious conscience by the bearers of the new message and its materialization in new national churches. So powerful was the Catholic tradition, so firmly attached to it were the masses everywhere, and so great, in spite of abuses and corruption, was the power of resistance of the established Church, that these new organizations could nowhere come into being unless backed up by the power of the state — in Germany and in England the lead was given by the rulers themselves. Everywhere factors of interest or political ambition, and, in the end, of power, even of war, can be seen coming into play, and in the light of the vicissitudes of the complicated struggles which were waged there is no sense in connecting the particular outcome in this or that country with its supposed 'national character' — as we saw was done so frequently and lightheartedly in the case of the Netherlands falling apart into two halves opposed in religion.

National character is in itself a meaningless term. And not only in the Netherlands, but in the whole of the European

33

theatre where the contest between Rome and the Reformation was staged, it is obvious that the outcome was decided by politics, by the incidence of power. The *cuius regio eius religio* of the religious peace of Augsburg (1555) — the principle according to which the peoples were to accept the religion adopted by their particular ruler, Count, Duke, Elector, etc. — can still be traced on a map of Germany showing the distribution of the religions today. And as to the main lines of the partition of Europe between Catholicism and Protestantism, the papacy fixed the *point d'appui* of the old Church in the South, while the King of Spain's championship made the Mediterranean definitely the base of Catholic power. Protestantism, for its part, soon came to rest upon the Northern seas — La Rochelle, England, Holland and Zeeland, Scandinavia. And so the Habsburg Emperors' last chance to subdue Protestantism in Northern Germany was lost when in 1628 Wallenstein had to give up the siege of Stralsund on the Baltic.

I recall this geographical explanation of the distribution of the warring creeds in Europe just as in my first lecture I pointed to the great rivers crossing the Netherlands from east to west as the decisive factor determining the North-South division in political status and in religion left behind by the revolt. But the process of 'Protestantization' that was made possible by the change of régime has a history of its own, and it will be worth our while to look into it a little more closely.

The term itself, which I used for the first time in the title of an essay published in 1930,[8] suggests pressure or compulsion, and it would indeed be a great mistake to think that liberation from Spanish rule was followed automatically by large-scale defection from the old Church and adherence to the new. What happened — and this too I pointed out briefly last time — was that the Sea Beggars, who from 1572 on held a dominant position in Holland and Zeeland, saw to it that power in the various towns of those provinces fell into the hands of reliable patriots, that is, according to their way of thinking, of Protestants; and a minority dictatorship was thus founded which in 1573, in spite

of the promises made the previous year, dissolved the organization of the old Church and prohibited any public exercise of the
Catholic religion. Protection was extended only to the new
Church, though to begin with it catered for an exiguous group
of members or sympathizers. But in all sorts of ways an attempt
was made to bring the majority, bereft as they were of their old
spiritual guardians, into the new Presbyterian organization.

Let us confine our attention for the moment to Holland and
Zeeland, where the new state of affairs had consolidated itself
during those heroic years 1572–1576 when the other provinces
were still under 'the Spanish yoke'. One town in Holland —
Amsterdam — had managed to resist the Beggar invasion and
had become a place of refuge for numbers of zealous Catholics
fleeing from the Beggar rule established elsewhere. At Haarlem
too, which was captured by Alva's son in 1572, Catholicism had
been restored to its old position. When the Spanish régime
suffered its temporary collapse in 1576 and all the provinces
united in the Pacification of Ghent, these two towns (Middelburg
in Zeeland was in the same position) had no option but to allow
themselves to be re-integrated into their province, but they did
so only on conditions. By regular conventions, called Satisfac-
tions, the rights of Catholicism within their walls were safe-
guarded.

The situation thus created did not last, any more than it
had in the case of the other towns which had in 1572 admitted
the Beggar forces on the same terms. In Haarlem, in 1579,
a procession on Corpus Christi day was attacked by a mob
supported by the Beggar garrison ; a priest lost his life in the
tumult ; and the toleration guaranteed to the Catholics by the
Satisfaction was withdrawn, as it was elsewhere. A number of
Haarlem notables addressed the States in 1581, asking for restoration of the Satisfaction. They professed themselves ready to
sacrifice property and life in common resistance to the Spaniards,
who had by then embarked under Parma on the re-conquest of
the Netherlands, and in confirmation of their promise they
pointed to the patience with which they and their fellow-Catholics

had borne the injustice of the overthrow of their rights, recognized so solemnly a few years before. The answer of the States was far from accommodating.

> As regards this patience of the Catholics mentioned in the address [so they said], the Hon. States are on the contrary well aware that it does not come from the heart, but is an enforced patience. The States know well enough how the Catholics act where they are masters, and the same would soon be the case here if they were in power.

One burgomaster, not a Catholic, and not a member of the new Church either, spoke up manfully in favour of the request.

> Following my conscience before God [he said], I hold that every church whatsoever ought to be permitted to carry on publicly such worship as in its conscience before God it considers to be good and just.

That, so he said, had been the principle for which we all contended when the troubles started in 1566. But indeed, since then the passions aroused by revolution and war had relegated the great ideal of toleration to the background, although it was to prove an inspiring force again when conditions became more or less stabilized.

For a long time to come, however, the warning uttered by the Catholic requesters that the suppression of Catholic organization and worship would lead to atheism, was neglected, and the policy of systematically and exclusively supporting the new Reformed Church was obstinately pursued, although, in fact, the masses who found themselves suddenly cut adrift from their former spiritual leaders were by no means readily absorbed into the new Church. Many still found comfort in the ministrations dispensed more or less secretly by Catholic priests. But the property of the old Church had been confiscated, and although the new Church was far from obtaining the disposal of all of it, its control of charity was one important means of bringing pressure on the poor to join it. The rich were gradually brought to do so by finding the road to office in town and province reserved for members of the new Church. And then there was the school system. Quite a number of resolutions could be quoted by which towns and provinces made the schools serve the interests of 'the true Christian religion', insisting on strict orthodoxy on the part of the teachers and making the Heidelberg Catechism the basis of all instruction. A regular system of spiritual compulsion, enforced for generations and in the early days of the rebellion enforced sometimes by methods of terrorism, was needed to turn the North-Netherlanders into anything like a nation of Calvinists. All through the first period of the war of independence the new Church embraced no more than a fraction of the population, and strong minorities of Catholics and of Protestant dissenters were never assimilated. So little did the change in religion proceed spontaneously from character or inclination!

Even more striking is the spectacle presented by developments in the eastern provinces. It was not until 1576 that these, like the provinces south of the great rivers — which indeed took the initiative — defied the King's authority and associated themselves with the Pacification of Ghent. In 1579 and the following years they acceded bit by bit to the Union of Utrecht (some of these north-eastern districts did so later than certain Flemish and Brabant towns or districts), which was a closer and more radical union than the Pacification and soon came to identify this second rebellion too with anti-Catholicism. When one looks a little more closely at what happened, one will notice that the motive force behind these developments in each province was a small, determined minority only, backed by the troops of the Union, which were mainly paid by Holland and Zeeland. In these two provinces, more or less settled conditions had already been established ; the Calvinist minority dictatorship sat firmly in the saddle, and owing to their command of the sea they were prospering in the midst of war. In the north-east, the town of Groningen, led by the Stadholder of the province, Rennenberg, seceded from the Union in 1580 — 'Rennenberg's treason' is what the incident used to be called in Dutch history books. But Rennenberg, as I pointed out in my last lecture, had the support of the most considerable part of the citizens. Their action was inspired by aversion to the growing anti-Catholic tendency of the Union. It is in the setting of a party struggle, of a civil war, that the defection must be seen to be understood historically. No doubt for the other side it *was* treason, and they could not but denounce it as such and thereby attempt to rouse public opinion on behalf not only of the new Church, but of the common country, making the most of the ignominy of the old Church's alliance with Spain.

In the following years, as you will remember, Parma, stopped by the river barrier from extending his victorious advance into the north-western provinces, did manage to recapture for the King and Catholicism the provinces east of the river IJsel and the Zuiderzee, where Groningen afforded him a foothold. Then, in the 1590s, when Parma had to divide his forces to intervene in the French civil war, the Stadholder Maurice, though unable to attack the Spaniards in their central position south of the rivers, by a series of masterly campaigns drove them out of that outlying north-eastern region.

And now, without asking the populations for their opinion, the new masters introduced into each town or district thus brought back into the Union, the Reformed Church organization which had in the meantime been set up in full working order. The 'Protestantization' of the people was now unquestioningly regarded as the indispensable guarantee of their loyalty to the States régime, and consequently as the first task incumbent upon authority. Whenever a town fell into the hands of the States, Catholic worship was at once suppressed and the churches taken over for the Reformed and 'purged' in accordance with their conceptions. Yet in the 1590s, even in Utrecht and the Western part of Gelderland, both long since freed from the Spaniards, the Reformed Church was still hardly established in the country-side. It was not until 1599, for instance, that the Court at Arnhem ordered 'that in the Veluwe district the altars, images, holy-water-fonts, etc., shall be removed from the churches, and crucifixes and chapels, placed in woods or by roadsides, shall be pulled down.' Even in the town itself, in the following year, the magistracy still had to prohibit the use, at funerals, of figures or crosses on winding-sheets. The mood in which the inhabitants of Groningen, after the capture of the town by the States army in 1594, underwent the Protestant régime imposed upon them was such that it was thought wise to construct a citadel dominating the town — as Alva had done to overawe Antwerp and other towns in 1567. Even as late as 1605, when Spinola, Parma's successor as Commander of the Spanish army in the Netherlands, undertook an attack on the eastern provinces from the neighbouring territory of some German rulers, the Protestant magistrates in Overijsel or Gelderland trembled to think how their citizens might react. When the negotiations for a truce were being set in motion in 1608, Maurice warned against the danger that the Archdukes in Brussels might take advantage of the cessation of war to enter into friendly relations with the Catholic populations in the north-east.

The process of 'Protestantization' made but slow progress. One difficulty that made itself felt everywhere was the lack of competent ministers of religion. Generally the former Catholic priests were left the choice between keeping silence on a modest subsistence allowance, or seeking admittance, after having satisfactorily passed an examination, to the Reformed ministry. In some provinces this plan was much more successful than in others.

In 1593 a commission appointed by the States of Utrecht — consisting of one nobleman, two Reformed ministers and one elder from the town of Utrecht — made a tour of the province, questioning the newly installed ministers as well as the former priests. Their report gives a vivid picture of the motley and sometimes extraordinary conditions prevailing. In the large majority of villages the old priests were still functioning. Many of them declared their willingness to comply ; but some were still obviously hankering after the accustomed usage ; others had come over part of the way, but had failed, whether through ignorance or through obstinacy, on some particular point. Of one priest, whom the commission regarded as 'an honourable

man, having little children, whose mother is dead', the report
states :

> In baptizing and marrying, this priest does not adhere to one usage,
> but accommodates himself according to the inclinations of the
> members of his flock.

Several priests refused to submit, and continued to dis-
tribute 'the popish sacrament' at Easter, or at least showed a
suspicious reluctance to marry their 'housekeeper'. One declared that 'he did not wish to have his conscience forced, by
the States or by anyone else'. The report continues :

> He has not yet married his housekeeper, although he has been
> ordered to do so by the Hon. States. He said expressly that he
> does not want to marry her publicly, adding that he would not
> mind leaving her, being well able to live without her, nay, he
> offered, scoffingly, to present her to anybody who might have a
> use for her.

For the correction of these and similar unsatisfactory conditions the commissioners looked to state intervention. So,
fifteen years earlier, when Flanders had not yet been subdued by
Parma, had the Synod at Ghent asked for measures to be taken
against the 'mass-priests' in the Flemish countryside ; so, at this
moment, were the Reformed Synods in all the seven provinces to
which the Union had been reduced admonishing States assemblies
and town governments to deal more severely with 'superstitions,
idolatries, abuses and profanations'.

> It would be particularly helpful in this matter [this is how the
> Utrecht commission put it] if all those in charge of churches were
> ordered by edict or otherwise to have their churches purged with-
> out delay of what remains of altars and other relics and rubbish of
> papism. Also, the superstitious ringing of bells at noon and in the
> evening should be put a stop to.

It is clear that after the first spontaneous phase under Spanish
oppression the progress of the Reformation had taken on an
entirely different character. It is clear that the majority of the
North-Netherlandish people abandoned the Catholic faith only
under pressure from above.

This lability of conditions in the religious sphere, which enabled the contending secular powers to bring about such re-alignments, did not, however, last indefinitely. It was itself a historically-determined phenomenon. As soon as the Counter-Reformation had got a hold on a Catholic population here or there, in Brabant, or in an eastern province, the latter proved immune to Protestant propaganda even when backed by the full force of the state. In the Netherlands the Counter-Reformation was long delayed by the troubles. It was only in the wake of Parma's conquests that it made its entry, and it finally got going in real earnest only under the Archduke Albert and Isabella. This explains why regions that were added to the territory of the Republic only after the Truce (that is to say, after 1621) have remained more homogeneously Catholic than any that belonged to the Union from the beginning. The larger part of the present province of North-Brabant and the Limburg town of Maastricht were not conquered by the Stadholder Frederick Henry until the 1620s and 1630s. These districts were never admitted to the Union or to representation on The Hague States-General ; they were held as 'Generality Lands', administered from The Hague. They remained, and still are, almost solidly Catholic.

A curious case is presented by two districts situated north of the great rivers, in the extreme east, Grol (in Gelderland) and Oldenzaal (in Overijsel). I mentioned Spinola's attack from the eastern borderland on these two provinces in 1605. Grol and Oldenzaal remained in Spanish hands all through the Twelve Years' Truce that soon followed (from 1609 to 1621), and were not recaptured for the Republic until after the Truce, in 1627, by Frederick Henry. They were therefore exposed to the Counter-Reformation influences patronized by the Archdukes, and it proved no easy matter to bring their citizenry back into the Reformed Church. Both towns, with their surrounding districts, are preponderantly Catholic to this day.

A number of reflections might be made. Let me confine myself to one final remark, the purpose of which will be simply to underline the special significance of what I have been trying to bring out all along.

To argue as if the Catholicism of the present-day Flemings and the Protestantism of the present-day Dutch (or of a majority of them) are evidence that the two halves of the Dutch-speaking people must have differed in character or in culture even before the religious divergence took effect, or was brought about, in the late sixteenth century, testifies to a thoroughly unhistorical attitude of mind, however numerous the historians who have in the past argued in that way.

III

Frederick Henry of Orange and King Charles I,
1641–1647
(1923)

THE interests of Orange and Stuart first became entangled
through the marriage of Frederick Henry's only son, William,
to Mary, the eldest daughter of Charles I, which took place in
May 1641 in the chapel of the palace at Whitehall. It is not
difficult to indicate the reasons that led Frederick Henry to seek
this alliance. He was actuated by purely dynastic considerations.
He hoped that if he could link the name of Orange with a royal
line it would mean an accession not only of prestige but of power
in the Republic. The prerogatives of the Stadholder were ill-
defined, and in the struggle with the burgher-oligarchy of Holland, high titles, military fame and the splendour of court life
played no small part.

When, in 1625, Frederick Henry had succeeded his brother
Maurice, he had had to proceed very carefully. It was a serious
time for the Republic. From its renewal in 1621, the war with
Spain had gone badly, adding fresh dangers to those left by the
bitter quarrels between strict Calvinists and Arminians for which
the Twelve Years' Truce is memorable. The new Stadholder,
whose sympathies had been with the vanquished party rather
than with his brother, was cautious in openly displaying his leanings. At one moment it seemed as though the stadholderate
would spontaneously adapt itself to the supremacy of the States.
Frederick Henry was not only courteous and affable ; he was
subservient. He adopted a genial tone with the patricians of
Holland, declaring that he had 'no taste for German pomp', but
that he was a Hollander like themselves, 'born at Delft'.[1]

With the first successes on the battlefield the position changed. Little by little Frederick Henry's authority in the state increased, and soon it appeared that he was far more intent on making his power felt than Maurice had been before him. Maurice had seized power, which lay ready to his hand, only when his passions were roused by a violent political crisis, and then only to let it slip almost heedlessly from his grasp again as soon as he had gained his end.

Not so Frederick Henry. He worked consciously and steadily, albeit patiently and cautiously, toward the strengthening of his position, and, again unlike Maurice, he had a son ; he worked not for himself alone, but for his house. He made use of all the resources offered him by the peculiar constitution of the Republic. By the distribution of offices he won for himself partisans in every quarter. The permanent committees that played such an important part in the administration of the Dutch Republic were devoted to his interests, and in more than one province he had his confidants, who at his will and through his protection could sway their respective provincial States assemblies.

In particular, Frederick Henry turned his earnest attention to the composition of the States-General. The deputies were usually appointed for long periods, and it was an easy matter for him to exercise considerable influence, at least upon the representatives of the inland provinces, most of whom were nobles and depended on his favour for the military careers of their sons and near relations. Far removed from their principals, who, moreover, were in session only for a few weeks in the year, they were able to follow their own, or rather, the Prince's, will much more easily than could the Hollanders, who, as the States-General met in The Hague, were always under the eyes of their masters, the States of Holland. When in the course of time, for the sake of speed and secrecy, the custom had crept in of allowing the Stadholder to decide important questions of foreign policy with a committee of the States-General, meeting in his 'cabinet', Frederick Henry had little difficulty in finding men for this body who were ready to follow his lead. In this way he came near to being possessed of supreme power.

In June 1634 this Secret Committee (*Secreet Besogne*), which had until then borne a purely informal character, was placed on a somewhat firmer basis. A resolution was passed authorizing the Prince to have minutes of the decisions arrived at in the Committee kept by the greffier of the States-General and laying it down that these decisions would be as valid as if they had been taken in the full assembly. The States-General did not, naturally, completely relinquish their control of foreign policy : it rested with them to 'defer', or not to 'defer', a question to the Committee. It must have been difficult, however, for it to resume a matter once 'deferred' because the secrecy applied also — indeed that was what mattered — to the principals.[2] So far did the Prince's influence reach already that the States often allowed him to select (to 'assume' was the current term) deputies for the Committee himself.[3]

For a number of years there had been very little difference of opinion concerning the lines of national policy, so that the Stadholder could be regarded as the natural leader. This had enabled him quietly to pave the way for his advancement to a position of real power. Curiously enough, at the moment of this important step, when the Secret Committee was established more firmly and at the same time largely fell under the Prince's control, there was already growing dissension over the plan of an alliance with France, the object of which was to be the final conquest of the Spanish Netherlands, which were then to be partitioned between the two powers. There were many who considered this a dangerous policy. *Gallum amicum non vicinum* was the cry raised at Amsterdam. Peace with Spain, leaving the Spanish Netherlands as a buffer between the Republic and France, seemed to these men preferable. But Frederick Henry managed to get the policy of war in conjunction with France adopted : the Secret Committee, just established, proved an efficient tool in his hands, and the decision, which was one of great consequence, in itself again strengthened, for the time being, his position. Richelieu's gratitude expressed itself by his addressing Frederick Henry by the title of 'Highness', whereas hitherto, like his brother and father, he had had to be content with 'Excellency'. This, too, was an important step, without which the next, the royal marriage, would probably have been impossible. Moreover, the confidential understanding with the French ambassadors strengthened the Prince's position in foreign politics.

Thus, from the moment when this question came to the fore, a renewal of the opposition to the Stadholder can be observed, but it was of an entirely different character from the movement in the days of Maurice. It was not directed merely against some definite policy; it was inspired no less by concern over the growth of stadholderly power as such. All over Europe sovereign rulers were struggling for absolute power with assemblies that held fast to their ancient privileges. In France Richelieu did the work for his King with marked success — Richelieu, who in 1635 had entered into such close relations with Frederick Henry, and who, doubtless of set purpose, did all in his power to reinforce the monarchical principle in the Republic. In England Charles I had been carrying on an arbitrary régime without a parliament, and when at length he was obliged to summon one, it was only to enter into bitter conflict with it. And it was with Charles I — a prince so much a monarchist that, speaking to a Dutch ambassador, he described the Dutch government, quite calmly and without a thought of discourtesy, as 'a populace without discretion' [4] — it was with Charles that Frederick Henry was now seeking an intimate connection, one that was still further to increase the prestige of Orange; by many at the English court it was even regarded as preliminary to a *coup d'état* whereby the Stadholder would be transformed from a servant of the States to soveriegn of the country.[5]

No more is needed to account for the fact that the regent class of the Netherlands, and especially of the wealthy trading province of Holland, did not take kindly to the English marriage plan. This royal connection did far more than had the French alliance to loose a storm of opposition against the Stadholder in his latter years. Indeed, what made it the more serious for him was the fact that the intimacy with the Stuarts was palpably at variance with national interests : it was so obviously a purely dynastic move. Neither Frederick Henry nor William II after him could in pursuing this policy count absolutely on that popularity with the Calvinist middle-class which was since the days of Maurice among the greatest assets of the Prince of Orange in their struggles with the States of Holland. The army, of course, never failed to support them, nor the nobility, especially the poor gentry of the inland provinces, who were closely connected with the army and who moreover looked to the Stadholder for help against the ambitions of the towns represented in their States assemblies.

It was through them that Frederick Henry, for his part, had so great a hold over the States-General. If in that assembly the smaller provinces generally stood by the Stadholder's policy and the centre of gravity of the opposition against him was always to be found in Holland, it is by no means necessary to assume that the interests of these provinces really were best served by the Stadholder's policy, which meant first, war with Spain, and soon after, as we shall see, war with England. It meant only that Holland, the wealthiest province by far, with the strongest and most self-confident burgher-class, represented that element in the Republic that was sufficiently independent to stand up against the encroachments of the Stadholder's power.

At the time when Frederick Henry on behalf of his son made overtures to Charles I for the hand of one of his daughters, Charles's leanings were much more towards Spain than towards Spain's enemies, France and the United Netherlands. In 1635 the plans of these two countries to divide the Southern Netherlands between themselves had had a very disquieting effect at the English court, and in 1637 the King declared to the Comte d'Estrades that he would do all in his power to oppose the conquest of the Flemish coast. True, as a result of the growing internal dissensions in England and the revolt brewing in Scotland, his power appeared to be extremely limited. He certainly had, with the help of the levy of ship money, equipped a fleet, but in 1639 it proved beyond his power to avenge the disgrace of the Downs, when the Dutch admiral Tromp had fallen upon the Spanish expeditionary fleet in English waters, where it had expected to be safe. The attitude of the English government about this affair had been so ambiguous that in Holland it was at first suspected and afterward generally believed that England had undertaken to support the Spanish enterprise.[6] The suspicion was in fact groundless, but Charles I was certainly anxious to curry favour with Spain. His favourite project in those days — it had been his father's before him — was to negotiate Spanish marriages for his children. Above all his wife, Henrietta Maria, a sister of the reigning King of France, strengthened him in this resolve, and her friend, the Duchesse de Chevreuse, who was a sworn enemy of Richelieu, acted as go-between. Under these circumstances, the French government could hardly regard the English court as anything but hostile. There is no conclusive proof that Richelieu actually supported the Scottish rising of 1639, but he certainly did maintain friendly relations [7] with the English parliamentary opposition when, in the following year, it was able to make itself felt again and still further paralysed Charles I's capacity for action.

It was in these days that the idea of a marriage between Frederick Henry's son and one of the daughters of Charles I was mooted once more. The subject had been first discussed with the Queen's mother, Marie de Médicis,[8] the Queen Mother of France — no friend of Richelieu's either — during her stay in Holland in 1638. In the following year Jan van der Kerckhoven, lord of Heenvliet, who happened to have been presented to Marie de Médicis, was sent to England as the Prince's private envoy, with secret instructions [9] to enter into negotiations about the project. He had made little progress when, in February 1640, Frederick Henry requested Aerssens van Sommelsdijk, who was then in England on a special mission on the part of the States-General, to come to an understanding with Heenvliet and to try to further the matter.[10]

It was Sommelsdijk's official mission to explain the motives that had led to the action of the States-General at the Downs ; at the same time he was to investigate the possibilities of a treaty with England. What he had had to report concerning the attitude of the court was not, however, very encouraging, and when Frederick Henry's request reached him he had just, in exasperation, begged the Stadholder insistently to arrange for his recall, as he suspected that his presence in England and the proposals he had to make were merely being used to force the hand of Spain, whose help was looked for against the Scots. Sommelsdijk was enough of a statesman to have protested vigorously, in a letter to Frederick Henry himself, when it appeared that it had been hinted to the King (apparently by Heenvliet in his zeal for the matrimonial plan) [11] that the Dutch ambassador was not merely to justify the battle of the Downs, as was prescribed in his instructions from the States-General, but also to apologize for it. At the same time he was too much of a courtier not to accede with zeal, even with gratitude, to the request to take over the marriage negotiations. (The regular ambassador from the States-General, Joachimi, who had been in England for many years and was by now a very old man, hardly took part in these matters. He was a refugee from Flanders and a States of Holland man rather than an Orangist.)

One might imagine that a Dutch statesman, especially one who belonged to the Orange party, that is to say, the party that believed in war *à outrance* with Spain, would try to use the marriage plan for an attempt to divert England from Spain. This was how the Orangist people regarded the matter.[12] Sommelsdijk himself did in fact express this point of view on a number of occasions.[13] But could he seriously have supposed, after the experience he had just had of the temper prevailing at the English court, that this could possibly be the result? The suggested connection would involve, not the conferring of a favour on the King by the Stadholder, but the reverse.[14] As early as January, when Sommelsdijk, although he had not then been asked to do so, was already doing his best to further Frederick Henry's

design, he had with striking lucidity pointed out this fact to
Charles I himself:

> By this marriage you will gain for yourself a first claim on the
> affections and interests of His Highness and the United Provinces,
> while if you seek kinship with a house of greater power than your
> own [Spain], you can expect nothing from their ambitions, but will
> only lose your daughter, whom you will force into wedding interests
> opposed to your own.[15]

The questionable character, from the Dutch national point
of view, of a dynastic relationship between Stuart and Orange
could not be better expressed. Again and again in generations
to come the danger was to arise that this relationship might place
the lesser of the two united houses in a position of dependence.
Heenvliet in fact had been instructed to assure the King in the
most respectful manner that the Prince, his consort and his son
would never forget the great favour of this connection, but that
he, Frederick Henry, would on the contrary 'acknowledge it by
his services whenever it might please His Majesty to let him
know his commands'.[16]

But Sommelsdijk at least wished to make one stipulation. He
wished that only the eldest daughter should be accepted. That
would at any rate rule out the possibility of a Spanish marriage,
for Spain would certainly not condescend to take the second
daughter if the eldest had been allotted to the Prince of Orange.
But, no doubt for the same reason, the English court was only
prepared to enter into negotiations involving the second daughter.
Sommelsdijk saw in this the design of the two Queens, whose
plan was to pave the way for a Spanish marriage for the eldest
by means of a Protestant alliance for the second daughter.[17] He
even feared, as he had done about the political treaty, that the
whole negotiation was meant only to put pressure upon Spain.[18]
If it was only possible to get a second daughter, he said finally,
then he was for a marriage with a French princess.[19] Certainly
a French connection was much more in keeping with the policy
represented by Orange at that juncture, but Frederick Henry had

set his heart on a marriage with a king's daughter and decided to take the second daughter if the eldest was not available.

Thus when the matter was settled in principle at the end of 1640, it was the second daughter of Charles I, Elizabeth, a child only five years old, who was designated as the future bride of William II. The final negotiations were carried on by a formal embassy from the States-General, which had been officially informed by Frederick Henry in December 1640 : the position of the Stadholder approached nearly enough to that of a monarch for the marriage of his son to be regarded as a matter of state. So Sommelsdijk, who was a member of this new mission also, could now give even more positive assurances that the friendship of the Prince of Orange meant the friendship of the Republic. Yet Frederick Henry at the same time sent Beverweert to France, where the English marriage project was naturally causing uneasiness, to explain that it was a private matter and had nothing to do with the policy of the Republic.

If the ambassadors, in January 1641, listened to English proposals for a treaty between the two countries, that was not really in conflict with the view expressed to France. The ambassadors were expressly instructed to do what they could to separate England from Spain, and it was the popular interpretation of the marriage plan that it would serve that very purpose. The question is only, how far did the royal negotiators actually represent the King's intention? or even, how sincere was the King himself when he assured his Parliament that he meant to go in that direction?[20] The prevailing opinion in the House no doubt was all for that policy. But was it not Charles's intention merely to use the name of Orange as a sop to irritated Protestant opinion, and this without loosening his contact with Spain?

Domestic difficulties were beginning to overwhelm the King. Shortly before the arrival of the Dutch ambassadors, after over eleven years during which he had ruled without a parliament (except for the so-called Short Parliament of April and May 1640), he had had to summon another parliament, and this assembly (the Long Parliament as it was later to be called), using to the full the

King's impotence as shown against the Scottish Covenant army in the north of England, had at once opened a deliberate attack upon the monarchical régime. Charles's advisers, Strafford and Laud had already been arrested; Windebank and Finch had fled. Yet Charles did not for a moment think of adopting a Protestant, anti-Spanish policy, which would have swelled the pride of his new parliamentary advisers. On the contrary, to him the marriage still was what Sommelsdijk had led him to hope it would be : a way to gain the good offices of the Prince of Orange. And as things then were, this was a prospect not to be despised.

Great as it was, Charles I had certainly an exaggerated idea of the power of the Stadholder.[21] He thought, and Sommelsdijk did nothing to disabuse him, that the Prince could manipulate the foreign policy of the Republic at his will, and that he would be in a position to give effective help in the English domestic troubles. Charles was now willing to give his eldest daughter to the young Prince of Orange.[22]

Thus, even before it took place, the significance of the marriage was entirely changed ; but Frederick Henry was in no wise daunted by that. At the very moment when Sommelsdijk was beginning to realize that the upheavals and divisions in England were too serious to allow a political treaty to be thought of, the marriage united the Stadholderly power in the Republic, not with England as a whole, but with one of the parties contending for power, and with that which was for long to fare the worst. On February 12 the contract was signed.[23]

When young William of Orange came over and the marriage with Mary took place (early in May 1641), the royal family was going through the deep humiliation of Strafford's trial. Mary herself, in spite of her youth, had been present with her parents during the tragic proceedings in Parliament.[24] A few days before the marriage ceremony the Lower House had passed the bill of attainder against Strafford ; a few days after, it passed the Upper House. Even before William (who had to leave his bride behind for the time being) had left the country, the King had given his assent to the bill. It was indeed a far from propitious moment for a union with the Stuarts. The English people, who not so long before would have welcomed the Protestant marriage with enthusiasm as a sign that the King was turning away from Spain, now regarded it with suspicion, fearing that Charles had stipulated for help against his subjects.[25]

Sommelsdijk felt by no means sure that the marriage between the children would not in due time be annulled by the English, seeing the obstinate resistance to all requests that the nine-year-old Mary accompany her husband to Holland. Others, too, regarded this as suspicious. As long as 'the bride is not aboard',[26] ran the opinion of Reigersberch, the brother-in-law of Grotius, it was useless to hope for anything from the marriage ; and that, he argued, was to the advantage of England, which would be able to extort still further benefits. When, in October, the question of a new embassy to England arose, one ostensibly to negotiate an alliance but in reality to bring about the *domiductio*, Reigersberch feared that the English would want to 'make use of this goad a little longer',[27] and he expressed anxiety that negotiations carried on in such circumstances would not be very favourable to the interests of his country. But as regards the country where the girl wife was to reside, at any rate, there soon was to be no question any more. The course of events was such that Charles had no choice in the matter. In 1641 his cause went from bad to worse. Finally, at the beginning of 1642, civil war came. Charles had to leave London, and he sent his wife, Henrietta Maria, with the Princess Royal to their new friends in Holland.

In announcing the intended journey to the States-General Charles's resident, Sir William Boswell, said that Charles was sending his daughter over as a token of his friendship for the Netherlands and that her mother was coming to bear her company. As a matter of fact, fear for the safety of his wife, a Roman Catholic whose strong personality had made her the soul of the anti-parliamentary party, was the main motive of Charles's decision. The journey was a flight. Yet at the same time

Henrietta Maria meant, as we shall see, to seek help in the Netherlands.

Instead of bringing the dowry stipulated in the marriage contract, she carried with her the crown jewels, which she hoped to pawn in Holland. She was moreover to try to get war material shipped from the Netherlands to England and to obtain leave for English officers and men in the States' service to return for action under the King's standard.

The two royal ladies who landed in the Netherlands under such unhappy circumstances were received with great display. All that they now brought to the House of Orange was their royal blood. Frederick Henry was all the more zealous in seeing that this should receive due homage. If we are to believe a royalist writer of the period, he himself never entered the presence of his daughter-in-law, then a child of ten, 'but with a reverence more like a subject towards his sovereign than the freedom of a father towards his son's wife'.[28] In fact, he arranged in every detail the formalities with which the Princess Royal was to be treated now that she was delivered into the hands of the Orange family, and these were all calculated to lay continual stress on her rank.[29] On the English side too, great care had been taken that her rank should be maintained.

It was by no means a small household that was considered necessary for the King's daughter. It had been stipulated in the marriage contract that she was to be allowed forty English servants, in the appointment of whom the House of Orange had no say, although it had to bear the cost. At the head of her household, it is true, Charles I, acting on the powers he had under the contract, had placed a Dutchman,[30] that same Heenvliet who had been used by Frederick Henry in the negotiations for the marriage. But the ambitious Heenvliet — he was the son of a Leyden professor of theology and had himself bought the manor of Heenvliet — had given a pledge of his attachment to the English royal family. Shortly before — his first wife having died in March 1640 [31] — he had married an English widow of position, Lady Stanhope, and his ambitions were now centred in

English titles and English property. Lady Stanhope (she continued to bear that name after her second marriage) was appointed governess to the young bride.

The retinue of eighty persons which Mary brought with her from England was modest compared with the three hundred followers by whom, according to Aitzema, her mother was attended. Frederick Henry paid for the upkeep of her court with resignation — for it practically all fell on him. The States occasionally chafed at their share, especially when the Queen 'for her amusement' travelled through the province 'at the country's expense, with a retinue of 600 persons'.[32] (Such is the number given, but this probably included the Stadholder's court.)

The people were dazzled by the splendour of English royalty. In particular, the ceremonial reception at Amsterdam made an impression. To that town the Princess, accompanied by the Stadholder and his son, paid a visit in May. In the allegorical scenes that, according to the taste of the day, formed part of the celebrations, reference was made to marriages of Counts of Holland and Gelderland with English princesses; and thus already the Prince of Orange was ranked with the former sovereigns of the country. Vondel's voice, too, is heard in heartfelt jubilation; in one breath he speaks of the children of kings and those of princes as

> . . . those who by God to Godhead are ordained
> To serve the common weal.[33]

Even Hooft — the scion of an Amsterdam regent family — who in that year dedicated his *Historiën* to the Prince, not, of course, omitting a reference to the 'royal bridegroom', refers to himself as the Prince's 'subject', as though he had for the moment forgotten the sovereignty of the States.

All this was just what Frederick Henry had intended. But the situation was not without its ugly aspects. Not only did the royal child prove a far-from-docile member of the Orange household — before the year 1642 was out, there are reports of a violent scene in which she showed her mother-in-law her 'contempt, hatred, and dissatisfaction' [34] — but the effect on the public, too, was far from being unmixed. The people might revel in the display, but that did not alter the fact that the papist Queen was far from popular. Events in England were followed with interest,[35] and sympathies were almost universally on the side of the Parliament.

The religious factor alone was enough to account for that. Even Dr. Rivet, young William's tutor, had been unable, during his stay in England in connection with his pupil's marriage, to disguise his sympathies with the parliamentary party.[36] It is true that he never dared to give open expression to them,[37] but clerics less closely connected with the court were not so scrupulous. In particular the Synod of Zeeland expressed itself more than once, and its letters were very welcome to the Presbyterian party in its struggle both with Episcopalians and Independents. They were in fact inspired by the minister of the Scottish Staple at Middelburg (Spang was his name),[38] by means of whom the Scottish Presbyterians kept in touch with the Dutch Reformed Church. And, indeed, the Synod of South Holland, too, learned 'with joy' that the Synod of Westminster had put before Parliament 'a certain project of church government, agreeing practically on most points with the government of the Reformed churches in this country'.[39] Nor did the Dutch Reformed in those years, 1644 and 1645, confine their sympathy for the cause of their foreign co-religionists to words. The Dutch Church sanctioned a collection for 'the oppressed Protestants in Ireland', which brought in 300,000 guilders.[40] Later, when enthusiasm had cooled under the influence of the rise of the Independents and of the war with the English Commonwealth (in 1652), one pamphleteer recalls with bitterness that 'we prayed for them in the churches', and he reproaches the rebels because 'they had used the money collected for them in our country in the struggle against their lawful sovereign'.[41] Whether the generous donors in the years 1644 and 1645 would have minded that so much is a matter of doubt.

In any case it is natural that the bishops and their ceremonial should appear hateful to the Dutch Calvinists, and the papist Henrietta Maria was not the ambassador best fitted to make them acceptable. Thus it came about that it was especially the ministers of religion, in other respects the most loyal adherents of the House of Orange,[42] who shook their heads over the Stuart connection. In England the religious factor was bound up with the political issue in much the same way as had been the case in the Dutch war of liberation. Reference to this resemblance was one of the favourite forms of propaganda of the parliamentary party in the Netherlands,[43] propaganda that was certainly the more effectual in that it was known how Charles had looked to Spain as long as he felt sufficiently independent.

But this traditional Calvinist and democratic aversion to despotism was now linked with the republican sentiment of the regent class, which before long expressed itself in an unwillingness to make the liberal donations to the young couple upon which the Orangists had counted,[44] and which is reflected in the caustic observations of Aitzema on the pretensions of the English, their greed for money, etc. The Honourable Members bowed down to the Queen, they kissed the hem of her garment,[45] but none the less they felt uneasy about the royalist invasion, and this feeling was not lessened by the suspicion, soon to be confirmed, that it was not merely a harmless, if annoying, exhibition, but a move in the Prince of Orange's game.[46]

On the very day of the royal personages' arrival a dispute is said to have arisen ; the story is too characteristic not to insert it here.[47] A supper was held, attended by a number of the English visitors as well as by States' officers and Holland regents. The Prince's health was drunk before that of the States-General, an irregular proceeding at which the regents present showed their displeasure : the Prince, so they said, was their servant and stood in their pay. A French captain of horse retorted that a Prince who had just married his son to 'a daughter of England, granddaughter of France' should be ashamed to pass for the servant of brewers, bakers and feltmakers. Judicial proceedings were said to have resulted. The contrast between

E

Orange and the oligarchy is seen to be taking on a sharper edge!

The royal alliance certainly gave birth to a universal suspicion that the Stadholder was aiming at sovereign power.[48] All the more closely was his foreign policy watched. And here the oligarchy and the Calvinist commonalty — a rare occurrence in Dutch history — found common ground in their disapproval of his policy. Under the peculiar conditions of government in the Republic, only the States of Holland, as I have already pointed out, could offer any effective resistance. But on this occasion they could count upon much more moral support than in most of their conflicts with the Princes of Orange. Thus among the first fruits of Frederick Henry's dynastic triumph must be counted not only the fact that new life was infused into the opposition of the States of Holland to the stadholderate,[49] but also the fact that they appeared against him as the defenders of a national policy.

The issue was one of no small importance : it was whether, in the struggle between the King of England and the Parliament, which broke out openly in August 1642, the Netherlands should remain neutral or should range themselves on the King's side, at least to the extent of giving him secret support. Holland was powerful enough to secure the acknowledgement of neutrality as the official policy of the States ; [50] it was, indeed, unmistakably in the national interest. But Frederick Henry, on his part, was sufficiently powerful, supported as he was by most of the smaller provinces and by some officials and even colleges of the Generality, constantly to obstruct or evade the official policy. The result was that, although it was impossible to give the King the effective aid on which he had counted, so that in the end his ruin was not prevented,[51] the Parliament was nevertheless given abundant cause for violent resentment.[52]

The chief care of Henrietta Maria and her advisers during their stay in the Netherlands was to put the King in a position to defend himself, to help him with money, troops and munitions. The support given by Frederick Henry was certainly valuable. He was the only man of any power on the Continent prepared to exert himself on behalf of the King's cause — Henrietta Maria knew full well that she could expect nothing from her brother, the King of France, and his government. Without the Stadholder's help Charles I could not have held out so long. Indeed, Frederick Henry's services were far from small. Not only did he bear the burden of Henrietta Maria's retinue, but he took immediate steps to borrow for her on his own credit a sum of 300,000 guilders, and this at a time when his own income was no longer adequate for his standard of living.[53] As Captain-General of the States' army, moreover, he could render the King great service by allowing English officers serving under him to join the royalist army.[54] Thus it was that in August 1642 Charles's nephew Prince Rupert left the Republic with his brother Maurice and a following of some hundred officers. Frederick Henry even placed one of the country's warships at their disposal when it proved difficult to find a means of transport.[55] Moreover, in spite of the scruples of the responsible official,[56] he allowed guns from the country's arsenal to be sold to the royalists.

This was not enough. One of the main things the Queen had to do in the Netherlands was to raise a loan on the crown jewels, which were valued [57] at a sum of 1,265,300 guilders. It was no easy undertaking. The bankers thought the stones too large, and they did not in general care to do business with princes; but the greatest difficulty was that the Parliament had made a serious protest to Joachimi that the Queen had no authority to dispose of the jewels. Heenvliet, who represented the Prince with the Queen in Holland (the Prince himself had been with the army in the field since June), did all he could by interceding with men of experience and influence, but it soon became clear that the transaction was impossible unless the Prince was willing to raise a loan on the jewels in Amsterdam in his own name, and thus run directly counter to a protest of the Parliament. Heenvliet had once declared to the Queen [58] that it would not do openly to provide arms from the arsenals while preparations were being made for mediation between the contending parties in England, that this would be 'procéder contre

la foy publique et tout honneur'. Whether it was any more loyal
or honourable to do it in an underhand way is a moot point ; but
the raising of a loan on the crown jewels in Amsterdam in the
Prince's name — for Frederick Henry succumbed to the entreaties
of the Queen, faithfully repeated to him by Heenvliet — was done
more or less publicly.

Was Frederick Henry won over by the power of her pathetic
entreaties, or was he moved by the reproaches that Henrietta
Maria, proud and passionate, did not spare him? The promise of
fresh favours carried more persuasive power than the reference
to those already granted, now that the little Princess had been
delivered up irrevocably to the house of Orange,[59] and undoubtedly more also than the pressure the child herself had at
times to exert at the instance of her despairing parents.[60] If the
Prince and his Consort Amalia of Solms (for express mention is
frequently made of her zeal,[61] and it is well known how ambitious
she was) took so much trouble to satisfy the Queen, if they
suffered her vehemence and her threats, if they led the Republic
again and again to the brink of a breach with the Parliament and
were ready to bear the brunt of a bitter contest with the States
of Holland, it was above all because the prospect was held out
to them of a second marriage, a marriage between the Prince of
Wales and their daughter, Louise Henrietta.

Their daughter to be Queen of England — even in the perilous circumstances in which the Stuarts found themselves, this
seemed to the Prince and Princess well worth all that unpleasant-
ness and even the lowering of the prestige of Orange with the
Calvinists at home. While still in England, Henrietta Maria had
broached the idea with Heenvliet. Now, in conjunction with the
Queen's councillors, Goring and Jermyn, they worked together
continuously to win over the Prince. Jermyn, wrote Heenvliet,
was urging the affair of the jewels and the permission for officers
and soldiers : 'il mesle tousjours parmy son discours l'affaire que
V.A. sçait.'[62] He did not do it very delicately either, but said
quite bluntly, as Heenvliet reported, 'that the one thing would
be done in return for the other and not for nothing.' This was

why Heenvliet was always anxious lest the Queen should be dis-
pleased (at least if for a moment his personal interests are left
out of account),[63] and this it was that led him to 'make excuses'
for the States of Holland [64] and to speak so highly of the good
disposition of the Prince. And this also was why the Prince,
as he himself expressed it, did 'the impossible' in order to please
her.[65]

The most important question during the Queen's stay in
Holland (she returned in March 1643, after the loan on the jewels)
— the question, too, that led to the first serious clash of the
Prince of Orange and his adherents with the States of Holland —
was in connection with the export of the arms and munitions that
had been bought for the King in the Netherlands, and with that
question was bound up the question of the attitude to be adopted
towards Strickland, the envoy whom the Parliament had sent to
the Netherlands in September 1642 expressly to prevail upon the
States to forbid the traffic. Heenvliet was taken aback by the
Queen's excitement at the appearance of 'this person' — an excitement that grew to a pitch when the States-General received
him, not, it is true, in a full assembly, but through a deputation
from all the provinces — and listened to his message. The
crucial item in this was a complaint that a number of ships laden
with munitions for the King's army had been equipped in Dutch
harbours; several were at that very moment lying ready for
departure. The majority of the States-General had only reluctantly decided to receive the envoy. They had at first tried to
escape from the necessity by raising all sorts of pretexts, and
immediately after having given way, in order to soften the impression of their action, they had given a ceremonious reception
to one of the King's ambassadors who was passing through the
country.[66]

It is not surprising that the States-General dared not offer an
affront to the Parliament. Its dominance was now assured over
the greater, or at least, the more important, part of England, and
above all, it was powerful at sea — and the Parliament men were
at least as anxious as had been the Kings to watch over the trading

and colonial interests of England. In Joachimi's correspondence, for all that he avoided contacts with the Parliament as much as he could, there are repeated reports of complaints and threats laid before him by the new officeholders in connection with such matters. The Prince and his supporters, who were not in ordinary circumstances primarily concerned about the interests of Holland trade, did not now miss an occasion to point out how detrimental it would be to allow the English Parliament to come out on top. The Hollanders retorted that the Parliament's irritability over such issues was in reality due to the unfair and offensive treatment it received at the hands of the Orangist States-General. They insisted therefore that attention be paid to the complaints of Strickland, and knowing well that no determined action on the part of the States-General was to be expected in this matter, the States of Holland took the matter into their own hands and themselves ordered the detention of the ships to which Strickland had referred, all of which were making ready in Holland ports.

This roused the Queen to fury, and she was in no wise to be soothed by the circumstance that the Hollanders, once they had embarked on investigations, discovered also ships destined for the Parliament, and ordered that these should be detained with the others, because, they said, they wished to observe neutrality.[67] It was precisely this equality of treatment which she felt to be insulting. She called Frederick Henry to her assistance with the loudest complaints and reproaches.

The States [she declared to Heenvliet] had promised that the marriage alliance should not be the concern merely of His Highness but also of the state; but they are not acting up to this.[68]

The Prince, reminded in this way of the ambiguous assurances of Sommelsdijk, could hardly do less than admit that the Hollanders had been mistaken in their action,[69] but all the same, he could not change the policy of neutrality. Theoretically there might be something to be said for the view that it was only to the King that the Republic was bound by treaties,[70] but actually it was impossible to identify the King with England any longer now that the power of the Parliament had become so great and tangible a reality.

Small wonder, then, that throughout this affair Holland enjoyed the support of Zeeland, although in the States of this province the Stadholder, in his capacity of first noble and lord of the two towns of Veere and Flushing, had an exceptionally strong position. So high did resentment run over the way in which the States-General allowed themselves to be managed by the Prince, that there was some talk of a closer association between the two seaboard provinces, and even of secession. The Grand Pensionary of Zeeland and the First Noble's representative, De Knuyt, exchanged acrimonious words in the provincial States assembly. But all things considered, the Prince's policy was so impossible that he could not maintain it in the States-General.

On November 1, 1642, Their High Mightinesses issued a general proclamation forbidding the export of arms to either of the contending parties. Thus the principle maintained by Holland was definitely accepted as an article of federal policy, and Strickland had gained an important success.[71]

Yet the Prince continued to work against it in an underhand way, and as several of the smaller provinces and some of the administrative colleges of the Generality were devoted to him, he was able to do so with no little effect. The greffier of the States-General, the notorious Cornelis Musch, a great friend of Heenvliet according to the latter's own statement,[72] was invaluable as an agent for invalidating the resolutions ordering the detention of munitions ships which his masters, to keep up appearances, were every now and again obliged to issue. Strickland felt greatly aggrieved by his attitude.[73] He took to heart even more the treatment he was to receive, in the beginning of December, at the hands of Renswoude, one of the gentlemen, be it noted, who shortly before had been appointed to take part in a mediatory embassy (about which more hereafter).[74] Strickland went to him on one occasion when he happened to be 'President of the Week' (of the States-General) to talk to him about some ships at Medemblik which were to transport officers and two to three hundred men besides twenty guns. Without even looking at the note that Strickland had handed to him, Renswoude declared that Strickland could not prove the facts of his complaint and demanded the name of his informant. But, writes Strickland, no English or Dutch merchant would have cared to be mentioned as informant for fear of the displeasure of 'great ones'. So angry was he that he told his government he could be of no use in the Netherlands unless it was made clear that there must be an end of such treatment. Probably with a view to mollifying him, the Prince himself received Strickland when the latter came to him shortly after this incident with a letter from the Parliament.[75] But this roused the anger of Henrietta Maria — to such an extent that the Prince instructed his confidants to declare that Strickland had taken him by surprise and that he should not be received again.

Soon after this a far more serious clash took place between the Parliament's envoy and the States-General. The Queen had at last taken her leave — to the relief of the States-General, says the Venetian ambassador in England, and we can well believe him! But even her departure was accompanied by dissonance and friction. With the ship in which on February 28, 1643, she crossed to England, there sailed another, crammed full with arms and soldiers. Parliament men-of-war had intended to intercept her at the mouth of the river Maas. But she was escorted by a Dutch fleet under Tromp, who had to defend her, even after her landing, against a bombardment by a Parliament squadron.[76] Shortly afterwards Strickland approached the States-General with the complaint that there were twenty-four ships lying at Dunkirk (in the Spanish Netherlands) all ready to sail out against the Parliament, and that the Prince of Orange had already given passports to two of them to enable them to get through the Dutch blockade. The Prince's attitude in the face of the danger that Spain might use Dunkirk as a base from which to help Charles I by sending support to the Catholic revolt in Ireland had for a long time past given rise to suspicion. But the Prince explicitly denied the imputation now made against him, and the States-General, packed with his supporters, resented so greatly the insult offered to the Stadholder that it looked for a time as though the incident would lead to a rupture of relations between the Republic and the Parliament. Once more, however, matters were smoothed over. The Parliament (where Tromp's statement that he had let the two ships pass on the strength of a letter of the Queen was met with scepticism : he must at least have had oral instructions from the Prince, so it was thought there) allowed itself to be pacified by 'letters from Holland'. Soon the Orange party tried to bring about the breach in another way.

Attempts to mediate between the contending parties seemed to offer an opportunity. As early as January 1642, Joachimi as the Republic's ambassador in England had been instructed to make an offer of mediation. But Joachimi was not the man the royalists wanted. The States-General would have liked to give him the support of Heenvliet, who was at that moment still at the English court in the capacity of envoy from the Prince of Orange. Holland, however, refused to agree to this because mediation through Heenvliet would have been tantamount to choosing sides. The Prince of Orange endeavoured nevertheless to induce Joachimi to submit to the co-operation of Heenvliet 'either in my name or otherwise'.[77] but the States of Holland had taken the precaution of informing Joachimi of their objection,[78] and so nothing came of the Prince's efforts. And in truth, when one sees what Heenvliet's conception of the task of a mediator was, it is difficult to do otherwise than applaud the Hollanders' discernment. Heenvliet objected to Joachimi's way of carrying out his work as mediator in the open. He, Heenvliet, would have begun with secret attempts, in consultation with the King, to lure certain gentlemen from the parliamentary party by offers of titles, offices and other favours.[79] Joachimi never got a chance, because soon he had to report that the parliamentary party would not hear of mediation at all.

Yet, when Henrietta Maria arrived at The Hague, a plan had

immediately been mooted to send a special embassy for this very purpose. Holland alone, basing its policy on reports from Joachimi 'that no mediator from this country would be pleasing to the Parliament',[80] held up the proposal in the States-General, but in May the province had to come into line — not, however, without making reservations.[81] One of these, namely, that the ambassadors should not attempt to sow dissensions among the members of the Parliament, shows that there were apprehensions that Heenvliet's methods might still be adopted. In fact, the gentlemen delegated for the embassy, William Boreel and Reede van Renswoude, both Orangists, notoriously inclined toward the royalist cause.[82]

But it was a long time before they set out on their mission. At first the English royalists in Holland, much to the annoyance of the Prince of Orange, would have nothing to do with the peace mission.[83] Later it was once more Holland that obstructed it. It was hinted in the States-General that Holland thought the continuation of the civil war would be advantageous to its trade ;[84] and Boswell, Charles's resident at The Hague, in the bitterness of his heart, made the same observation.[85] But it is not probable that it was this conviction that led the States of Holland to sabotage the mediation. Their principal objection was, without doubt, that an embassy over which the Prince of Orange had so much influence would inevitably get too closely involved with the royalist party and would lead the Netherlands into difficulties with the Parliament.

These were questions of great consequence. The English marriage and the resulting complications had placed the Stadholder in sharp contrast to a broad public opinion on issues of vital interest to the state as a whole. As always, it was first of all the States of Holland who disposed of the political power needed to switch over from disapproval to opposition, and inevitably they directed their attack against the personal authority over foreign policy which the Prince had been building up before he had discredited his person by indulging in dynastic ambitions. Holland could no longer leave any of the hotly contested issues concerning England to the decision of the Secret Committee, in which its deputy could be voted down by the Prince's other 'gentlemen of the cabinet' while remaining bound to secrecy with regard to his own 'principals'. We saw above that already in 1642 the province had ventured privately to warn the States-General's ambassador, Joachimi, not to accept Heenvliet as joint mediator. This was rather a strong step for the province to take. But it was inevitable that in the face of the English entanglement Holland should try all means to wrest the lead of national affairs from the Stadholder. His abuse of Generality powers — 'abuse' because of his dynastic aim as well as because of the methods of pressure and corruption applied to the deputies of the smaller provinces — could be most readily countered by Holland taking its stand on the principle of provincial sovereignty. This is what the States of Holland now did, with shattering effect on the Prince's policy. The private warning to Joachimi had been applauded by that staunch republican Van Reigersberch as a welcome 'sign of public vigour'. Yet he had gone on to speak slightingly of 'particular views' as the motive force behind that action and to deplore that this vigour 'was nowhere to be found in matters of greater importance and weight'.[86] In the next year he had nothing to complain of any more.

In August 1643, in fact, the States of Holland drew up a new instruction for their deputies on the States-General, upon which these gentlemen were to take an oath. It was intended to tie them more strictly than before to the directives of their States. In particular they were instructed not to act on a number of points without such directives, in the assembly of Their High Mightinesses *or elsewhere*. Among the points specified were:

> Peace or truce, war, negotiations with other potentates about alliance or aid, lands or cities . . . also the sending abroad of ambassadors or any notable deputation.

All the eighteen towns voted in favour, without any reservations; only the 'member of the nobility' (a committee of some five or six men representing the entire order and casting one vote of the total of nineteen) made difficulties. Aitzema takes care to point out in passing that the 'member' — meaning the entire delegation — of the nobility 'depended entirely upon the Prince'. The States of Holland overrode that opposition. It is clear that by means of this instruction they killed the Secret Committee instituted nine years before, and that this is what they meant to do. The lord of Mathenes, the nobleman in the Holland delegation in the States-General, had objected that 'it is necessary sometimes to secrete matters among a few'.

> But that [Aitzema comments] was the very reason why those of Holland wanted the instruction, because under that pretext, as they said, the most important matters were settled by the Prince with some gentlemen 'assumed' by him.[87]

It is idle in this connection to blame the Holland States party for having sacrificed a promising unitary institution to provincial particularism. Too often, unfortunately, the States-General, and especially this otherwise so useful Secret Committee, had appeared to the Hollanders not as the true representatives of Union interests, but as the tools of an ambitious Stadholder. How generally concern was felt over Frederick Henry's policy is shown by the fact that in nearly all the provinces attempts were made to follow the example set by the Holland instruction, but only in Gelderland was something similar brought off; everywhere else the Orange party managed to block the way.[88] This does not necessarily mean (to repeat the caution) that in those provinces there was any real sympathy with Frederick Henry's foreign policy. Aitzema tells a story that gives plain evidence of the contrary for the province of Overijsel. A man who went there in October 1643 to apply for the office of Bailiff of Salland, and who carried with him letters of recommendation from the Prince, discovered

> that the Overijsel towns, both on account of the English marriage and because they did not like His Highness favouring the King of England more than the Parliament, would not be much impressed by this recommendation and that it might do him harm rather than advance his cause. For which reason he kept the letters by him.[89]

The fact remained, nevertheless, that the Prince could still count on the deputies of most of the provinces in the States-General, and the struggle therefore continued with increasing bitterness. To begin with, Holland could not prevent the mission of Boreel and Renswoude. The province endeavoured to obtain that a third man of less pronounced Orangist proclivities should be added to the delegation.[90] But nothing came of this, and it was difficult for Holland to persist in its opposition when, in 1643, the position in England seemed to have altered so much to the disadvantage of the Parliament that Joachimi declared that the embassy would be able to accomplish something, while Strickland refused to make any pronouncement. Thus in October 1643 Holland agreed to the departure of the envoys, and early in the following year they at last set out.

It is no more than natural that the leaders of the parliamentary party received the envoys with suspicion. The war was suddenly taking a turn in their favour again : they had concluded an alliance with Scotland ; Charles was in grave danger. In the beginning of December 1643 a letter was intercepted, in which one of Charles's councillors wrote to a royalist at The Hague to urge the necessity of sending the mediators.[91] Even before this, however, it was well known in England that the mediation emanated from the Orangist States-General, and that both the envoys extraordinary were declared adherents of the Prince of Orange and had already shown themselves inimical to the Parliament. Also, it can hardly have been a secret that Renswoude carried on a regular correspondence with the Stadholder's court.[92] Thus, when the ambassadors were at Oxford, where the King had his court, we find the Scotsman Baillie writing that they would be able to accomplish nothing, 'for they are taken here [in London] for the Prince of Orange's creatures'.[93]

It is not surprising that the envoys met with a better reception in Oxford than in London, where the parliamentary leaders had done their best to isolate them.[94] Baillie complains loudly that, taking advantage of a moment of discouragement after the disaster of Newark, Renswoude and Boreel created dissension in the

Parliament, and between England and Scotland.[95] In fact, the
ambassadors themselves admit in their report — which, however,
as Holland was sure to examine it closely, can only have been
written with a minimum of frankness — that they were persuaded to stay a little longer in London so that the 'good' people,
i.e. the peace lovers, might not lose hope of some arrangement.[96]
After another journey to Oxford they came back to London and
stayed there for months, but all they got was empty compliments,
and they were treated at times with a good deal of impatience.
Among the public wild rumours were afloat concerning the evil
intentions of the so-called mediators, who felt themselves to be
in so false a position that they begged to be recalled. The
States-General, however, instructed them to make one more
attempt. Without doubt the Prince of Orange and his royalist
friends had come to think that they would yet be able to do
service to the King's cause.[97] So they went — it was now 1645
— for the third time from London to Oxford and back again.
On this occasion the suspicions of the parliamentary party [98]
led to an unpleasant incident, which was very much resented
by the ambassadors, and it was in a very bad humour that, in
April 1645, they delivered their farewell speech to the Parliament,
a speech that added fuel to the flames. In it they made it very
clear that they held the parliamentary party to blame for their
failure, and in London the conclusion was drawn that the States-
General had at last decided to range themselves openly with the
King.

Certainly the report that the ambassadors presented to the
States-General on their return seemed to point to that conclusion,[99] and it is difficult to escape the impression that in this
they were faithful to the intention the Orange party had from
the first attached to their mission. At any rate, we know from
letters that have been preserved by chance [100] that in April, while
the envoys were still in England, the Prince of Orange was
already discussing with an emissary of the King, one Dr. Goffe,
how to make the best use of their return in order to get the
States on the side of the King,[101] and that after their return they

were working, in close touch with the Stadholder's court and with the same Dr. Goffe, to overcome the opposition of Holland to their war policy. Goffe was delighted at their zeal. The Prince of Orange himself spoke of them in the highest terms to the Englishman : 'Ils se crèveront', said he, if they do not succeed in accomplishing some good.[102] And Goffe declared that their report was so clearly in favour of the King, that no better plea could have been made for his case by one of his own subjects.[103] As for Boreel, his 'mind was set on serving the King', and he was determined to do something in the States 'which shall be very high and bold'.[104]

But the bold plan did not succeed. What no doubt paralysed Frederick Henry's action was that he could not, as he would have done a few years before, deal with the report in his 'cabinet', with some 'assumed gentlemen'. Everything came before 'the full assembly' of the States-General, and it was not so easy there to dispose of Holland's neutrality policy, with which most of the deputies at heart sympathized. The Prince, however, had not given up hope of reaching his goal by devious paths. As late as June he was still assuring Goffe that everything would come right :

> Hee [Goffe writes] had given Sir William Boswell his taske, to propose the liberty of their Havens and hiring of ships, and the Ambassadors theirs to urge the necessity of granting of Letters of Reprisall to the many complaints received in England from their owne people, and then he added : Croyés-moy, par ce moyen ils seront menés insensiblement dans une guerre.[105] [The word 'insensiblement' speaks volumes.]

But this was equally unsuccessful. The late mediators had already tried, in 'poincten van consideratie', to draw attention to the harm caused to trade by the Parliament's supremacy at sea.[106] But the Hollanders, who must have smiled privately at the ardour of the Stadholder's party for their trade interests, managed to get the States-General to refer these matters, too, to the provinces and thus to postpone them. However, the Orangist deputies in the States-General certainly succeeded in making the

Parliament suffer a few pinpricks. When, for instance, Strickland came forward to clear his masters from blame for the lack of respect shown to the ambassadors during their stay in London — a great deal was made of the 'insults' offered them by the Parliament — he was, at the instance of Boswell, denied a hearing. Whereupon, however, the States of Holland received him, and he was able to express himself freely to this body over the partiality with which the ambassadors had conducted themselves in England. Holland was not so easily intimidated as Dr. Goffe and the Prince had anticipated, and still less so since several other provinces, somewhat hesitatingly to be sure, ventured to join in the opposition to the unpopular Stuart policy of the court.[107]

Even apart from the general question of war or peace with Spain, which began to be acute again in 1645, this was not the only point of foreign politics on which the Prince and the States differed. In 1644 and 1645 a war raged in the Baltic, in which Holland, almost dragging the States-General along, threw the weight of its powerful influence on the side of Sweden. That Holland's trade interests required this policy leaps to the eye. Denmark controlled the Sound and took advantage of this position to exact tolls that no country felt so heavily as did the Netherlands. Added to this was the fact that in the wider European policy Denmark had for a long time been inclining toward the Hapsburg party. But the King of Denmark was an uncle of Charles I, and in the plans made untiringly by the latter's friends for his relief, an important part was assigned to Denmark.

The outbreak of the northern war was a disappointment to the royalists, who had all through 1643 and 1644 been counting on help from Danish troops.[108] Especially when the war turned to the advantage of Sweden, Frederick Henry thought it his business to save Denmark, but the States of Holland were not to be restrained. The Prince's warning that his plans against Antwerp would be endangered by a new war — and this was the only argument of which he could make open use [109] — had little or no influence on Holland, which did not particularly desire the conquest of the great commercial town on the Scheldt. On the contrary, at the beginning of 1645 the Hollanders threatened to withhold all contributions to the campaign in the Southern Netherlands, if they were not allowed to carry out their northern policy. Frederick Henry, burdened with the odium of his dynastic policy, could not prevail against the powerful public opinion that was with the States of Holland in this matter too. However, with the help of Zeeland, which was more dependent on him than any other province, he obstructed Holland's policy as much as was possible, and his attitude so embittered the Hollanders that one man felt called upon to warn him 'not to strain this rope too much lest greater ill arise therefrom'.[110]

The public of that day had its suspicions, which were to be confirmed in the following year,[111] as to the incentive for this new outburst of zeal for the Stuart cause. At the beginning of 1644, when the two mediators were on the point of crossing to England, a French diplomat at The Hague wrote [112] that a number of people were of the opinion that Renswoude had a commission to open fresh negotiations with a view to a marriage between the Prince of Wales and Louise Henrietta of Orange. There is no evidence that this was so : no trace of it is to be found in the archives of the House of Orange ; in Renswoude's own letters the subject is not mentioned, and in the correspondence with the English his name does not occur. But the first letter of Renswoude which has been preserved is not until April 7,[113] and it is apparent from what he writes to Huygens on more than one occasion that he had other channels for keeping in touch with the Prince while he was in England. In any case, it is a fact that he and his colleagues had hardly arrived in Oxford, when the subject of the marriage, which had been allowed to lapse [114] in 1643, when the King's prospects seemed more cheerful, was again broached in a letter from Jermyn to Heenvliet.[115] And so while the Netherlands envoys were 'mediating' under an instruction which expressly forbade them to listen to proposals for an alliance until the contending parties were reconciled,[116] Charles I and Frederick Henry were busily negotiating not only about the

F

second marriage scheme, but, in close connection with this, also about a political alliance. In 1641 the English court had been content with a marriage alone, relying on the assurances of Sommelsdijk that in this way the royalists would win the friendship of the States. Now, with the wisdom of experience, the English wanted to make a formal alliance with the Dutch Republic the price of the marriage.

The plan in the form in which it was presented to Frederick Henry in June 1644 by Dr. Goffe contained two alternatives: [117] if France was willing to participate, it was to be a triple alliance, whereby the Republic would provide ships for the transport of French troops to England; if France was not willing to participate, the Republic was to conclude a truce with Spain, in order to have its hands free, and to send the English troops in Dutch service over to England by whole regiments. Frederick Henry replied immediately that a truce with Spain was impossible without France, in view of the 1635 treaty with the latter country. Negotiations about peace were already being carried on at Münster between Spain and the two allied powers, France and the Dutch Republic. Indeed, a month or two before this date, the French plenipotentiaries for the congress at Münster had written from The Hague, that the Prince of Orange was too conscious of the unpopularity he had brought upon himself by the English connection to risk a peace that would make it easier to get on without a Captain-General.[118] To conclude peace or a truce without France, which would thus become alienated, with the express purpose of forging a still closer bond with the Stuarts, would be too hazardous. But it did not seem at all impossible that France would participate. Since the death of Richelieu in 1642, a more favourable attitude towards the Stuarts had grown up in that country, and Charles was not without hopes in his negotiations with Mazarin.[119] Thus it was that in 1645 the Prince of Orange had accepted the English conditions that he should try to induce the States to declare against the Parliament, and that he should have a force of three thousand fighting men raised and sent to England; but only in conjunction with France.[120]

But we have already seen that the danger spurred the States of Holland to a successful resistance. The triple alliance between France, the Republic and Charles I, on which the English royalists had set their hopes, came to nothing. Yet another member of the Stuart combination, Denmark, as we have already seen, was put out of action by Holland, despite the endeavours of Frederick Henry. Circumstances, moreover, favoured Holland. France's co-operation was often lukewarm. If Frederick Henry did not always display sufficient energy in the struggle with the States of Holland in May and June 1645, this was attributed, by the mediators then back from England, to 'private discouragements' he had suffered at the hands of France. They advised, therefore, that the Queen of England should try to use her influence with the Queen Regent and Cardinal Mazarin.[121] But fate was against the whole scheme. The Stuart cause itself went down with a rush. On June 24, 1645, the army of Charles was routed at Naseby. From Lord Digby's papers captured on that occasion the Parliament was able to prove, as it had indeed suspected for a long time, that the King had been negotiating with the Catholic Irish rebels — thus robbing him of the last remaining vestige of honour in Protestant eyes.[122] During the period that Charles wandered about before the final surrender to the Scottish army in May 1648, he had practically no army any more, only irregular bands, of which the principal was after a while the one commanded by the most romantic of all Cavaliers, Montrose.

Frederick Henry became only the more eager to offer help, but it could now be nothing but the old policy of unauthorized actions and obstructions pursued as far as he dared.[123] It was a curious position. Not only had the Stadholder considered himself justified in making use of the envoys, supposed to be mediating in England in the name of the States, for intrigues with the royalists, and in making plans, without any reference to the States, with the ambassadors of Charles I and with France, he even presumed to withdraw a few ships from the blockade of the Flemish coast and to place them at the disposal of the Queen of England.[124] But his real concern at the end of 1645 and the beginning of 1646 was the equipment in Holland or Zeeland of a considerable fleet for the transport of troops, French troops or such as the Duke of Lorraine [125] was prepared to provide. At first it was hoped that the peace in the Baltic (September 1645), which brought a stream of ships back to Dutch harbours, would provide a good opportunity. Particularly in Zeeland, where the Prince's servant (his representative as First Noble) De Knuyt, was lending his help, the English agents hoped to get a good fleet together.[126] Again, nothing came of the Prince's efforts. In the early months of 1646 some ten ships were being equipped in Amsterdam at French expense and were doubtless intended for the English adventure. The States of Holland, acting upon complaints from England, induced the States-General, which had been long inactive, to put an end to this undertaking.

All Frederick Henry's great plans were linked together. The support that was to be given to Charles I must be based on the alliance with France. France in its turn must help Frederick Henry to win a share of the Southern Netherlands, either by war or by peace with Spain, for early in 1646 there was talk of a reconciliation between France and Spain with the Southern Netherlands as a prize to be paid for by the evacuation of Catalonia. The French obtained the Prince's agreement to this scheme not only by holding out the prospect of an independent position for him outside the dominion of the States [127] (preferably in Antwerp), but also by hinting that, if only they had their hands free in relation to Spain, stronger co-operation might be expected from them in the restoration of Charles I.[128] To the States these plans were not only objectionable in themselves, but they were particularly disturbing because they so clearly tended to increase the power of the Stadholder. Allied to two great monarchs, one of whom, the French King, would have become an immediate neighbour of the Republic, master of a new and important territory, the States could no longer have stood up to Frederick Henry.

But the Spanish-French plan for peace on the basis of an exchange, too, was exploded, for suddenly it became clear that it had never been more than a feint by which the Spaniards intended to create dissension between the States and France. The States were indeed greatly alarmed by the rumours that the Spaniards let purposely transpire, while the Prince, for his part, when he found that he had been taken in, could do nothing but hurry to the States-General and deny all knowledge of the transaction. This did not really clear him in their eyes.[129]

This proved the final failure. Frederick Henry could not carry through his policy. In April 1646 the negotiations for a marriage between the Prince of Wales and the Stadholder's daughter were definitely broken off.[130] In May, as we saw above, Charles I gave himself up to the Scots. About this time the piquant details of Frederick Henry's secret negotiations with the Stuarts, which had come into the possession of the Parliament with the papers of Lord Digby, became known in the Netherlands. Dr. Goffe's reports about his conversations with the Stadholder — some details of which I mentioned already — appeared in a Dutch translation.

The Holland regents, in studying this most confidential correspondence about their Stadholder's foreign intrigues, must have found their own thoughts expressed in the prayer of thanks with which the English Puritans introduced the publication.

> God's blessings [so they could read there] appear in the discovery of the enemy's counsels as well as in the dispersal of his hosts.

The self-confidence of the leading province was considerably strengthened. Holland could now only with difficulty be persuaded to provide a meagre sum for the new campaign in the Southern Netherlands. The great scheme, so much was clear, was doomed to fail in every detail. The Prince, discouraged, old before his time, felt his authority totter.

All through those years the storm of opposition against Frederick Henry's dynastic policy had been gaining force. Annoyance at the involvement with the unfortunate Stuart family, a settled suspicion that every suggestion made by Frederick Henry was inspired by his determination to acquire sovereign power — these were the sentiments that gave impetus to the anti-Stadholder movement. In 1646 matters had gone so far that three members of the States of Holland dared to tell the Stadholder to his face that in his dealings with France his sole object was to oppress Holland, and when the Prince refused to take them seriously, their principals came and repeated the accusation.[131] The French plenipotentiaries at Münster, who were trying to keep the Republic from engaging in serious negotiations with Spain for which the Hollanders thought the time had come, and who in 1646 were continually travelling back and forth between Münster and The Hague, noticed with the greatest displeasure that the reality of power now rested with the States of Holland.[132] Already in April[133] they feared that Frederick Henry, anxious for the future of his House, would prefer to give way and allow the States to conclude a separate peace with Spain in direct contravention of the treaty of alliance with France (of 1635) by which the contracting parties had undertaken to make peace only jointly.

And so in fact it turned out. Amalia of Solms saw greater advantage[134] in accepting the proposals of Spain, which would bring to the family, according to the French ambassadors, '3 ou 400,000 livres de rente'. Considering how little chance there was of a return of the sums advanced to the Stuarts, the temptation must have been very great. The increasing helplessness of the old Prince certainly explains in some degree Amalia's choice as well as his. Young William, his son, soon his successor, did not think the game lost yet ; he resisted the change of policy as much as he could, and was furious with De Knuyt, who had arranged the bargain with Spain (empowered thereto by the Princess, although he did not forget to line his own pocket in the transaction).

The truth of the matter was that Frederick Henry's dynastic policy in conjunction with the Stuarts and France had called into being forces that he could not control. At the end of his life the whole edifice of his great scheme was crumbling, while the States of Holland stood triumphant.

IV

William II of Orange and the Stuarts, 1647–1650
(1923)

WILLIAM II had not wanted to give way as his parents had, and when his father died, in March 1647, it might have been supposed that he would still manage to accomplish something, for peace with Spain had not yet been concluded. He had in fact, while his father was still alive, been in close communication with the French ambassadors, who did not fail to appeal to his ambition, giving him to understand that his greatness depended on France, and that France was prepared to do everything to maintain, nay even to advance, his interests.[1] When he became Stadholder this relationship naturally became even more intimate, and the French vigorously urged him to prevent the treaty of 1635 from being broken.[2]

But although the young Prince made a few attempts proving that he still cherished the plans his father had abandoned in despair and was anxious to avert a peace that would mean their complete breakdown, his French friends soon evinced their bitter disappointment in him. It was clear that 'ce bon petit Prince', as De la Thuillerie scornfully calls the twenty-one-year-old youth,[3] could not stand up against the States of Holland. 'Neither determination nor prudence' — in these terms does Servien characterize William's conduct in the critical conflict with the States in this first phase of his stadholdership. In May 1648 the Count d'Estrades writes bluntly that he has received a most unfavourable impression of the young Prince : he does not seem to care about the inroads made on his authority by the States, lost as he is in frivolity and debauchery ; advice is wasted on him, for all his time is spent on hunting and playing ball. And so about this very time the peace with Spain was made.

But strangely enough, no sooner was the separate peace an accomplished fact than William II seemed to throw off his indifference. Brasset records, on July 13, 1648, a firm resolution made by the Prince two days previously, to apply himself seriously to business from that day on,[4] and although at first sight one is inclined to smile at a promise of amendment announced so emphatically beforehand, it is certain that during the two years of life that still remained to him William II cut a very different figure. Although there are reports of wine and women even in this latter period, there is no further mention of indifference, of lack of ambition or of courage. On the contrary, from that time forward William II threw himself with youthful impetuosity and rashness into the task of undoing the peace and resuming with France, not only the plans for partitioning the Southern Netherlands, but also the scheme for the restoration of the Stuarts.

There appeared to be more hope for the Stuarts in 1648 than there had been in the years immediately preceding. The increasing power of the party of the Independents, who had the disposal of the army under Cromwell and Fairfax and opposed the introduction of a stiff-necked and intolerant Calvinist theocracy by the Presbyterian Parliament, seemed to offer a good chance to Charles I in his captivity. After having in the first place made advances to the Independents, he unexpectedly attached himself to the Presbyterians, and a new civil war broke out in which Presbyterians and royalists joined forces. Their main hopes were centred in a Scottish army under the Duke of Hamilton, but there were serious disturbances in the south of England as well. In the beginning of June, a number of ships belonging to the parliamentary navy declared for the King, and sought a refuge on the roadstead of Helvoetsluis. At first the young Duke of York, who had lately fled from England, tried to secure the command of this fleet, but the lack of unity among his counsellors caused such confusion that the Prince of Wales was called to the rescue. He arrived at Helvoetsluis on July 21, and to his brother's great indignation deprived him of his command.

The Prince of Wales had spent two years in France, where his mother was still continuing her vain efforts to induce Mazarin's government to render some effectual aid. Mazarin's main idea was to prevent any party in England from achieving a complete victory which by restoring unity might renew England's power, and for this reason he was inclined to encourage resistance to the Independent army, which he feared most of all. But just at this time, owing partly to the defection of the Dutch Republic, partly to the domestic disturbances of the *Fronde*, France was in no position to spare money or troops for an English expedition. Once more all the hopes of the royalists were centred in a Prince of Orange.

An envoy from the Scottish Committee of Estates, dominated at that time by the royalist Presbyterian party of Hamilton, had just had to report from Amsterdam that the States would not hear of an alliance with Scotland against the English Independents — no wonder when it is remembered that even loyal adherents of the Prince of Orange, as we shall see presently, placed no faith (and rightly) in the power of the Hamilton party — and that William II himself was not equal to his position.[5] This was about the time of the Prince's resolve to begin a new life. It soon became clear, in spite of the pessimism of the Scot, that William was indeed ready to render all the help that lay in his power. It is true that he could not move the States of Holland. He even frankly admitted this to his brother-in-law, warning him not to expect any action that would be too directly opposed to the declaration of neutrality, and also not to count on financial support from the States.[6] All that could be expected was the kind of help his father had always given — whereby he had almost ruined himself without averting the fall of the luckless Stuart family. Together with that same somewhat incalculable Duke of Lorraine on whom hopes had been set even in Frederick Henry's day, the Prince raised troops, which were encamped for the time being at Borcum, and for whose use he chartered a couple of ships in Amsterdam. This transaction took place in consultation with the English royalists.[7] At the same time the

Prince arranged for the purchase of munitions for the Scottish army,[8] up to a sum of 30,000 francs.

This was the first business into which William II threw himself heart and soul after his resolve to improve his manner of life, and his own servants observed it with profound concern. A man like Heenvliet, to be sure, served without offering criticism and was content if he won the gratitude of the Stuarts.[9] But the letters in which De Wilhem, the member of 'His Highness's Council' who was commissioned to carry out the work, describes these activities to his brother-in-law, Huygens, are one long lamentation. De Wilhem ventured to warn his master against 'getting more deeply involved in the English labyrinth', but no attention was paid to him.

In particular De Wilhem complained most bitterly of the incapacity and intractability of the servants of the Prince of Wales and of the infinite confusion prevailing among his counsellors.[10] Culpepper was the man who had the most influence with the Prince of Wales in those days, and predominance on the whole was with the party that, following the lead of the Queen and her confidant, Jermyn, placed all its hopes in the Presbyterians. True Episcopalians, such as Sir Edward Hyde and Sir Edward Nicholas, had already been attached by the King to his son, but they were not yet making their influence felt. It is certainly remarkable that De Wilhem, as strict a Calvinist as any of the Prince of Orange's followers, was so little impressed by the policy of working with the Presbyterians. In any case, his judgement was right. He realized that little reliance could be placed in the Hamilton party, which was losing ground even in Scotland, and he shook his head over the imprudence of exposing the Prince of Wales in such a hopeless enterprise. For after fruitlessly cruising about the English coast for a week or two with his ill-disciplined fleet,[11] young Charles — he was eighteen at the time — did indeed make preparations to go and place himself at the head of the Scottish army. But he was still in The Hague when the news came that there was no longer a Scottish army: Cromwell had annihilated it at Preston (end of August

1648). The 30,000 francs worth of munitions too, which had just been dispatched, would now, says De Wilhem, probably fall into the enemy's hands; the troops at Borcum were disbanded, and the Prince of Wales with his ill-assorted retinue — Catholics, Episcopalians and Presbyterians; English, Irish and Scots — lingered on at The Hague at the expense of his brother-in-law of Orange,[12] his fleet blockaded at Brill by a parliamentary fleet under Warwick, and gradually disintegrating through lack of funds.

William II was himself of too active a nature not to be impatient at the ease with which the English Prince accommodated himself to his idleness.[13] As for the States of Holland, they would not have been sorry to see the parliamentary Admiral seize the opportunity and destroy the weaker royalist fleet at one bold stroke,[14] but when he neglected the opportunity, they could hardly do otherwise than observe neutrality. Soon afterwards Rupert Prince Palatine was placed at the head of this fleet, and he with his indomitable energy succeeded in preventing further decay, even though there was the greatest difficulty in finding money and making the fleet seaworthy again. All sorts of ambitious plans were built on the possession of this force — the last almost on which the royalists could completely rely — but practically the only way in which Prince Rupert was ever able to use it, after he had set his course for Ireland early in 1649, was for privateering expeditions against English merchantmen, and this soon became the only source of income for young Charles in his exile.

The disaster at Preston had sealed the fate of Charles I. Scotland still maintained its independence: now that those Presbyterians who under Hamilton had thrown in their lot with the Stuart cause were beaten, power was in the hands of the implacable Presbyterians under Argyll. This party for the time being worked with the Independents although it did not really have any more in common with them than had the Hamilton Presbyterians. But in England there was now no longer any power capable of withstanding Cromwell. In December 'Pride's

Purge' expelled all oppositional elements from the Parliament, and in January the King appeared before his judges.

The Prince of Wales, who, at the pleasure-loving court at The Hague, with his brilliant Palatine-Bohemian cousins and the beautiful sisters of his brother-in-law of Orange, had forgotten his political troubles amid gaieties, now had a rude awakening. On January 22, 1649, he received reports from which it became clear that his father's life was in jeopardy. The next day he appeared in the States-General, where Boswell spoke for him, saying : 'J'ai horreur de dire, qu'un prince d'Angleterre vient requérir intercession pour la vie du Roi son père.' At the proposal of Holland it was resolved to send across without delay Joachimi, who was on leave in the country, and Pauw van Heemstede. Everybody realized that adherents of Orange would not be the best advocates to soften the hearts of the Independents. Without heeding storm and ice the envoys sped to London. It needed some insistence, although they were treated with due courtesy, to obtain access to the Parliament, which listened to their plea for the King's life in silence. The next day, January 30, 1649, O.S. (February 9, N.S.), Charles I was beheaded at Whitehall. A few hours later the Parliament issued a solemn warning that no man was to presume to claim the title of King of England.

The deed made a profound impression in the Netherlands. The nation, its own revolution already but a memory stored in the glorified annals of the past, saw with horror 'the hosts of hell' building 'their throne in England's realm', as Vondel expressed it. Even those who hitherto had been on the side of the Parliament, be it on grounds of freedom or of religion, expressed detestation. Such is the testimony of Aitzema,[15] the chronicler, and there is no doubt that it deserves every credence. Strickland, so it is said, dared not show his face in the streets.[16] The ministers of religion were vehement in their condemnation of 'the atrocious deed'. No doubt they had little sympathy with the Episcopalian doctrines, and even Catholic leanings, of the Prince of Wales and his counsellors, but for a long time past they had looked on the looming spectre of Independentism with the greatest uneasiness. The Zeeland ministry, under the influence of Spang, and Voetius himself, the 'Pope of the Dutch Reformed Church', as he was sometimes called, were no less vigorous in their protests against Independentism, that is against freedom of worship (at least for Protestants), than against Episcopalianism. The religious sympathies of the Netherlands Calvinists were entirely with the Presbyterians, who had now suffered defeat in England. The *odium theologicum* is clearly seen in the address in which four Hague clerics felt it their immediate duty to offer condolence and comfort to the son of the King who had been deprived of his life. After vigorous manifestations of horror at 'this unheard-of parricide, that accursed destruction of the holy, anointed head, and that never sufficiently to be deplored murder of this one King of the Reformed Faith', the reverend gentlemen declare that from this can be seen 'what it is to be an Independent'.[17] But they were reprimanded very sharply by the temporal power for their interference in politics. The States of Holland told them in unmistakable terms that they were not in future to address *en corps* foreign potentates, that they were not to discuss the affairs of Great Britain from the pulpit, and that they were not to carry on correspondence across the sea.

For in the midst of the general excitement, the States of Holland were unyielding in their adherence to their guiding principle, that it was essential to keep on friendly terms with the parliamentary party, and all the more now that this party had the whole country at its feet. Aitzema remarks caustically that the States party was absolutely determined to keep in with the winning side. Indeed this was the wordly-wise maxim, one that we have already seen the French government establish as the unshakable *raison d'état*,[18] and one that was so obviously in the interest of the Netherlands that the other commercial province, Zeeland, in spite of the Prince of Orange's influence there, continued in these days to go hand in hand with Holland. All the other European powers too — with the exception of Sweden, where the somewhat unbalanced Queen Christina indulged in a short-lived outburst of noble indignation — took it as their guiding principle. As for France, with which the Prince of Orange would so gladly have allied himself in order to set things right in England, that country was entirely powerless just at this time on account of its own *Fronde* risings.

However, it was certainly not only their inclination to *Realpolitik* that ruled with the States. These men, who did not really sympathize with the religious aims of the Presbyterians any more than with those of their own Calvinist clergy, must have cherished a certain secret admiration for the bold republicanism of the Independents. Aitzema himself cannot refrain from remarking on the folly of the public, who were now all 'full of compassion over the death of the King, *one* person — and had looked on with dry eyes while *thousands* had lost their lives in England, Ireland and Scotland, during the English disturbances'.[19] And he refers to 'Libertinists' who put awkward questions about the consistency of people like the Calvinist ministers, who were now so indignant, although their sixteenth-century predecessors, too, had, after all, offered armed resistance to their lawful king. No doubt, so he goes on, it was objected that the English republic was only established by a small section of the House of Commons. But in the United Netherlands the revolution was not even begun by any States assembly or by a section of any parliament, but by some rabble at Flushing in Zeeland and at Enkhuizen in Holland. . . .

That there were freethinkers who dared to say such things, and not under their breath either, we need not assume only on the authority of Aitzema. A student of the University of Utrecht published a refutation of Professor Boxhorn's *Dissertatio de successione et jure primogenitorum*, in which it had been argued that innocent sons of kings possess a right to succeed to the throne which cannot be invalidated by the deposition of their fathers, whether guilty or not. How does the professor — so the Utrechter would like to know — rhyme this with his loyalty to the state from which he draws his salary and which would not be an independent state if Philip III's right had not been invalidated by the 'abjuration' (or deposition) of his father. He goes on to state as a general proposition that kings do not rule by the grace of God, a phrase without a meaning, but by the grace of the people — which the writer assumes to be acting through a States assembly, for he is clearly a regents man. And he is not a little surprised to see that in free states and republics there still are men who think so highly of royal authority.[20]

When the well-known lawyer Dirk Graswinckel published a little book, or rather, when an older book of his was reprinted for the occasion, the ultraroyalist views expressed in it drew further opposition. A pamphlet appeared in which a cultivated and well-read man pleaded in temperate terms for the principle — indeed a typically Netherlands principle, as he does not fail to remind his readers — of royal power limited by the interests of the people. And he concluded very sensibly that those who meant well by the King ought now to wish that he had listened more to his people and less to his court.[21]

One can be certain that views like these were pretty generally current in regent circles.

All this does not alter the fact that the rise of the Independents, and their impressive judgement on the King, did more than anything else to bring about a great revulsion of public opinion in the Netherlands in regard to English affairs. The Calvinists, who had been in sympathy with the Parliament in its struggle with the King, were distinctly inimical towards the English Commonwealth. William II might well think that a policy of interference with the domestic affairs of Great Britain, although even now there were certainly no signs of any active desire for it, would be less unpopular than it had been in the days of his father, particularly as the Scottish Calvinists or Presbyterians, too, seemed at that very moment to be reverting to the monarchy.

Yet here a serious complication presented itself. The Presbyterians, frightened by the danger of Independentism, were reverting to the monarchy, but Charles II was by no means eager to meet them. He would no doubt have been ready to join the

Hamilton party, although even that was not at all to the taste of
the majority of his English advisers. But the Marquis of Argyll's
party, which had come into power after the fall of Hamilton,
was considerably more obnoxious. It consisted of the most rigid
Presbyterians, unwilling to make the slightest concession to the
policy of the Stuarts, or even to put an end to the persecution of
those who had formerly served them, or were tainted with Episcopalian leanings. It is true that the execution of Charles I had
aroused great and universal indignation in Scotland also. The
Scottish Parliament moreover, immediately after the receipt of
the news from London, had proclaimed his son King of Scotland.
It did, however, attach conditions to its proclamation, which in
the main came down to this, that Charles II was to give certain
personal assurances in the matter of religion, and that he was to
swear to both the National Covenant of 1638, which established
the Presbyterian church order for that realm and required severe
persecution of men of different persuasions, and the Solemn
League and Covenant of 1643, which was intended to introduce
Presbyterianism into the King's other realms as well. In other
words, it was demanded of Charles II that he should embrace
the policy that had been so unacceptable to his father and all his
father's faithful followers that they had preferred to face civil
war. Small wonder that in the King's English council there was
strong opposition to acceptance of the Scottish demands. The
unfortunate result of the naval expedition in August of the
previous year had weakened much the influence of Culpepper
and the other Presbyterians. It was now the turn of the strict
Episcopalians, such as Hyde and Cottington. Charles II indeed,
who, so far as his nature allowed him to believe in anything,
believed in the full royalist programme and in the Episcopalian
Church, did not relish the prospect of submitting to the Presbyterian yoke and entrusting himself to the people who, as it was
said in the terms of party feeling, had sold his father to his
executioners. Particularly so long as there was an alternative
course open to him.

In Ireland the Lord Lieutenant, the Marquis of Ormonde, had

not only managed to stand his ground, but he had just concluded a peace with the Catholic insurgents ; he was confident that he would soon be able to restore to their allegiance to the King the towns that were in the hands of the Parliament, and that he would then have at his disposal an army to make an attempt on England itself. In February he sent an envoy to The Hague to invite Charles to come to Ireland, and one can imagine what a temptation this idea must have been to the young King. It was really a resumption of the old plan of Charles I and Strafford to establish the royal power in England with the help of Catholic Ireland. In case of success, young Charles, instead of being, under the royal title, bound in religion and in politics by the Covenants, would become the autocrat his father had dreamed of being. The greatest obstacle was that, in spite of the assurances of Ormonde, the position in Ireland still appeared very uncertain, and consequently several English councillors preferred Scotland. There were, moreover, in The Hague, Scots of various shades of opinion who advised an acceptance of the Scottish conditions, among them even several nobles of the Hamilton party who had been banished by the present government. Of the Scots it was only Montrose — the representative of absolute royalism, the man who had fainted on hearing of the execution of his King — who unhesitatingly urged the choice of Ireland, and there was no one to whose urgings Charles gave way so easily, however fiercely the Presbyterians might hate this man. It was not until April that the envoys of the Scottish government arrived to negotiate with 'the proclaimed King' about his reception.

One cannot wonder that in these circumstances the Prince of Orange must have greatly preferred to see his brother-in-law depart for Scotland than for Ireland. For anyone who was trying to make the King's cause palatable to the people of the Netherlands that plan had all the advantages. It was one thing to recommend an alliance with the free Presbyterian kingdom of Scotland, but a very different matter to plead for support for an Episcopalian Stuart, dependent on Catholic Ireland and aiming at autocracy. The chaplains of whom the Scots wanted Charles

II to rid himself were equally repugnant to the Netherlanders ; one of them, for instance, used to preach vigorously against the Calvinists in general.[22]   The Scots themselves counted on William II's advocating their cause with the King and used all possible influence with him.

The fullest and most authentic account in this connection is that of the Scottish minister, Spang, whom we met before.[23] He went from Veere to The Hague in March, at the request of his friends in Scotland, and had a personal interview of over an hour with the Prince.[24]   It appears from Spang's detailed report that the Prince was very well informed as to the confused state of affairs in England and Scotland, and that, although he naturally gave a sympathetic reception to the Presbyterian spokesman, he was well posted in the arguments of Charles's English counsellors and gave a fair exposition of them.   Above all he saw clearly the dangers of the fierce intolerance of the party in power, and he feared, too — surely not without ground — that to embrace the Solemn League and Covenant would damage the King's cause by alienating the Catholics and Episcopalians in England.   Yet he concluded by promising that he would advise the King to accept both covenants, and he assured Spang on the following day that he had done so.[25]   When the envoys of the Scottish government themselves arrived at the beginning of April, they were able to report immediately that they hoped to get their demands accepted with the help of the Prince of Orange.[26]

Lord Byron, Ormonde's envoy, was of the opinion that the Scottish sympathies of the Prince of Orange and his mother were to be ascribed in the first place to the renewed suggestion of a marriage between the King and one of Frederick Henry's daughters.[27] No positive evidence that this was so can be found. But there is no doubt that Amalia of Solms actually gave open support to the Scottish envoys,[28] while Sophia of Bohemia, afterward Electress of Hanover, declares in her *Mémoires* (a doubtful source, however, for the years she spent at The Hague) that the old Princess at a somewhat later date, 1650, threw suspicions on her, Sophia's, orthodoxy, in order to make the Scots the more readily conclude to the suitability of her, Amalia's, daughter for the dignity of Queen of Scotland.[29] And of course we know only too well how very largely Amalia's policy was decided by the matrimonial prospects of her children. Byron, however, somewhat later commits himself to the rather surprising statement [30] that William II by no means allowed himself to be talked round by the Scottish lords, but that he had a higher opinion of his, Byron's, principal, Ormonde, than of any of them and desired to maintain friendly relations with him. This probably means simply that the Prince, who wanted to take up a propitiatory and mediatory attitude, thought it worth his while to cultivate the Irish party as he did the others, and was prodigal at least in protestations.

Meanwhile it is very probable that William did not always follow a consistent course in this difficult question. Even Henrietta Maria and Jermyn, of whose advice William II always thought very highly, considered that the Scots were too exacting. And the Queen of Bohemia and her daughters, too, were opposed heart and soul to the policy of submission to the Covenants, a policy that was loathed by the most famous of her sons, Rupert, who at this time was at sea with the royalist fleet. How much more attractive to chivalrous minds was the idealistic royalism of Montrose or even the unbending Episcopalianism of Hyde. In November the Queen of Bohemia writes to Montrose that her niece, the Princess Royal, 'still keeps steadfastly to our side'. All the English influences in his cosmopolitan court and in his cosmopolitan family acted on the Prince to the detriment of the Scots. Nevertheless it is certain that in June, when Charles was already in Breda and on the point of setting out for Ireland, the Prince once more brought serious pressure to bear on him to induce him to accept the Scottish demands.

And indeed, however much one may sympathize with the point of view of the English royalists, who not only felt deeply wronged by the negotiations with the Presbyterians, but the noblest of whom abhorred an alliance with them as a line of action both insincere and humiliating, it is natural enough, and it speaks something for his independence, that William II took into account in the first place not English but Dutch conditions. That the States-General wanted an arrangement between the King and Scotland is most positively asserted in all the contemporary sources.[31]   Strickland hits the nail on the head when he observes that the Prince is doing his best to bring the King and Scotland together, 'hopeing by that means to carrie all heere'.[32]

In 1649, however, when there was still a possibility of a choice between Scotland and Ireland, William II, for all the obligations under which he had laid the King, did not succeed in keeping him back from Ireland.   Nor did the Scots by any means make things easy for Charles.   Compliance with their demand to introduce the Presbyterian religion into England and Ireland would cost the King the support of the only true friends he had.   In Scotland, moreover, the persecution of the real royalists was being relentlessly pursued ; above all, the execution of the Marquis of Huntly in the beginning of April was extraordinarily painful to the King.   During this same period the Scottish envoys arrived at The Hague, and the first demand they put forward (and in the most offensive manner) was that the King should banish Montrose from his entourage.

It is not to be supposed that the States of Holland could have been prevailed upon to give any practical help if Charles had chosen the Presbyterian path.   *They* were not in the Netherlands the admirers of that ecclesiastical system.   But in any case, when the King applied to the States-General for transport ships and a loan of £200,000 to further his expedition to Ireland,[33] at the same time explaining exhaustively why he could not give ear to Scotland's call, the request fell on deaf ears.   The Prince of Orange had supported the request even though he had advocated the alternative course, but a policy that was to cost money could not easily be carried out against the wishes of Holland, and Holland would not hear of it.[34]   When at last, in June, the King set out on his Irish expedition, William II had once again to put his hand in his own pocket to prevent Charles from being retained by his creditors.[35]

Yet all this trouble was for nought. It went ill with Charles's cause in Ireland from the moment that Cromwell set about subduing the island. The King himself, after long delay in France, never got any farther than Jersey, where he waited for months in the most straitened circumstances, and where eventually in September and October the news of Cromwell's complete triumph reached him.

> It is obvious [writes De Wilhem to Huygens] [36] that God wishes to make him understand that Scotland is the only way to his restoration.

In fact there was nothing else left. But the Scots had not become more tractable. It is true they were ready to renew negotiations — they had even sent envoys to the King in Jersey — but always on the same conditions. It was now agreed that the negotiations should be resumed at Breda through the mediation of the Prince of Orange.[37]

The King accepted the proposal of these negotiations on January 21, 1650, N.S. On the following day he wrote to his trusted Montrose that he none the less wished him to proceed with his proposed expedition against the Scottish government. Montrose, the unconditional royalist, now represented Charles's only alternative, but the way in which Charles sent him out against the Scottish Presbyterians at the moment he himself was entering into negotiations with them is a striking example of his duplicity.

The position of the mediator in these negotiations was clearly no easy one. After consultation with his mother in France, Charles arrived at Breda with his destitute retinue early in April. Feelings between his English adherents and the Scots had not improved since 1649. The English were in a suspicious mood even regarding the Prince of Orange. They knew that the Scots were counting on his support and that some of their spokesmen had spent the whole winter in The Hague in order to bring their influence to bear on the Prince.[38] According to an English Republican, who had wormed his way into the retinue of Charles II and who from there wrote vivid reports to the government in London,[39] the King's followers comforted themselves with the thought that he would after all feel fairly independent with respect to his brother-in-law, for William had so completely ruined himself in the service of the Stuarts that little more financial support could be expected of him; besides, in his own country he had serious difficulties to contend with, and his position was hardly secure.[40]

There is no doubt that, just as in 1649, the Prince did his best to induce the Scots to be more reasonable. Even the English royalists, for all their malicious talk, recognized that fact. According to the Republican spy, William made use in these efforts of the services of the Dutch Calvinists, of Dr. Rivet (who was at that time rector of the university founded by Frederick Henry at Breda), and of Voetius himself. The Dutch Calvinists were, as the Englishman says, 'nothing so rigid' as the Scottish, and Voetius was expected to lend his name out of complaisance toward the Prince.[41] But the Prince's overriding desire was that an agreement should be arrived at, he cared not on what terms. The English Republican, who watched the doings at Breda with a strong sense of their humorous aspects, perpetually alleges that the Prince's chief motive was determined by the fact that the upkeep of the King and his retinue fell entirely on him and his already overburdened fortune — that therefore he wanted to be rid of Charles at any cost.[42] It is not improbable that this consideration counted (although just at this time the Prince obtained the use of a very large sum),[43] but as has already been explained, an agreement between Charles and the Scots fitted in with William's general policy, in which an alliance of the States-General with the Stuarts against the English Commonwealth formed so important a part. In any case, it is certain that the Prince urged his brother-in-law to an acceptance of the most important demands of the Scots: one or two documents have been preserved [44] in which he puts before the King his ideas on a possible answer to the Scottish delegates, and according to these Charles was to take his oath upon the National Covenant, as well as upon the general Solemn League and Covenant, and personally to conform to the Presbyterian form of worship all the time he was in Scotland.

And so, to the bitter disappointment of Charles's English followers, the negotiations ended by his giving in. He still made a few reservations, but the main points he accepted. Montrose and Ormonde were repudiated, and with them Episcopalianism. In the beginning of May Charles signed the agreement. Dr. Rivet, who also took counsel with the Scottish ministers as to the manner in which, in accordance with the treaty, the Anglican chaplains were to be removed from the King's entourage, was present at the signature.[45] Loyal royalists learned with indescribable bitterness that the King had adopted for himself and his subjects a religion in which he had no faith, and that he had undertaken to cast off all those who had ruined themselves for him and for Episcopalianism in order to be received as the mock king of the hated Scottish rebels. His mother herself repudiated the suspicion that she had 'urged him to sacrifice his honour and his conscience'. Royalists in England were discouraged.

And even before he left the Netherlands, Charles received news that was to bring home to him acutely the false position in which he had placed himself. Montrose had fallen into the hands of the Scottish government. It is not improbable that his expedition might have had a better chance of success if Charles himself had not by his negotiations with the Covenants smothered the desire of wavering Scots to join Montrose's ranks. In any case, no mercy was shown to the captured hero. Despite the King's commission, he was hanged and quartered as a traitor. No greater ignominy could have been shown to Charles. The news reached him while he was staying with his sister and brother-in-law Orange at Honselaarsdijk,[46] immediately before he was to embark. For one moment it caused him to hesitate.[47] What would his own life be worth if he put himself into the power of these inexorable fanatics? But it was too late to turn back. Towards the middle of June he embarked on a Dutch man-of-war, commandeered for the purpose, with a couple of others, by his brother-in-law. With him sailed a party of

English Presbyterians and moderate Scots, whom the true Presbyterians regarded as nothing short of 'prophane', and whom on his arrival (still further concessions having been wrung from him *en route*) he was forced immediately to dismiss. He was irretrievably delivered into the hands of the unbending clerical party, and it was to spare him no humiliation.

And Charles had not the Scots alone to reckon with. There was the English Commonwealth. The English spy to whom I have referred before wrote to his principals, as soon as he knew of the conclusion of the agreement, to warn them that the royalists would now move heaven and earth to get foreign troops into Scotland in order to use that country as the back door for an attack on England. 'Therefore if you be wise, shut the back door this summer, and then you will be safer next' [48] — advice that Cromwell was to follow in less time than Charles needed to get hold of foreign auxiliaries. For although his brother-in-law Orange, in whom, as ever, his main hopes were centred, still managed to help him to get some more funds,[49] he had his own opposition to reckon with before he could think of mobilizing the resources of the Netherlands on behalf of the Stuarts.

The history of the last year or two had proved that the opposition of Holland was enough to cripple all political action on the part of the Stadholder. In order to grasp that fact, we must go back to the moment when the news of the execution of Charles I reached The Hague. From that moment, the middle of February 1649, there was as violent an onslaught on the policy of neutrality established in 1642 as there had been in 1645, and from that moment, too, the States of Holland, with the same success as before, had put up an obstinate resistance. The Hollanders did not allow themselves to be upset for one moment by all the excitement about 'the regicide'. From beginning to end they made it their business to keep on good terms with the actual rulers in England. It was not in the first place a feeling of spiritual kinship with the Republican party that prompted their attitude. It was above all a dispassionate appreciation of the interests of their own province. True, it might be argued that those interests would be endangered rather than helped by the conquest of Scotland by the English revolutionaries. The French, as has been observed already, realized quite clearly that the disunion of the island kingdom fitted in best with their interests, and events were soon to prove how dangerous for the Netherlands particularly a strong and united Great Britain, be it under Cromwell or under the Stuarts, could be. In fact, the commercial interests of the moment played an important part in the political considerations of the Holland party — as they always did — and that meant, of course, avoiding irritating the Commonwealth, which was powerful at sea. There was, moreover, the fact that it must have been difficult for the States of Holland, realistic as they might try to be, to take an unprejudiced view of a question that, owing to the dynastic policy of the House of Orange, had become so essentially a party question. Had the States of Holland and Orange been of one mind they might perhaps have played off the Stuarts against the Commonwealth — it would have been a dangerous policy at any time! — but the Hollanders naturally preferred not to have any dealings with a Stuart whom Orange when it suited him might play off against them.[50]

In the meantime the Orange party had immediately attempted to make the proclamation of the Commonwealth the opportunity for a break. Naturally it hoped to be able to carry the States-General with it in its dangerous policy. The Lord of Renswoude, the Utrecht Orangist whose performance as 'mediator' in England will be remembered, happened to be 'President' for that week, while the greffier, Musch, whose duty it was to 'extend' — that is, to resume and formulate — 'resolutions', could always be counted on. Together these gentlemen did their best to push through a resolution that Charles II should be acknowledged formally as King of Great Britain. Holland and Zeeland — urgent commercial considerations again made this latter province shake itself free from Orange control — opposed this proposal tooth and nail, and succeeded at length in modifying it so far that Charles was to be addressed merely by the general title of King, a title to which, of course, since his proclamation by the Scottish Parliament, he had an unquestionable right. The two provinces also succeeded in preventing the éclat of an ostentatious recall from England of the ambassadors who had been sent in a vain effort to save the King's life. Pauw van Heemstede, who had to return for private reasons, gave great offence to the Orange party by reporting that he had been treated with the utmost consideration by the new rulers in England. But he had been merely an envoy extraordinary; the great point was that Joachimi was allowed to stay. And, in fact, why should he not stay? The ambassadors of France, Portugal, Spain, were not recalled either, even though for the time being the English Commonwealth was not recognized by any other state.

But the Dutch Republic was a house divided against itself. Each party succeeded in making it impossible for the other side to carry out its policy, and the result was a grievous lack of cohesion in the conduct of foreign affairs. The States-General could not recall Joachimi against the wish of Holland, but it could prevent his being accredited to the new government. To all the ambassador's urgent requests for more definite instructions no other reply was made than that he must observe and not enter into any negotiations. This attitude naturally roused ill feeling in the new rulers of England.

Then a sensational event took place in The Hague. In May, Doreslaer, a Hollander in English service, was appointed by the Parliament as ambassador to the States in addition to Strickland. A few days after his arrival he was murdered in cold blood by some Scottish royalists from Montrose's following. The States of Holland did what they could to have the perpetrators of the deed, which had taken place in their territory, brought to justice, but without success, and the occurrence naturally made a profound impression in England. The Parliament addressed a very sharp note to Joachimi, who replied by expressing in writing his horror at the event. This roused the indignation of the States-General against him, because it implied a recognition of the Republican government. The ambassador, consequently, could not move a finger, and at the same time the States-General persisted in their refusal to receive Strickland, who now presented himself again with new credentials on behalf of the English Commonwealth. Here again the opposition of two forces resulted in a negative policy, although in manœuvring as they did the Orangists were keeping their aim in view. Their idea was that in this way, simply by doing nothing, it would still be possible so to poison relations with England that a conflict would become inevitable.

In fact, this question of recognition grew to be the most dangerous of all. Holland could easily enough, as we have seen, prevent any help being given to Charles II on his expedition to Ireland. But although Holland could obstruct, it could not compel. And so Strickland, in spite of all his importunities, eventually even by using the threat that he would have to leave the country, could not obtain admittance to the States-General. This was taken very much amiss in England. Strickland himself, as far as can be gathered from his letters in the well-known *Thurloe State Papers*,[51] was inclined to be satisfied with the deference shown him by the States of Holland, which had received him as Resident of the Commonwealth of England as soon as he turned to them.[52] He was perpetually urging his masters, the Council of State, to encourage the Hollanders in their line of action by giving them satisfaction on the blockade questions that were always cropping up. In this respect the English government was at times willing enough to be accommodating, but the threat to recall Strickland, in other words, definitely to break off diplomatic relations, was none the less seriously meant. The States of Holland, therefore, who were no doubt impressed by Cromwell's victories in Ireland just at that time, proceeded to act in a way that bitterly offended the Orange party, but was all the more enthusiastically welcomed by Strickland.

So far the Hollanders had been trying to bring the States-General to view things in their way by long arguments presented by extra-numerous delegations, but now the Holland deputies requested the 'recording' of a formal and vigorous protest.

What makes this document so interesting is that it contains an accusation against the deputies of the other provinces which one will rarely find expressed so pointedly. The protest is directed, not against these other provinces, but against their 'deputies' who were holding up the admission of Strickland '*under pretext of* having no instructions'.[53] The deputies of the other provinces (with the exception of Zeeland, which was still acting in harmony with Holland in all these matters) felt not a little aggrieved at thus being regarded as 'such agents who, knowing the wishes of their honourable principals in matters of state of this importance, would delay the effect of them instead of reporting and acting upon them in due time and place'. This was perhaps more than the Hollanders had meant to hint. Strickland indicates more exactly what was in their minds. The important thing to them was that the attention of the provincial States assemblies to which the protest would have to be sent should be directed to the question. Those States, he explains, 'who live remote and know noe more then their deputyes informe them', did not see through 'the mystery of iniquitye' that was being enacted in The Hague. This is the view that I have set out already : that the deputies of the landward provinces let themselves be used by the Stadholder for the purposes of his personal policy, perhaps not exactly against the intentions of their respective States assemblies, but in the comfortable knowledge that these lived too 'remote' to check their doings very accurately. And we have here proof that the Hollanders believed firmly enough that this was the case to expect their protest to have the effect that these gentlemen would for once be called to order by their principals. As a matter of fact, both Aitzema and Strickland testify that the protest created a good deal of uneasiness among the deputies attacked. But the power of the Prince, the dispenser of countless jobs, not only in the army, let itself be felt sufficiently by their principals as well to see that the deputies were not disavowed.[54] Holland's protest did not in the end result in anything. It appeared convincingly that the Prince of Orange could influence the States-General to carry through a policy that served no single Dutch interest, that indeed most obviously ran counter to Dutch interests.

Under these circumstances, then, the States of Holland decided on a step of incalculable import. In the beginning of December 1649 it was proposed in the Holland assembly [55] to send a 'commissioner' to England on behalf of the province, and in fact, on May 21, 1650, Mr. Gerard Schaep of Amsterdam crossed to England in that capacity with an instruction dated May 5.[56] The aim of this mission, which is indeed clearly stated in the instruction, must have been twofold. In the first place, Holland, whose inhabitants had so many interests to be looked after in England, wanted to have an agent there who could accomplish more than the regular Union envoy, Joachimi, who now was nearly ninety years of age, and whose hands, as we have seen, were tied by the States-General. Then, Holland wanted also, particularly now that there was the danger of Strickland being recalled, a channel through which to keep in touch with the Commonwealth administration in England and to mitigate somewhat the ill feeling caused by the attitude of the Orange party. Thus, to look after commercial interests and to counteract the war policy of William II was to be the task of Gerard Schaep. If Holland was not meekly to submit to the dynasticism of the Stadholder's policy and allow the country to be plunged into a senseless war, a step of this kind was inevitable, but that it might have a serious effect on the unity of the Republic, even though it was not a violation of the Union of Utrecht,[57] needs no arguing. The Prince of Orange spoke with the greatest concern about it to the French ambassador, describing it as a manœuvre that if it were not thwarted, would result in the complete disruption of the Union.[58]

Solicitude for the Union was always the fine-sounding shibboleth by which the Princes of Orange, who could do what they liked with the States-General, tried to impress public opinion. In reality, it was the opposition Holland offered to his English policy which William II could not brook. It is of course incontestable that in those days the Union was tottering on its foundations.

The conflict between Holland and the Orange party was almost more than the makeshift constitution could bear. But I trust I have made it clear that it was the Prince's action in the English question, together with the unrepresentative, even corrupt, character of the States-General, which was the main cause of the crisis ; Holland's attitude was fundamentally a defensive one. The constitutional slogans were not the issue of the struggle ; they were the weapons with which it was fought.

At this very time the conflict was beginning to concentrate round the question of the disbanding of troops. Now that there was peace, Holland wanted to diminish the military charges so as to be able to set about clearing off the public debt. Although certainly not negligible in itself, this question became one of crucial importance mainly because of its connection with the great conflict of opinion over foreign policy and who was to have the deciding of it.

Here the English question, which under Frederick Henry already had been the principal factor in causing the revival of the States' opposition to the Stadholder, was still the most prominent. Aitzema, after having spoken about the difficulties in connection with the reception of Strickland, says : 'This in time caused a difference between Holland and the Prince, which was increased by the questions of economy and reduction of the army.' It is to be noted that Aitzema, too, regards the English question as the main cause of the breach. An even more definite expression of opinion in this sense came from the Spanish Ambassador, Brun, who watched with anxiety the course of the party struggle that for his King, too, would result in war or peace.

> It appears [he wrote a few weeks after matters had worked up to the crisis of the famous attempt on Amsterdam (about which more soon)] that the event in Holland has occurred in retaliation for the action of the States in sending a resident to England, and not on account of the troops.[59]

It is true that the English question was not the only one in the realm of foreign politics, but it was indissolubly bound up with the others. In the mind of the Prince it had long been connected especially with the question of the peace with Spain and with the attitude toward France. The plan that occupied his mind (as we already know) was to undo the work of Münster, to renew the alliance with France for the partition of the Southern Netherlands and for the restoration of the Stuarts to the throne of England.[60] In this he followed the tradition of his father, but without the latter's caution. In itself already his scheming with France behind the back of the States with a view to breaking the freshly made peace was much worse than anything Frederick Henry had ever done. But moreover, William's secret negotiations had the highly objectionable purpose of drawing France into the Dutch domestic quarrel.

In October 1648 he had already made an opening through the instrumentality of Aerssens van Sommelsdijk, the son, but Mazarin had his hands full with his own *Fronde* difficulties and the whole year 1649 passed by without anything being achieved. In the next year matters at first wore a more promising look — not for long, in fact — and now William came with positive proposals. Probably there is no document in the archives of the House of Orange that redounds so little to its credit as does that of February 1649[61] in which William II, in his own imperfect French, wrote down his ideas on the subject of his co-operation with France as an instruction for an envoy of his own to the French government. France was to be assured that he had sufficient influence in the six small provinces to venture to count on their support for his war policy against Spain. Without mincing words he calls on the support of France against the opposition of Holland. He reckons with the possibility that a schism might break out in the Republic, in which he and the six provinces would find themselves opposed to Holland — and not even a united Holland. If France then should be willing to recognize the six provinces as a state and come to their assistance with money, he would be able to quell Holland with the army and lead the whole Republic into the war.

Of course the States of Holland had no knowledge of this

startling document, but the Hollanders must have had a suspicion of what was going on. In more than one case the Prince's intentions came to light clearly enough. In December 1649, for instance, he had managed to prevail upon France not to call back its troops in the service of the Republic, as it was entitled to do under the treaty of 1630. Why was he so anxious to retain them? Because for his plans against Holland he could rely on French troops more than on Dutch.[62] For that same reason the States of Holland would have acceded eagerly to the first request for a recall, but the French government supported the Prince against Holland. Indeed the whole dispute about disbandment turned largely on the foreign troops, which the Prince, with a view to his dynastic and anti-national policy, would not have on any account dismissed.

Compared with the almost treasonable relations with France into which William II had entered, the mission of Schaep, the boldest step that the States of Holland permitted themselves, was innocent enough. If this act of his adversaries nevertheless more than anything else moved William II to undertake his *coup d'état* of July and August 1650, it was, therefore, on account not so much of its constitutional impropriety as of its political tendency. Naturally the Orange party made grateful use of the Hollanders' straying into diplomacy to reconcile public opinion with the Prince's resort to force of arms, but for that purpose the Orangists had badly to distort its significance. Although the French Ambassador immediately on hearing the news was ready to declare [63] that the task of the 'commissary' was to bring about an alliance between the province of Holland and the Commonwealth of England, there is no single indication that this actually was the case. The Gelderland Orangist, Van der Capellen, gives an account of a rumour [64] to the effect that 'Bicker, De Witt, and others', through the medium of Schaep, had carried on 'a secret correspondence with the Parliament in England', but he is obliged to add that there is 'no evidence of it'. As a matter of fact, such stories were circulated of set purpose. About the time of the attempt on Amsterdam a pamphlet was published in which a letter from Schaep is printed, dated July 14, 1650, with a complete draft-treaty between Amsterdam (not even Holland!) and the English Commonwealth, which undertook to furnish troops. This was a barefaced fabrication. It was part of the plot against the great city. It made some impression at first,[65] but soon people began saying that the Prince ought to lay proofs on the table.

Of course, with their opponents in so close a bond, a working alliance between the Republican parties in England and the Netherlands would have been quite natural. Nor is there any doubt, as has already been indicated, that the Hollanders wished Cromwell every success in his military enterprises both against the Scots and the Irish.[66] Their desire to keep on good terms with England went so far that the States of Holland did their best to suppress the writings of Salmasius and Graswinckel against Milton's *Pro populo Anglicano defensio*.[67] The correspondent of the *Briefe Relation* [68] even gives an account of somewhat reckless utterances he has heard from Hollanders :

> If the rest of the provinces will be slaves, they will not. If the bundle of arrows must be unbound, they of Holland know into what quiver to put their arrows with safety and advantage.[69]

Remarkable language certainly, but obviously more an expression of irritation and fear than the reflection of a responsible political plan. A main characteristic of the regents of Holland was their caution. Their tactics had all the weakness that is usually the accompaniment of a defensive attitude. In order to act offensively they would have had to be better organized under a universally recognized leader. Men like the Bickers of Amsterdam and De Witt of Dort certainly made their weight felt in the States of Holland, but the only position that offered an opportunity to a real leader to develop himself to the full — the position of grand-pensionary — was held by the timid, pliant Cats.[70] The States generally left the initiative to their opponents, who, whatever else they lacked, had the advantage of being subject to a strong personal leadership.

Thus it happened that at the end of July 1650 the crisis took the States party unawares with an act of aggression on the part of the Prince. He had, after all, to risk the *coup* without French aid, of which, as the *Fronde* troubles were still continuing, there was no likelihood. It is not necessary to repeat here all those familiar happenings, the capture of the six members of the States of Holland, the attempt on Amsterdam, all undertaken on the authority of a most irregular and very vaguely worded resolution of the States-General. It is enough to observe that in none of the struggles between the House of Orange and the regent party was the sympathy of the people so little on the side of Orange. The German captain of horse who snapped at one of the arrested gentlemen, 'whoever has the army on his side is master',[71] was not unfair to William II's cause. It was military force that decided the issue.

It is true that the Calvinist clergy on the whole worked for the Prince,[72] and probably the agreement that the Prince had brought about between Charles II and Presbyterian Scotland at Breda had still further strengthened the Calvinists' zeal. The Reverend Maximilian Teellinck, for instance, a Zeelander, expresses himself quite vehemently in the dedication to the Prince of a little book by his father Willem Teellinck, *Den Polityken Christen*, which he published just about this time. After having glorified Maurice and Frederick Henry and anathematized their adversaries, he extols William because in him was *the wisdom of God* (I Kings 3 : 28) and because he opposed the peace (of Münster), *a girdle marred, profitable for nothing* (Jer. 13 : 7), finally to explode :

It cannot be denied, there are only too many *sons of Belial* [Judg. 19 : 22], Papists, Arminians, enemies of religion and of the state, in our midst who dare *bring a railing accusation against* [Jude 9] Your Highness . . . as if Your Highness, who have in all this proved yourself to be *wise in heart, and mighty in strength* [Job 9 : 4], would have had no other aim than to make your own authority *increase* and the authority of the state *decrease* [John 3 : 30]. . . . *The Lord God of Gods, he knoweth, and Israel he shall know* [Josh. 22 : 22], with all true patriots, your *witness is in heaven*, your *record is on high* [Job 16 : 19], that suchlike never occurred to your princely heart.[73]

No less instructive than the ecstatic praise is the defensive tone.

The commercial classes in any case can hardly have looked forward but with the greatest uneasiness to the Prince of Orange's being able to carry out his military plans. We have seen how Zeeland, where the Prince had great personal influence, but where at the same time the commercial interest was almost as predominant as in Holland, had ventured to make a stand against his English policy in 1649. That was no longer so in 1650. Zeeland was again obeying the demands of the court. As Aitzema puts it, in his most unflattering manner : some of the 'principaelste' of the Zeeland delegates 'tried as usual to comply as much as possible with the Prince's wishes to serve their private interests and intrigues.'[74] Particularly significant is the unanimity with which the inhabitants of Amsterdam stood by their regents during the siege.[75]

One might have thought that the failure of the attack on Amsterdam would have offered a splendid opportunity to the States party once and for all to square accounts with the ambitious Stadholder. But here the party's lack of organization told. Van der Capellen says scornfully that he 'had expected more wisdom and courage from these gallant spirits.'[76] Indeed, particularly the lack of unity among the Amsterdam magistrates, some of whom used the opportunity to oust the Bickers from power,[77] makes a pitiable impression.

Thus in spite of his initial defeat William II managed not only to find a way out of the impasse, but also decidedly to strengthen his position, and he made use of it with more talent perhaps than he had displayed hitherto. There are signs more than enough that his *coup d'état* instilled feelings of fear in his opponents : for some time they left him a free hand. The small provinces swallowed their objections to his action [78] and vied with one another in offering him resolutions of thanks. Aitzema relates that the States of Groningen had passed a resolution to the effect that the envoy of the English Commonwealth ought to be received, and that their delegates dared not now table this proposition in the States-General.[79] The English Republican whom I have so frequently quoted observed it all with the greatest annoyance. Writing in the beginning of September,[80] he refers to

> the miserable base business of Amsterdam, whereby hath been discovered the baseness of som Provinces, and the weakness of other, and by both their ripeness for slaverie, and readiness to succumb. Certainly that gallant spirit, which possest those people when they bravely (to their hitherto lasting honour) vindicated that libertie from the oppressions of the most potent Prince of Europe, which they have now tamely given up into the hands of their own servants, hath made a transmigration into our Nation.

Indeed the records that are left of the conduct even of the Hollanders in the hour of crisis do not impress one with respect for their strength of character. The imprisoned gentlemen were left in the lurch without much opposition. Several of them addressed humble letters to the Prince which are far from edifying.[81] Gerard Schaep, too, wrote from London to the secretary of the Frisian Stadholder, William's cousin, in the hope that 'sinistre opinies' that were cherished about him at the court would be given up.[82]

Nevertheless it would be very wrong to believe that the crisis had placed William II in an unassailable position of power. It is certain that he was preparing himself for a vigorous attempt to carry out his foreign plans when death took him by surprise. But it is equally certain that Holland immediately thwarted him again when, as early as August, the question of war was brought up once more.[83] The States had bent under the force of the storm, but they were by no means broken. They were probably still as little fitted as ever to take an energetic initiative against the Prince, but under their new leaders, now that the old ones had been forcibly removed, they were no less adept in the tactics of parrying and checking.[84] The English Republican, writing from Leyden, anticipated that the Prince would succeed in moving the States-General to a war with the Commonwealth if

Cromwell was not successful in Scotland.[85] There was a close relation between developments there and in the Netherlands. The Scots themselves expected much from William II.[86] MacDowell, as resident of the King of Scotland, made tremendous efforts, and the Hollanders hardly dared protest against the vehemence with which he expressed himself against the English Republic in official documents.[87]

The battle of Dunbar, however, where the Scottish army suffered a crushing defeat (September 13, N.S.), was a fresh setback to the English policy of William II. The position certainly became more perilous than ever when, in October, the English government, which now felt itself to be stronger, turned Joachimi out of the country in reprisal for the refusal to receive Strickland. An actual break in the diplomatic relations between the two states had taken place. But without doubt Dunbar renewed the courage of the Prince's opponents in Holland as well. On September 24 Sir Edward Nicholas, one of the most eminent of royalist exiles, writes from The Hague that party feeling against the Stadholder is increasing daily.[88] William II had by no means done with the opposition in Holland. The actual battle would yet have to be fought when he decided the moment had come to press for a decision on the all-important point of foreign policy.

Nobody can tell what the outcome of that battle would have been. On November 6 the Prince, but twenty-four years old, died of smallpox, and the States of Holland, led by the staunchest Republicans, suddenly found themselves masters of the field, not only in their own province, but in the Republic.

V

William III and the Crisis of 1672

WILLIAM III is a great figure in the history of Holland, in the history of England, in the history of Europe. From 1672 Stadholder of Holland and of four other provinces and Captain-General of the Union of the Seven, from 1688 till his death King of England; a tireless advocate, and in fact the leader, of European resistance to Louis XIV and his efforts to establish — to use a term of the time — 'a universal monarchy'.

All that William III came to be, and all that he achieved, was rooted in his birth. A lineal descendent of William the Silent, bearer of that name of Orange which meant so much to the people of Holland and Zeeland, he was at the same time a grandson of Charles I of England. Orange might be no more than a tiny principality, but the royal blood added a particular distinction to his position in the Europe of his time. The King of England was his uncle, brother of his mother; the Elector of Brandenburg (the Great Elector, as history knows him) was also an uncle, married to the sister of his father William II; he was even closely connected with Louis XIV, for his mother was the great King's cousin, daughter of a sister of Louis's father. Henry IV, the grandfather of Louis XIV, was William III's great-grandfather.

All this is not to say that William III's greatness was just presented to him. On the contrary, what fascinates us in his career is the struggle. In his elevation to the high offices of his ancestors, in the fearful crisis of 1672, we are struck by the tremendous drama, the miraculous turn of events, the commonalty rising in its wrath and forcing the faithless regents to place the son of the old family in the position in which he would be able to save the country and prevent its being delivered to France.

Obviously the work of God, using the people as his instrument
— so said William's adherents, then and later. A criminal grab
at power, said his opponents, an action accompanied by an unparalleled campaign of slander, disfigured by the brutish excesses
of the bewildered mob, which seemed like the introduction to a
successful resistance only because the French army had already
been checked by the Line of Inundations covering the province
of Holland.

No less dramatic, no less the object of vehement contention,
was the way in which in 1688 William III achieved his second
elevation — to the English throne. In the Republic this time
opinion was less deeply divided. Responsible circles, that is, the
States assemblies, had hesitated before placing the country's army
and navy at the Prince's disposal for that risky undertaking, an
expedition to England; the public had, as usual, taken a more
downright complicated view of the problem. But in fact the
danger threatening the country from the co-operation of Louis
XIV and a Catholic King of England was so serious that agreement was quickly reached. The adventure succeeded beyond
expectation, and everybody admitted that the result was an
immense strengthening of the Republic's position in face of that
everlasting menace, the monstrous growth of Louis's power. At
the most there were murmurings that in the situation now
created by William, the Republic was definitely reduced to playing second fiddle to England; and also that the royal Stadholder
had now developed into so considerable a personage that extra
care would be needed to keep the Republic a republic! But in
the other camp, in France, among the English Jacobites, William's
successful attempt to drive out his father-in-law James II and
seat himself on his throne came to be regarded as an example of
the criminal deeds to which ambition can drive a man. The
upholder of an idea, the prophet of a crusade, the defender of
Protestantism and the Liberties of Europe, was there seen as an
unprincipled self-seeker and usurper.

These were the two pinnacles in the drama of William III's
life: 1672 and 1688. But before, in between and after, there was

always a struggle — a struggle with vacillation or disapproval, with opposition, at home (whether in Holland or in England), a struggle with the enemy — always, that is to say, with Louis XIV. Out of that struggle there rises before us a character — a character not crushed but steeled by pressure ; a character living by some few strong convictions. Not in all respects a lovable character — self-willed, easily roused to impatience by contradiction or a show of independence, too passionate to be nice in the choice of means when opposition must be subdued. Nevertheless, a statesman, that is to say, a man who could, when it was necessary, control himself, using his formidable will-power to bridle his own impetuous inclinations. Time and again one sees him ready, in the vehemence of his first opinion, to break through all obstacles or be smashed in the attempt ; but all the time he is acquiring the painful art of making concessions to an opposition he despises, of biding his time, of compromise.

I shall not try to present you with an idealized sketch of William III. To gloss over his shortcomings, to smooth out his sharp edges, would detract from the striking effect made by his historic personality. Nor shall I try to magnify him at the expense of his adversaries.[1] He does not need it ; in that way too the dramatic tension would be lost from the story. The greatness and sincerity of men like De Witt and Van Beuningen constitute a precious part of the Dutch national tradition. William III was right ; but they were right too. Their contrasting opinions in the field of foreign policy were conditioned by the difficult — I might almost say the impossible — position of the country : of the small country between the so much more powerful kingdoms of England and of France.

Born a few days after his father's death, William III had grown up as a pretender. He could not lay any hereditary claim to the high offices of his forefathers (the Stadholderate of Holland and of some other provinces, and the Captain-Generalship of the Union). Sovereign power (speaking for the province of Holland) was indisputably in the hands of the States of Holland, and these had been treated so brusquely and had

been so deeply offended by his father shortly before his death —
and this without William II having succeeded in breaking them
— that among them, among the councillors and burgomasters
of the leading province, the name of Orange evoked very different
sentiments from those of gratitude or veneration.

Feelings were indeed sharply divided. The first violent
crisis had occurred in 1653, when the first Anglo-Dutch war was
going disastrously for the Dutch, and the country (to quote
De Witt, who had just assumed the office of Grand Pensionary
of Holland) 'was as if blockaded and besieged.' The people
were inclined to impute this state of affairs to the 'Stadholderless'
régime, and clamoured for 'a head'. But 'the people' is a vague
term. Was it really 'the people' against 'the regents'? De Witt
himself bears witness that hardly one in a thousand of 'the
common rabble' was free from that opinion in that anxious
summer. But 'the common rabble' is not identical with 'the
people'. Which class he intended to indicate it is hard to say
exactly, but so much is certain, that the position held by the
regent oligarchy in that society was by no means an isolated one.
The comfortable citizens, a broad group round the regent class
or immediately below it, felt on the whole a closer connection
with the regents than with the humbler citizenry, and shared their
opinions and prejudices. Then there were, more particularly,
the Catholics, the Arminians (expelled from the Reformed
Church in 1619), the Baptists, and other sects, all of whom might
expect a greater latitude from the ruling regent group than from
an Orangist régime, which would have the enthusiastic support
of the ministers of the Reformed Church. It was, above all, the
orthodox members of that Church, hardly the most numerous
group among the population, but, compared with the others
mentioned, the most active, animated with the greatest self-
confidence, who looked up to Orange ; and although a foreign
danger was the most effective way of rousing the public, grievances against the regents on account of the usual abuses of
oligarchic rule, but also of the firm hand with which they bridled
the ministers of religion, and of their toleration of all sorts of

unorthodox doctrines — such grievances lay always slumbering in the minds of the commonalty, ready to wake up at moment of tension.

A pamphleteer of 1653, belonging to De Witt's camp, scoffed :

> It will be hard for a later generation to believe that a brave people in war-time sought salvation in a little boy still wrapped in swaddling-clothes!

Such downright republican, anti-monarchical sentiments had hardly been heard in the first generations of the Stadholderly Republic. But since the connection of Orange with Stuart ; since the marriage of 1641, of which William III was the off-spring ;[2] since Frederick Henry's and William II's attempts to drag the Republic into foreign adventures for the purpose of bringing about the restoration of the luckless Stuart family ; and especially since 1650, that is to say, since the surprise attack on Amsterdam undertaken by William II, and his arrest of the six members of the Holland States, a consistently anti-Orange and republican doctrine was in process of being evolved.

De Witt — I am recapitulating well-known facts — saw no other way of putting an end to the first Anglo-Dutch war than by getting the province of Holland to deliver to Cromwell a promise never again to appoint a member of the House of Orange to the Stadholdership, and to prevent such an appointment to the Captain-Generalship of the Union by an adverse vote in the States-General of the Seven (where, in all matters of importance, unanimity was required) : the Act of Seclusion, 1654. The assertion that De Witt was making use of Cromwell in order to have a pretext for getting the exclusion thus passed by the States was party slander ; he had consented to the transaction only because Cromwell made it an absolute condition for peace, and the war indeed no longer offered any prospects. This was the conclusive answer to the complaints and reproaches levelled at Holland when the secret came to light. It is true that in his elaborate defence of the conduct of the negotiation — the famous Deduction, which appeared in print before the end of the year under the name of his masters the States of Holland — De Witt set out a boldly republican argument. One-man rule, so he asserted, had always, in the days of the Counts of Holland already, been a source of dissension. And gratitude? Were they to employ the scion of the House of Orange out of gratitude for what his ancestors had done for the country? Well, these high-born personages had been liberally paid for their services while they lived. That debt had been acquitted. And as an appendix to the little book De Witt added a list, drawn up by two clerks of the Chamber of Accounts of the province, of all the payments shown in the documents as having been made to members of the illustrious family, and amounting to 19,694,000 florins.

This was the atmosphere in which — against which, I might say — the young Prince grew to manhood. Naturally, arguments of this kind could not damp the ardour of his adherents. As the years passed, and the moment approached when he would be able to enter the scene in person, the contrasts became more bitter. The restoration to the throne of England in 1660 of his uncle, Charles II, had already had that effect. With his uncle no longer a wanderer on the Continent, but a king indeed, the adherents of the young Prince felt sure that the Seclusion could not be maintained for ever. But for De Witt and his fellow-republicans, the Restoration in England introduced, on the contrary, a new and dangerous element into the situation. They feared that the Prince of Orange might allow himself to be used by his uncle the King as an instrument to serve English interests in the Republic.

This was not so wild an idea as we might be inclined to think. In the seventeenth century personal relations of dependence or loyalty, dynastic connections, could still easily transcend feelings of duty towards the national community or the state. This appeared only too clearly in 1666, during the second Anglo-Dutch war, in the affair of the captain-of-horse Buat, formerly a page to the young Prince, a man of French descent but married to a daughter of the late Greffier of the States-General, grand-daughter of Cats, the famous poet and Grand Pensionary. Buat, in consultation with English agents, set on foot a regular plot, with ramifications in Holland regent circles, in order to bring about the elevation of 'mon petit maître' (as he called William III) and a peace with England — on the terms desired by England! It appeared again after the unmasking and execution of Buat, when the unsuccessful conspirator was extolled by the more vehement Orangists as a martyr and De Witt execrated as his murderer. For the time being, nevertheless, the discomfiture of the plotters, soon followed, after the spectacular incident of the raid on Chatham, by the successful conclusion of the war with England, resulted in the republican system feeling itself master of the situation. It was in that mood that the States of Holland in 1667 passed the Eternal Edict, by which the Stadholdership was for ever abolished, and on which each individual member of the governments of the voting towns and of the committee of noblemen of Holland had to take an oath.

For all that, it was impossible to ignore young William entirely. He had already been declared 'Child of State'; the States of Holland, in return for coming to the rescue of the finances of the family (which were in a sorry plight as a result of the support given to the Stuarts in their misfortunes by Frederick Henry and William II), obtained a thorough purge of his court of English influences; they were also allowed to assume the supervision of the boy's education. De Witt personally instructed him in the fundamental principles of government, of the régime, in other words. The prospect of his being appointed to the Captain-Generalship on reaching his majority was held out to him as part of the transaction; only the combination of this military function with the political one of the Stadholdership — the combination on which the strength of his predecessors had been based — remained barred, definitely as it seemed, by the Eternal Edict.

But then, in 1672, the French attack that had long been threatening burst upon the country, and Charles II took part in it as Louis XIV's ally. The French army invaded the country from the only direction from which it can be invaded, from the east, and in a few weeks' time had penetrated as far as the town of Utrecht; Holland was protected — for how long? — by the Line of Inundations (the 'Water Line'). And now panic led to an irresistible popular movement. The States of Zeeland first, then those of Holland, had to bow to riotous demonstrations by the citizens. The Eternal Edict — five years old — was torn up in spite of all the oaths guaranteeing it, and the Prince was appointed Stadholder. He had already been appointed Captain-General before the war actually broke out, and the restrictions then imposed upon his powers were now swept away. De Witt, just recovered from the wounds inflicted upon him when an attempt on his life had been made, resigned in a dignified manner.

But popular excitement continued unabated. Orangist pamphlets went on coming from the presses by dozens, and in them De Witt and the Wittian regents — the Loevestein faction, as they were called after the castle where Maurice and William II had imprisoned several of these gentlemen, among them Grotius in 1618, and De Witt's father in 1650 — were decried as traitors, out to sell the country to France. But Charles II, who had from 1670 on plotted with Louis XIV the destruction of the Republic, was excused; was he not the uncle of the beloved Prince? It was the Loevesteiners who had insulted and provoked him. The De Witts were made responsible for the previous English war (the second) as well: the descent on Chatham in 1667, led by De Ruyter, the admiral, and the Grand Pensionary's brother Cornelis, as deputy of the States-General, was depicted as a cowardly, treacherous attack. The painting which Cornelis had presented to the Town Hall of Dort in commemoration of this glorious feat of arms had been mentioned by Charles in his declaration of war as one of his grievances, and now the Orangist mob acted enthusiastically upon his hint. They broke into the Town Hall, tore the picture to pieces, cut out Cornelis's head and nailed it to the gallows. The Rotterdam regent Kievit, an accomplice of Buat's, who after the discovery of the plot had fled to England (in 1666, in time of war), now, after William had become Stadholder, made a triumphant return and was received as a hero. All this while Charles II, his protector, was making war upon the country in alliance with Louis XIV. De Ruyter was on the high seas, and managed with a great effort to hold off the combined English and French fleets. But in Amsterdam a crazy mob was attacking his house in order to give vent to their twin feelings of veneration for Orange and for Charles II.

The English king meanwhile dispatched envoys to his ally Louis, who was at that moment residing near Utrecht, in order to come to an agreement about the projected partition of the Republic. When these gentlemen, Arlington and Buckingham, stepped ashore at a little town west of Rotterdam — meaning to break their journey to Louis's army headquarters to see the Prince in *his* headquarters behind the Line of Inundations — they were lustily cheered : 'Long live the King of England and the Prince of Orange! The devil take the States!'

Small wonder that the English gentlemen were in high hopes regarding their mission to the Prince of Orange! They were to suggest to him (De Witt had foreseen this quite correctly) that his best course would be to submit to his uncle, who meant so well by him : had he not stipulated with Louis XIV that the two of them, after having each taken his share of the Republic, should leave to William III the sovereignty over the rest? *Sovereign* he was to be! How much better than Stadholder! And while Arlington and Buckingham were staying at the camp near Bodegraven they heard the young noblemen who surrounded William III, and who expected to come to greatness all of a sudden in his wake, discuss the fine plan with approval, adding that, to crown it all, a dozen of the States gentlemen should be hanged!

I have gone into these details in order to illustrate the dangerous aberrations in which party passions had involved a large part of the Dutch people. From 1641 on, the connection with the Stuarts had tempted the Orange party on to 'unnational' paths. This helps to explain the distrust with which De Witt regarded the young man to whose hands its future had come to be entrusted. At the back of it was not only oligarchic animosity, there was also the fear that the Prince of Orange would, in the interests of his powerful uncle of England, undermine the country's independence. That William III might have done so is clear. The English expected him to. The mob, who cheered them and reviled Cornelis De Witt and De Ruyter, was blind. The young courtiers stood ready, like Buat and his conspirators six years earlier, to place their Prince above the national interest.

But now listen to the answer William gave to the English tempters. They noted it down themselves. He began by stating that he had been empowered to treat with them by the States — thus already, in his introduction, emphasizing his attachment to the States and his recognition of their sovereign authority — to treat, but only on a basis tending to the severance of England's alliance with France. The proposition that had been laid before him, involving cession of territory, he called altogether extra-ordinary, concluding that 'we' (by which plural he once again stressed the connection existing between the States and himself) 'we would rather die a thousand deaths than submit to such conditions'. The English envoys thereupon tried to make their demands a little less offensive (that is how they themselves put it) by substituting the term of 'giving towns in pledge' for that of 'ceding' them. But the Prince declared he was convinced that the States would never agree to this, and as for himself, he could not in conscience advise them to do so.

> We desired him to bethink himself well [so the report continues] not only to remove the war out of his country, but to establish to himself a sovereignty over it, wherein both the Kings would secure him from all danger both abroad and at home. He replied he liked better the condition of Stadholder which they had given him, and that he believed himself obliged in conscience and honour not to prefer his interest before his obligation.[3]

William III was twenty-one years old when he spoke these words. One has only to remember the critical military situation to feel admiration for the firmness of his attitude. But if, in addition, one reflects that in resisting the English temptings he was at one with advisers like Van Beuningen and Van Beverningh, leading figures in the States of Holland, and that he was going directly against the evil tradition which had had only too great a hold over his party, and against the mood prevailing at this very moment among his excited adherents — then especially one will realize that the test of the crisis was revealing a character of uncommon courage and self-reliance. This declaration of independence issued to his uncle the King by the young Prince not only benefited the country, to which the widespread infatuation with regard to Charles II was as much of a menace as were the power and militant policy of Louis XIV; it also laid the foundations of William's own greatness. Had he consented, he would have remained a little Prince of Orange, protégé of the Stuarts. Now he could become their rival, the man to whom the opposition in England were eventually going to turn.

It was not long before Charles II had to reckon with William so seriously that he made another attempt to win his attachment. The King had by then already withdrawn from the war, in 1674, without realizing any of his original ambitions. The situation had undergone a profound change through the intervention of the Emperor and the Elector of Brandenburg on the side of the Republic. The French had evacuated all the Dutch territory they had occupied in 1672, though the state of war between the Republic and France lasted until 1678. Now, in 1677, Charles arranged for his nephew a marriage with Mary, the daughter of the King's brother, the Duke of York. This too proved a miscalculation; William did not allow himself to be deflected from the straight line of his policy by this marriage either; no more than in 1672 by the offer of (a sham) sovereignty. So the result of the renewed connection with the Stuarts was not to compromise him in the eyes of the English opposition (as Charles had intended); on the contrary, it strengthened his claim to meddle in English affairs, until in the end, in 1688, he could intervene, on the double ground of his own blood-relationship with the royal family and of his wife's rights, in order to overthrow the Catholic despotism which the Stuart régime had come to be.

But the year 1672 is of such fundamental significance, it sheds light on William's personality from so many angles, that we must for a moment return to it.

We saw the force of that personality come out in the unshakable determination with which he opposed a tendency in his own party decorating itself with his name and indeed rooted in traditions formed during his minority. A feebler nature would have been swept along. But if he stood firm against that tendency on the one particular point which I told you about, this does not mean that he was wholly impervious to it. He did things in 1672 which can only be explained by the influence of that party spirit, and which, indeed, prove, as I hinted before, that in order to attain his aims he was not over-nice in selecting the means.

The popular bitterness and suspicion against De Witt and his adherents had by no means been allayed by the nullification of the Eternal Edict and the appointment of William III to the Stadholdership. These feelings were not exclusively inspired by the awful shock of the sudden danger in which the country still found itself. There was also a widespread dissatisfaction, which now exploded into violence, with the narrowly oligarchic character of the States government.

We must not too readily describe the anti-oligarchic movement, bursting forth in the exceptional circumstances of the threatening military situation, as 'democratic'.

True, theories were formulated in several pamphlets intended to give a legal or historical foundation to the commonalty's uprising against the oligarchy. Here and there demands were put forward for a share to be given to the citizens in the election of their town corporations, and through them of the States. The year 1672 has its significance on account of these stirrings of democratic tendencies. But they were unable to transform themselves into realities. Even in 1748, when such aspirations came to the fore with still greater insistence, they still failed to do so. Both these movements, sheltering under the name of Orange, can be regarded as rehearsals for the Patriots' Movement,

I

which in the 1780s attempted to carry through the democratic programme *against* Orange.

One thing, however, was made plain in 1672, and that was the feeling of the citizens that the state was their concern as well, that it did not belong only to the regents. But when it came to putting their ambitions into practice, all they could think of was to force through, for this once, in these altogether exceptional circumstances, a change in the personnel of the town corporations (and ultimately therefore in the States), a change which the Prince would have to carry out for them. *He* was their man, it was for *him* to do it. After which they would retire into their quietness and obedience (the great virtues of the commonalty in the eyes of the oligarchy). There is a moving quality in the confidence they had in this young man, but it is not democracy as we understand it.

The most vividly written, perhaps, of all the pamphlets of 1672 is one in which the old allegory of the ship is employed (the ship *Hollandia*). The crew violently push the unfaithful steersman, who sets the course for France, away from the rudder (De Witt is meant, obviously, and the allegation is pure slander), and compel the skipper (that is, the States) to have a try with a young fellow on board, William, William's son, who has so far kept in the background. And it was a wonder to see how naturally the art of steering came to him!

> The oldest sailors said, with tears in their eyes : 'Look, this is the way it was done of old ; this was how they steered in a storm. From father to son the Williams have known that art.' When the unfaithful steersman, bursting with spite, exclaimed : 'Shall a boy come along and teach me how to steer and turn?', one of the men, who was not of the most patient, rejoined : 'What do you talk of boys? He has learnt steering better than you have, who hired yourself out as a steersman without ever having been taught.'

One can feel here how deeply rooted was the respect for the principle of heredity. The popular movement did not want democracy, it wanted a dictatorship based on popular approval. Attempts were no doubt made occasionally, as I have hinted already, somewhat timidly, to attack the oligarchic system in its foundations. They did not meet with the slightest sympathy on the part of William himself. That the regents should govern the towns after their own pleasure was for him as natural as it was inevitable. What he wanted was only that they should have to count with *him* in the conduct of the general affairs of the country. In his eyes the popular movement had its use for strengthening his hold upon these — for that, and for nothing else.

The regents and most of the well-to-do citizens regarded the popular movement simply as sedition — the rabble in revolt against the social order —, and they now looked anxiously to the Prince for protection, even though in the preceding years they had done what they could to keep him out of power. But during that summer William did not in the least mind their fears or the serious disturbances that did indeed take place. Let the States first empower him to effect a 'change of law' — the technical term for an exceptional purge of the regent personnel — such as his predecessors had been empowered to undertake in earlier crises, in 1618 and in 1650. The States were naturally very reluctant to fall in with his wish. But when, for instance, two gentlemen of the Rotterdam government arrive at the army camp at Bodegraven to implore the Stadholder to come and restore order in their town, he keeps them waiting while he goes on conversing with some ministers of religion. When their turn comes, the Prince is already in the saddle. He keeps his hat on and lets his horse cavort so much that the burgomaster and alderman from Rotterdam have to jump for safety. Finally he spurs his horse on and rides off, shouting over his shoulder 'I can't come. I have told you often enough : I can't come.'

One move which he made in this policy of intimidation (for that is what it was) was of a very questionable nature indeed. He had received a letter from his uncle in which the King laid the full responsibility for the war squarely on the shoulders of De Witt and his insolence, and now William and Fagel, his devoted collaborator, De Witt's successor in the Grand

Pensionaryship, decided to publish this letter. On the King's part it was, of course, a barefaced piece of war propaganda ; but how is one to qualify the publication by William III and Fagel? That mendacious imputation could not but act as fuel on the flames of popular indignation against the traitor, against the unfaithful steersman, and this was what it was intended to do by the Prince and his counsellor. That that popular indignation should shortly afterwards find vent in the massacre of the brothers De Witt was certainly not what they had intended, but even so the publication of the letter was far from playing fair. And far from edifying, too, was the cold-blooded manner in which the Prince and the Grand Pensionary went on to make use of the horrible crime in their system of intimidation.

But in this way the States were now made to give in. The Prince obtained his authorization. In the 'change of law' that followed he was able to thrust all Wittians out of the various town governments, and consequently out of the States, and replace them by what the pamphleteers of the States party called 'yes-men'. And now that the popular movement had served its purpose, the Prince resolutely quieted it down. The scoundrels in The Hague who had prepared and executed the massacre of the De Witts were not prosecuted. The alderman Van Banchem, who, as all the world knew, had played a leading part on that day, was promoted. When later on he got into difficulties with the law on account of his malpractices, William still comments, apologetically, that the man had always been a good friend of the House of Orange. In Rotterdam, Kievit, the traitor of 1666, was readmitted to the town government. Wishes or plans for democratic reform that had been laid before the public here and there were silenced. It was the Prince who would govern, with a docile oligarchy.

This was from now on to be the aim of his governing system : to see that the oligarchy should be docile. It is the unattractive side of William III's régime. The people remained without any regular influence, but the oligarchy was brought under the control of the Stadholder as much as possible. In every unit of political power a clique was formed of adherents or henchmen who coaxed the majority along in the Prince's sense by means of pressure or, to use the term then current, *douceurs*. In many Holland towns the regents came to hang on the Prince's slightest nod. 'There is as much liberty left here', said one embittered republican, 'as in any town of France.'

The system was applied most rigorously in the three provinces that had been occupied by the French in 1672 and liberated at the end of 1673 and the beginning of 1674: Utrecht, Gelderland and Overijsel. In these provinces were introduced the so-called 'Government Regulations' as the price of their readmission into the Union. Under these, the whole of the regent class retained their unassailable authority as far as the citizenry was concerned; in all local matters the regents were still all-powerful as of old. But in affairs of wider importance, especially where foreign policy and the army were concerned, the vote of these provinces at the States-General was now largely at the disposal of their Stadholder, who under the Government Regulations practically appointed their representatives on the general assembly. William's whole policy, not only in these three provinces, was directed, through a complicated and dark system of corruption, to establishing control over the States-General.

It goes without saying that his domination over the assembly, although at times very real, was never complete. Yet, when it came to the point, there was only one province which had preserved any considerable liberty of action, or rather, some towns in that province had, and above all Amsterdam. For that province was Holland. In spite of the fright experienced by the regents in the summer of 1672, and in spite of so many 'yes-men' having taken the places of independent republicans, Amsterdam and one or two more of the Holland towns were the first to have the courage to form opinions of their own about the great issues of war and peace and matters connected therewith.

For William III these issues were everything. I have now given you a glimpse of his system of government from the inside; and it does not appear very attractive. But when one asks : what purpose was behind all this? — the greatness of the man again springs into view. William III was not a democrat, but who was in the seventeenth century? He was no reformer, but he had not been called to power in order to institute reforms? In an unparalleled crisis — 'in a storm' — he had been placed at the rudder so that he might 'steer' — and that is what he did. There is no sense in asking whether in fact he did it so much better than De Witt had done. He had one advantage over De Witt, and for the moment that was all that mattered : his coming into office was enough to restore confidence. With him at their side the States were again able to exercise their authority. Courage revived, and obedience. Yet it is clear that his significance did not reside in his name only. If that had been so, the result could have been no more than a breathing-space. Young as he was, his advent meant that a ruler of un-common stature had taken charge.

He was sensible enough to make use of the services, and listen to the advice, of experienced regents like Van Beuningen and Van Beverningh, both experts in foreign policy (and the latter, note well, the man who less than twenty years before had concocted with Cromwell the Act of Seclusion!). But from the first, nevertheless, he followed his own judgement with an amazing self-confidence. The conversation with Buckingham and Arlington gives the measure of his force. He said exactly what needed to be said, clearly, to the point, without one super-fluous word, but with those great words of 'honour' and 'con-science' charged with conviction — and, I am inclined to add: putting those unprincipled courtiers firmly in their place. The interview with the Rotterdam burgomaster and alderman makes less pleasant reading, but that this coolly insolent young man knew what he wanted, these gentlemen, offended as they were for the rest of their lives, cannot have had any doubt. That century still believed in the magic power of princely blood, a power which enabled its possessor to rule. William III believed in it himself. He would have cast the thought in religious terms : God had called his family, and now himself, to serve the Netherlands, and more than that, the cause of Protestantism in Europe. The miraculous turn of events after his elevation — miraculous in appearance even when we can find matter-of-fact explanations — strengthened both the belief of the public and his own. And it certainly constituted an enormous force.

So we are driven back to his birth in order to explain the secret of his career, but birth conceived in a way that stimulated his sense of duty and responsibility and his capacity for action. Never did William III betray what he felt to be his mission, which was to offer resistance to Louis XIV's power policy. His first care must be to keep the Republic ready. But it was clear that the small country was powerless to do anything decisive by itself. His second care, therefore, was to detach England from the side of France. The peace of 1674 was not enough : England must be brought over into the anti-French camp. The Republic had already won the support of Spain, of the Emperor, of Brandenburg, but without England no European coalition was complete. To draw Charles II, his cynical and frivolous uncle, who believed in nothing, whose only concern was 'not to go on his travels again', on to the side of the Republic against France — this was what William III was consistently trying to effect. When, after the evacuation of Dutch territory by the French in 1674, war-weariness in the Republic kept growing with every campaign in the Southern Netherlands — for that unhappy country had once more become the theatre of war — William III wanted obstinately to hold on, always hoping he would succeed in his next attempt. He was a man of one idea, unable to admit that he might be chasing a chimera. At this particular moment the regents were really more clear-sighted. The 'yes-men' of 1672 broke away from his lead ; Van Beuningen and Van Beverningh, even the faithful Fagel, realized that peace had become inevitable. The Peace of Nijmegen of 1678, concluded against William III's wishes, did lead, as William had forseen, to bitter recriminations against the faithless Republic on the part of its Continental allies, and during the next ten years Louis XIV turned these divisions to his own advantage. But that does not mean that it would have been possible, in 1678, to go on with the war.

In any case Nijmegen proved to be no more than a temporary setback. William III had by no means thrown in the sponge. Even now he still fixed his hopes on England.

But a new chapter is opening in his career. I have allowed the fascination of his personality to lead me into a somewhat detailed account of his first appearance on the political scene. The first half of my next lecture, too, I shall devote to the part he played personally in the drama of England's always more or less reluctant participation in the European struggle for power: 1688, and the preparation, in the years before his death in 1702, of the final and decisive effort of the War of the Spanish Succession, which he did not live to direct.

The rest of that next lecture I shall use to link up the entire episode with the great problem dominating the whole of the history of the Low Countries since the split in the late sixteenth century with which I began this series: the relationship between the Northern and the Southern Netherlands.

VI

William III and the Liberties of Europe — The Northern and the Southern Netherlands in the Revolution Period

As I said last time, William III did not throw in the sponge after the disappointment of Nijmegen in 1678. He still fixed his hopes on England, and his determination, which was on the whole crowned with success, to bring England into the struggle for the European balance of power was to dominate the rest of his life.

Van Beuningen, who had been sent to London as the ambassador of the States-General, came to the conclusion in 1682 that nothing was to be done with Charles II, who let himself be paid by Louis XIV for remaining neutral. His presuming to form that opinion and so to thwart the policy of action infuriated the hot-tempered Stadholder. The attempts made by Amsterdam to safeguard the peace in consultation with d'Avaux, the French ambassador, are understandable when one remembers how unfavourable the international situation was — and this not only because of the unreliability of Charles II. But William decried the men of Amsterdam as traitors, and it looked as if a conflict like that of 1650 was pending. Van Beuningen had to make his exit from the political stage ; but Amsterdam did not therefore give in. William resigned himself ; he mastered his passion and a reconciliation was effected. With Louis XIV becoming ever more overbearing, with the Edict of Nantes revoked, with the Catholic King James II doing his best in England to undermine the Protestant and Parliamentary constitution, everybody began to feel that the international situation demanded harmony at home.

1688 appeared to be a second miracle, like the one of 1672.

James II expelled, Parliament and the Established Church re-affirmed in their rights, and all this without civil war, at the expense of nothing more than a campaign for the subduing of Ireland : it was possible only because William, through the unwavering consistency with which he stuck to his line of policy, had gained the confidence of the English opposition, that is, of the leading elements of the English nation. And so his great aim was realized, and England did join in the struggle against Louis XIV. The new war had already started. It was the first that was not to bring Louis any gain. The Peace of Rijswijk in 1697 was a draw.

But how tremendous a task, meanwhile, was facing William in England! And this in circumstances with which, even though his attention had, from his youth on, been directed towards England, he was unfamiliar.

On the banner that was borne before him when he landed at Torbay the time-honoured motto of the House of Orange '*Je maintiendrai*' (I shall maintain) was followed by 'the Liberties of England and the Protestant Religion'. But what were these 'liberties' of England? The contest for supreme power between King and Parliament, which had in 1642 brought about the civil war, had not, after the interregnum of Commonwealth and Protectorate, really been settled. Now, in 1688, factors came into play that could not but add to the influence of Parliament with respect to the Crown. William's intervention had been undertaken in response to the request of some members of the Upper House. The task of settling the new state of affairs was left to a freely-elected Parliament, whose sanction was needed for William and Mary's ascension. Yet, even though they owed their position to the choice made by Parliament, William and Mary entered upon all the traditional rights of royalty. These, it is true, might seem to be limited by the Declaration of Rights drawn up by Parliament, which they accepted, but this document was of a conservative tendency, and was in fact only directed against the specific malpractices the nation had just suffered at the hands of James II. The main issues were left in a state of vagueness as before, and, as might be expected, William tried, here no less than in the Republic, to keep the conduct of foreign policy in his own hands.

At first he got his way. But in the long run, after Mary's death in 1694, when he wore the crown alone, and especially after the Peace of Rijswijk in 1697, he came into sharp conflict with Parliament. He had done what he could to keep out of the party struggle. One might think that the Whigs were his natural allies — the Whigs, who stressed the Protestant affiliations of the Church of England, and who had been the first and the most vehement in opposing the Stuarts. But William was at least equally attracted by the monarchical tendency in Tory thinking, and he did his best to win them over. In any case he wanted to avoid a party government, and indeed the development of political life in England was hardly ripe for that; the cabinets were still too much the King's personal affair. And as for William, the party contests aroused his impatience. Those questions did not interest him.

On the whole it may be said that England did not interest him. He needed the country against Louis XIV, but he did not feel at home there. The Stuarts, with all their shortcomings, had been truly English. Charles II, pleasant in intercourse, witty, had been genuinely interested in science, in literature. The new King made an impression of stiffness, reserve, coldness, on the English, and indeed it was only in the company of his Dutch friends that he thawed : there was Bentinck, with whom later on the relationship cooled off when the King showed preference to another and younger nobleman, Keppel. But even to Holland town regents William could open his heart in a way he never did to English courtiers or politicians, and indeed these latter would have been not a little offended had they known of some of his utterances. In 1689 Witsen, burgomaster of Amsterdam, came to England as a member of the delegation which had to confirm the new alliance between the two Maritime Powers, and he witnessed the Coronation in Westminster Abbey. William asked him what he had thought of 'that comedy', and scoffed at 'these foolish, old, popish ceremonies'. It could not have been more Dutch, that reaction! The friction which he experienced in England some years afterwards made William even more conscious of his Dutch origins. In 1692, in the week when The Hague was holding its annual fair, he sighed to his secretary Huygens, son of the great poet and brother of the great scientist : 'I wish I were a bird and could fly over!' There was in his relations with Dutchmen a personal, a human, element which was lacking in those with Englishmen.

And stiff and cold as William might seem, he was in the depth of him very much a human being. Under the surface of the Prince, the Stadholder, the King, there burned a fire. The passion behind his conduct of politics had itself a human touch. His whole heart was in his feeling of responsibility towards the great cause he served, and in his detestation of Louis XIV's system of domination. Whoever stood in his way there, he looked upon as an enemy ; with anyone who supported him he could throw off his reserve. What he disliked most in the English was that their thinking was so little European. In the Netherlands, too, he had met with plenty of objections and hesitations and even opposition. But now, as far as the Dutch were concerned, the situation had been cleared, the great choice had been made. England had been brought in, and a main cause of controversy had been eliminated. Indeed, even before 1688 there had been a number of Dutchmen who had understood him and his policy, and who had supported him whole-heartedly, among them Fagel, the Grand Pensionary, who died just about the time of the English expedition. The letter William III wrote on that occasion to the dead man's brother (in Dutch) came straight from the heart.

> I cannot sufficiently testify to you with what sorrow down to the inmost of my soul I have learnt of the sad death of the Grand Pensionary. I am losing the truest friend I can have in this world and certainly the Republic the most devoted subject.

With Fagel's successor, Heinsius, a similar relationship grew up. The correspondence William conducted with him from

England, or while campaigning in the Southern Netherlands, is the best source we have for his policy in the last period of his life. (To him too he wrote always in Dutch; only with the members of the nobility — Bentinck, Ginckel, and the rest — did he correspond in French.) He expressed himself in those letters to Heinsius with complete unrestraint. Complaints about the English climate — his health, which was never strong, suffered, he felt, from its effects — bitter sallies against 'this people'. Speaking to Huygens, he let fall on one occasion: 'I am sure that this people has not been made for me, nor I for it.' It was always the indifference of the English for what lay closest to his heart — the co-operation of Europe against the French danger; their naïve feeling of being safe behind the sea, and their foolish illusion that England was a world by itself. When, in April 1699, he was able to announce that he was coming to Holland the following month, he added from the bottom of his heart: 'For which I am longing as a fish for water.'

In fact his disagreements with Parliament had at that moment come to a head, and it was the Tories who were causing him difficulties — the Tories, who were much more insular (or 'isolationist') than were the Whigs. For the Tories — that is to say, for the landed gentry — the Continent hardly existed, and they did not feel that their beloved Church of England had anything to do with the Continental Protestants. In the eyes of the High Church men these latter were not a whit better than their own detested Presbyterians. These Tories were now, under the influence of their resentment at William's international views, forgetting their monarchical principles, and were not scrupling to use their strength in Parliament to whittle down the royal authority in the field of foreign policy.

William's conduct of affairs had indeed been extremely high-handed. After the Peace of Rijswijk the prospect in Europe was far from reassuring. On the contrary, the great crisis, which would have to decide between a balance of power or French hegemony, seemed only now to be imminent. This was connected with the precarious life of the unhappy King of Spain, the last of the Spanish Habsburgs, Carlos II, whose death had been expected really from his birth in 1661 on, and who now at long last seemed to be dying in real earnest (it took him in fact until 1700). His death would pose the problem of the succession in the decadent, but still enormously extensive, Spanish empire : Spain, the American colonies, Milan, Naples and Sicily, the Southern Netherlands. Through his marriage with a Spanish princess Louis XIV was able to claim the entire succession for his son, or for a grandson ; but the claim of the Austrian Habsburg, the Emperor, was at least as good. A great war seemed unavoidable, but exhausted as Europe was after a series of wars, attempts were made to prevent a rupture by resorting to a partition. It was above all William III and Louis XIV who worked for this end, and it is curious to see this short-lived *rapprochement* between the two antagonists.

That vital English interests were at stake in the modalities of such a partition goes without saying. The Mediterranean, South America — these were extremely sensitive points for English commerce, and of course important strategic considerations were also involved there. The arrangements with Louis XIV for the Partition Treaty of 1698 and, when this had been nullified by the unexpected death of the little Bavarian prince who had, by way of lightning conductor, been assigned for the succession, those for the second Partition Treaty of 1699 as well, had been discussed by William with Portland, that is to say Bentinck, and with the States-General, but he had omitted to consult not only Parliament but even his English ministers.

Parliament took their revenge by opening an attack on everything that affected William personally. His gifts of land in Ireland and elsewhere to Dutch favourites were first questioned. These Netherlands gentry masquerading as Englishmen, with their brand-new estates and titles, were a thorn in the flesh of the old English nobility and gentry. Next, Parliament — which since, after all, it was peace, had made a point of economizing on the army — presumed to dissolve the Dutch Guards' regiments that had been in English service since 1689.

I am so angry [William wrote to Heinsius] about what is happening
in the House of Commons in the matter of the troops, that I can
hardly concentrate my thoughts on anything else. I foresee that
I shall have to come to extreme decisions and that I shall see you in
Holland earlier than I had intended.

He was thinking in real earnest of abdicating and leaving
England for ever. However, he controlled himself. But the
cup of his humiliations had not been emptied yet. In 1700
Carlos II, as I said earlier on, died. And now William had to
look on, inwardly raging, but without letting the world see it,
while Louis set aside the (second) Partition Treaty, so recently
concluded, and allowed his second grandson, Philip of Anjou,
to succeed — in accordance with the will left by Carlos — to
the sovereignty over the entire, undivided, Spanish empire. It
filled William with impotent wrath to see how blind were the
English (and even a good many of the Dutch) and how they
applauded this solution. For to their gullible minds it meant
'no war' and they did not look beyond the moment. He even,
in his capacity as King of England, had to recognize Philip V —
bitter necessity! The States-General did so likewise. It looked
as if Louis would carry it off and William's entire life's work end
in failure. For though he was no more than fifty years old, he
could not disguise to himself the fact that his end was not far
off. Everybody noticed his worn-out appearance, his deeply-
sunk eyes, the cough that tormented him relentlessly. But his
energy was unabated.

It was the cruellest trial of a life during which he had met
with so many trials that he had to prove his energy in self-control,
in passively waiting. He never for a moment shared in the
illusionist mood prevailing in England — and to which many
in the Republic too gave way, now that England's resignation
left no practical alternative —, but to go right against it might
have done irreparable harm. His unpopularity, and the unpopularity of his Dutch bumpkins, constituted for the moment
an insuperable obstacle. A waiting policy was indicated. There
was always the hope that Louis himself would play into his

hand, and for that eventuality it was necessary to be prepared and on the watch. In the meantime a blank face must be presented to the Tories, attempts must be made to win them over by concessions. The watchword was, in other words, to lie low until the moment came.

And indeed the moment did come, soon enough. Philip V, King of the Spanish empire — that could seem sufferable, even though he was a Bourbon, as long as it could be assumed that he would indeed be a King. But it soon became plain that he was nothing more than his grandfather's vassal. Great was the commotion, first, of course, in the Republic, but then also in England, when the Southern Netherlands were occupied, in the name of Philip V, no doubt, but by French troops. Then in 1701, when James II died at the French court, where he had found a refuge after his flight from England, Louis XIV addressed the exile's son as King of England. This was like a blow in the face of William III. There was no possibility of living on terms with Louis, that was the conclusion drawn in wide circles ; he would never stop ; all his affectations or protestations of moderation were deceit.

Our generation, which has witnessed similar phenomena, however different in appearance, can readily understand the sudden reversal of the public mood. The protagonists of 'appeasement' were themselves abashed. Everyone had now to admit that William III had been right in denouncing the French danger. Supporters flocked around him. Away with cutting down expenses! Away with neutrality! The army and the navy were made ready, negotiations were set on foot with the Emperor, the rival pretender to the Spanish inheritance, who had not for a moment thought of recognizing Philip V, but on the contrary had already resorted to warlike action in Italy.

So the Grand Alliance came into being. Before the end of 1701 it was concluded at The Hague. Marlborough, the great man of the period now beginning, had been sent over by William III to undertake the relevant negotiations. The new allies demanded of Louis XIV that he should meet the Emperor's claims and at the same time give guarantees for the safety of the United Netherlands and of England. In practice this meant that he was challenged to consent to a partition after all. It was out of the question, of course, that Louis would consent. Another great European war was inevitable, the War of the Spanish Succession.

William died in March 1702, while preparations were being made. Riding in the park of Hampton Court, his horse stumbled. He fell off and broke his collar-bone. At first the accident did not seem serious, but soon complications set in. His household, and the patient himself, understood that the end was near. Stoical to the last, yet at the same time sensitive, the Stadholder-King took leave of his friends. Bentinck was there — it was a reconciliation in the face of death — and they shook hands — 'for the last time', as William whispered in Dutch.

What must be our final reflections after my very cursory survey of that crowded life? That William bequeathed to Europe another great war, after so many? In the sphere where lay his task, war was not the aim but an indispensable means. The aim was the liberties of Europe. That generation knew no other way to safeguard these than by means of the balance of power. To us that is an antiquated notion, but with the conception of the liberties it was intended to safeguard we are, on the contrary, acutely familiar.

The War of the Spanish Succession lasted until 1713, when peace was concluded at Utrecht. Its long duration was due to the fact that after a few years the relatively moderate conditions laid down by the Grand Alliance had to give way to the demand that Louis's grandson should hand over to his Austrian rival the whole of the Spanish empire with all its dependencies in various parts of the globe. The final settlement at Utrecht meant a return to the idea of partition. Looked at in detail, some of the arrangements made at Utrecht were curiously artificial, and in practice unworkable. But I shall not now go into that. The main thing is that this war, and this peace, did indeed put an end to the idea of a 'universal monarchy', of French domination over Europe, which had all along been the ambition of Louis XIV's government. The European balance of power, it can be said, was preserved, and the future of European liberties kept open.

This is what we remember above all when we consider the historic figure of William III. In his position as Stadholder and, generally speaking, in his relations with domestic politics, what strikes us is his dictatorial behaviour : headstrong and high-handed. When he died, there was in the Republic certainly as much of a feeling of relief as of sorrow, and this in a much wider circle than that of the regents. He was in no sense of the word a democrat ; he had not easily borne opposition ; his birth had meant a great deal to him. But what he had fought against in Louis XIV was the despot, the man who looked upon the state as an instrument for his own greatness — and he was far from being such a man himself. The tradition of his house seemed to him to designate him — and so it was understood by the people too — to promote the general interest, and at the same time to protect the ancient liberties, that is to say, the rights of individuals and of groups. In this latter respect his interpretations were often arbitrary enough, although this part of the Orange tradition did mean something very real to him in his conception of his task ; in any case his adherents were soon to gloss over his contradictions and shortcomings so that the tradition could survive him unimpaired.

But the true significance of William III lies in his faithful service to the cause of European liberties. This term 'European liberties' does not allow of a very exact definition. It can best be explained negatively as the rallying-cry of those who resisted political and spiritual domination by any one power, by any one tyrannical system. In that resistance, moreover, there grew up a certain awareness of common European interests. That William III took this with profound seriousness cannot be doubted. And it is in this that we can feel very close to him ; here his life's work can still be an inspiration to us.

William III had embodied in his lifetime the policy of preserving what was the indispensable guarantee for the safety of the small Dutch Republic and its Protestant system, the European balance of power. In reality Dutch public opinion was most of the time engrossed by the aspect of that larger conception which touched it most nearly, the fate of the Southern Netherlands. Indeed William III himself, in his letters to Heinsius surveying the situation created when Philip of Anjou took over the whole of the Spanish monarchy, said more than once in so many words that his principal concern was 'to prevent the Spanish Netherlands from falling into the hands of France'. After his death, when it fell to Heinsius, without the aid of a Stadholder (1702 to 1747: Second Stadholderless Period, is what we learn at school), to guide the country through the great coalition war of the Spanish Succession, that major preoccupation was no longer purely negative, but began to assume a positive shape.

The French were driven out of the Southern Netherlands by the Anglo-Dutch forces under Marlborough as early as 1706 (battle of Ramillies), and the Austrian Habsburg pretender's claim to the country had then of course to be recognized. But the Dutch now looked upon it as their 'barrier', and they were anxious, not only to secure the right to maintain garrisons in a row of fortified towns along the southern frontier of the Austrian Netherlands, but also to lay hold on the nerve centres of the country's internal communication system so as to make it economically dependent too ; to turn it, one might say, into a kind of Generality Lands. In 1709 they extorted from the Whig government a promise that England would, at the peace, help them to obtain from the new Austrian overlord of the Southern provinces terms intended to realize that conception. Their English ally was not very keen to let the Republic monopolize the Southern Netherlands, but England had far-flung ambitions elsewhere — in the Mediterranean and in Spanish America — and although the way these ambitions tended to protract the war caused great heart-burnings in the Republic, the Dutch leaders were, however reluctantly, willing to give them full scope in order to get the promises they wanted with respect to the Southern Netherlands. In 1711, however, the new Tory Government repudiated the promises made in 1709 and soon arranged a peace with France behind their ally's back. In the end the Dutch did get their barrier, but the provisions of the Dutch-Austrian Barrier Treaty of 1715 fell far short of what now appeared to have been the illusions of 1709.

Looking back, it can be seen that the War of the Spanish Succession laid the foundations of English world-power, while at the same time it brought to an end the period in which the Dutch Republic had been able to play a really effective rôle in the affairs of Europe. That war and its conclusion revealed the Republic's dependence upon England, caused not only by its small size and limited resources, but by its vulnerable situation on the Continent. It had been made clearer than ever that the Republic's safety depended on the Southern Netherlands, where the Barrier Treaty now gave it certain rights, but which were left, after all, in alien hands, and whose people remained passive in these international contests. Worse than that, the Flemings and Brabanters were inclined to resent the presence on their soil of Dutch garrisons (in fact largely composed of foreign mercenaries), and even more the economic privileges which their self-styled protectors had managed to obtain for themselves.

This brings me back to that disastrous event in Netherlands history to which I devoted my first and second lectures : the separation in the late sixteenth century of the Northern and the Southern provinces. In the first half of the seventeenth century, even in the days of De Witt, there had still been fleeting thoughts of reunion, but the difference between the religious systems that had triumphed in the North and in the South respectively had always doomed to failure such projects as were formed. Now the very word 'barrier' seemed to degrade the people of the Southern Netherlands, and stamp their country as a thing with no interests or will of its own, a mere convenience for the benefit of the Dutch. The events that had, throughout the reign of Louis XIV, perturbed Europe and the Northern and Southern Netherlands in particular, had made it clear that the sixteenth-century split had left both in an exposed position and too weak to maintain themselves separately. The barrier arrangement could not really remedy that state of affairs.

As a matter of fact, this Dutch defence system on Austrian territory collapsed early in the second half of the eighteenth century, when the Austrian Emperor, sovereign of the Southern Netherlands, and Louis XV of France drew together. This might seem another way of covering the safety of the Republic, but in actual fact it proved unreliable. Even before the French Revolution broke out little was left of this Franco-Austrian understanding. Then, at any rate, France resumed her expansionist policy with greater ardour, and at first with greater success, than ever under Louis XIV. And the Austrian Netherlands were among the first spoils.

By 1793 a great European coalition had been formed, as in the days of William III, to contain this startlingly dynamic France, a coalition to which Austria, England and the Dutch Republic all belonged. But Austria was not really vitally interested in that outlying dependency, the Southern Netherlands, England was slow to throw her full strength into a land war, and the Dutch Republic was no match for France, especially now that the latter country was posing as the champion of freedom and in most countries many were ready to acclaim her as such.

In Holland, just before the Revolution had started on its career in France, there had been an active movement of democratic reform, directed this time against the House of Orange. The old order, of which the Stadholdership had now become the symbol (for the regent class, at one time so suspicious of its ambitions, was now sheltering behind it), had been restored, with Prussian and English aid, in 1787. This restored Orangist régime, lacking in imagination as well as in energy, was not equal to the task of holding the Southern frontier, which was immediately threatened when the French occupied the whole of the Austrian Netherlands ; and when in January 1795 they broke into the seven provinces, it collapsed at once. (Let me remark in passing that this was the only occasion in modern times when the Northern Netherlands were invaded from the South : the rivers could not fulfil their usual protective function because they froze over solidly enough for the ice to carry men and horses and guns — a very rare occurrence.) The Stadholder, the pitiful William V, fled to England, and in one town after another little bloodless revolutions were effected, new men taking the place of the old regents. The personnel of the States too — first Provincial, then General — was changed, and the Batavian Republic, which was recognized by the French Convention, was proclaimed.[1]

For the future of the Dutch community it was highly important that this change was effected without the direct interference of the French, and that the Batavian Republic, and even the Kingdom of Holland under Napoleon's brother Louis which succeeded it (1806–1810), were able to manage their domestic affairs by themselves. Quite apart from how we regard the achievements — some important reforms were in any case carried through — this was in itself a matter of importance for the future. But it must always be remembered that self-government was confined to domestic matters. In international affairs The Hague had simply to follow the lead of Paris, and this meant, above all, that the country was dragged along in the interminable war with England, which crippled its trade and colonial possessions and left it in the end more economically exhausted than it had ever been by the wars of the *ancien régime*.

In 1810 Napoleon deposed his brother, who had identified himself too much with his Dutch subjects for the Emperor's liking, and the country was annexed to the French Empire. Unassailable as the position of the great conqueror still seemed, there were those who in their hearts persisted in regarding him as a usurper. When in 1812 (in Russia) and then in 1813 (at Leipzig) he met with disaster, a small group composed of pre-Revolution regents and nobles, but supported by men of 'Batavian' principles and antecedents, proclaimed at The Hague their country's independence, under the sovereignty of the late Stadholder's son, constituting themselves into a provisional government. It was a well-timed act, and a courageous one ; Van Hogendorp, the leader, has deservedly remained a great name in Dutch history. Russian and Prussian troops were already crossing the eastern frontier but French troops were still holding the centre of the country. William V's son was waiting in England. He now came to Holland, was welcomed by the Provisional Government at The Hague, and then, in front of a large and enthusiastic crowd in Amsterdam, announced his acceptance of the sovereignty (which in the old Republic had rested with the States-General), the sovereignty, as he put it, under the restraint of a wise constitution. That he could figure as William I, not VI, at the expressed desire, and amid the acclamations, of the nation, instead of being introduced by the victorious army of the allies, was a fact of real importance.

The fate of the Southern Netherlands — of Belgium, as the country was now being called — was very different, as it had been all through the period of the Revolution. Annexed to the French Republic in 1794, it had been, for fully twenty years, part of the strong-centralized French state, first a Republic, then an Empire. The numerous ancient bodies, provincial and municipal, which under the Austrian régime, even after the innovations of the Enlightened Despot Joseph II, still dispensed justice and carried on local administration, had been swept away. Antiquated and riddled with abuses as they were, these bodies had been the last refuge of self-government. While the Austrian central government had been gradually extending its power and with it the use of the French language, these provincial courts of law, provincial States assemblies, municipal councils and magistracies, had still retained Dutch as their official language. Now, suddenly, a new judicial system and a new administration were introduced, strictly subject, not to Brussels, but to Paris, from whence directives came ; and even in the lower ranges of the judicature and of the administration Frenchmen penetrated. French law was introduced and the Dutch language was proscribed for official use from the lowest grades upwards.

Education was adapted to the needs of this alien régime

imposed upon the country. In the elementary schools it was impossible to use any language other than Flemish (Dutch) as a medium of education. For that reason the new rulers could never work up any interest in these schools ; they were badly neglected and by the end of the period illiteracy had increased. Meanwhile, in the Batavian Republic, an Education Act was passed in 1806, by which elementary education, thus far left to the church and to private, largely charitable, enterprise, was placed on a firm national foundation. This Act survived the revolutionary period and remained of outstanding importance down to the middle of the nineteenth century. In Belgium secondary and university teaching had been taken firmly in hand by the French and thoroughly gallicized. The well-to-do classes in Flanders and Brabant, especially if they were thinking of careers for their children in the law or in administration, had to have them educated in French ; soon, indeed, there was no choice left. French became the medium of instruction, Frenchmen flocked into the new French *départements* to help turn the next generation of the better-born into little Frenchmen. Naturally the Flemish and Brabant upper classes still knew Flemish. They spoke it in their intercourse with the lower orders, in its strongly-varying dialectical forms ; they even spoke it among themselves, on homely occasions and in relation to homely affairs. But French came more and more to be the only language for polite intercourse and for cultural and public purposes.

The profound cleavage between the socially and economically powerful French-speaking classes and the people ignorant of French — that cleavage so characteristic of nineteenth- and early twentieth-century Flanders, and not entirely overcome today (I shall have more to say about this later on) — was largely created by the twenty years' annexation to France and the merciless centralizing tendency of the French state.

One result was that the popular classes of the Dutch-speaking provinces of Belgium were, through being confined to their native language or dialect, more completely shut off from contact with any form of higher culture or any public discussion of national affairs than is usually the case (and was, even at that period) in a normal unilingual society.

Indeed, these twenty years were, for the Southern Netherlands, a period of complete subjection and political passivity, coming on top of two centuries of a régime, milder, no doubt, but also foreign, and which had also left the native-born leading classes no say in the destinies of their country as a whole. No wonder there was not — indeed there could not be — anything like the upsurge of public spirit, of which Van Hogendorp's proclamation of independence, and the enthusiasm that greeted the return of a member of the House of Orange, had given so striking an example in the North. We must not forget, certainly, that in November 1813, while these stirring scenes were taking place in The Hague and Amsterdam, the French troops still in the neighbourhood were no more than a rearguard section of the strong force with which Napoleon was still holding Belgium. But even if immediate circumstances had favoured a similar enterprise there, where were the men who might have taken the initiative and whose names would have appealed to the popular imagination? What happened was that Belgium had to wait until the allied armies had cleared the country of the French and the French régime, and when that had been accomplished, in the late spring of 1814, Belgium was placed under a provisional allied administration until the great Congress gathering in Vienna had decided what was to be done with it.

Everyone knows that the solution reached by the assembled powers was to unite Belgium with Holland in a Kingdom of the Netherlands — to unite — indeed, to amalgamate ; that is to say that the two peoples were to live under one constitution. For that purpose the fundamental law which the Dutch had just evolved on the basis of William I's pledge of November 1813 was revised by a Dutch-Belgian Commission, and one representative assembly was set up.

This solution — of a reunion — was largely inspired by England — by Castlereagh. Austria was only too pleased to waive her claims to a possession in that critical north-western corner of Europe in return for a compensation in Italy. But to England it could not be a matter of indifference that there should be, opposite her shores, this weak spot in the European system. To statesmen who knew their history it must have been obvious that this weakness had its origin in the disruption of the seventeen Netherlands over two centuries earlier, and the experiences through which that generation had just passed could not but make it seem likely that France would, sooner or later, under whatever régime she might be living, again try to take advantage of it. The barrier system had not proved satisfactory. All that I have said about the problem in the days of William III and Louis XIV, and later on during the Revolutionary period, was still applicable. What could be more reasonable than to correct what had been so patently an error of history!

But again, everybody knows that the reunion did not work, and that as early as 1830 an insurrection in Brussels led to a renewed separation and to the foundation of the Kingdom of Belgium, with Leopold of Coburg as its King.

The fact is, of course, that the considerations of international policy which had determined the English government's attitude towards the question in 1814 could not so exclusively dominate public opinion in the two countries immediately concerned. I have told you enough about the estrangement between the Dutch and the Flemings (and then there were the Walloons!), the estrangement following upon the separation over two hundred years earlier, to make it understandable that the reunion could not be really popular either in Holland or in Belgium. In Holland, no doubt, there was the King, who was all eagerness, to whom indeed the reunion was the fulfilment of ambitions he had cherished as a young man, during his father's lifetime, in the early years of the French war, in the 1790s, when international relations were in a flux and everything seemed possible. He was not entirely without support. In Holland some of the leading men in his government believed in the reunion, as did some intellectuals. In Belgium, curiously enough, it was the new classes of industrialists, officials and lawyers, all of them

French-speaking Walloons or gallicized Flemings, who on the whole welcomed William, while the mass of the Flemish people, following their bishops, regarded the Calvinist King with suspicion. In fact, of course, William's political programme was in no sense specifically Calvinistic ; it was liberal, in the sense then attached to that word.

But these are extraordinarily complicated questions. I shall just touch upon them in a lecture to come, and the story of the failure of the great experiment I shall have to dispatch very briefly. The main purport of that lecture[3] will be to show that the renewed separation in 1830, enthusiastically greeted in Belgium as the final solution and accepted as such even in Holland, with relief rather than with regret, left in fact very grave problems in being. I am alluding — as you may guess — to the unsatisfactory position of the Dutch-speaking population of the Flemings in the newly-created wholly French-dominated Kingdom. Soon after 1830 there arose the Flemish movement, which gathered strength as time went on, especially after the First World War ; as a matter of fact it is at this moment a major factor in Belgian political life. I have since my early years been very closely connected with it — I still am. The history that I shall offer you when dealing with these problems will be permeated with the personal memories of a lifetime.

VII

Historical Appreciations of the Holland
Regent Régime
(1954)

THE struggle between the Holland 'regents'[1] and Orange — the Holland regents acting from their bulwark, the States of Holland, based securely on the Amsterdam town hall — presents one of the most spectacular aspects of the history of the Republic of the United Netherlands in the seventeenth and eighteenth centuries.

In the first decades of the Republic's existence these two powers had not been at variance. The crisis that opens the contest is the famous one occurring during the Twelve Years' Truce (1609–1621), culminating in the execution of the old 'Advocate' of the States of Holland,[2] Oldenbarnevelt, in 1619. After that there still were periods of harmonious, or tolerably harmonious, co-operation, but rivalry and suspiciousness were never completely overcome. In 1650, 1672, 1683, 1747 and 1780 they gave rise to new crises, until in 1795 regent sovereignty and Orange eminence together were brushed aside by the Revolution.

The history of the Republic presents itself stiffly framed within unshakable constitutional forms. From start to finish the towns in Holland (to speak only of that province; the other provinces each knew different arrangements, but all alike were wedded to them immovably) were administered (or 'governed', as it was put at the time) by corporations (*vroedschappen*), consisting of from twenty-four to forty gentlemen who sat for life, filled vacancies through co-optation, and every year appointed burgomasters and aldermen. The citizens had no say in the election of their rulers or in the conduct of affairs. Order was maintained by civic guards drawn largely from the lower middle-class, but officered by members of the regent class. In 1581 the States of Holland passed a decree forbidding the town governments (that is, its own component members) to consult the guilds about matters on which the town delegates would have to pronounce in the assembly.

The States of each province exercised the rights of sovereignty in that province. The Holland assembly consisted of eighteen town delegations, appointed and instructed by the town governments, and the committee of noblemen (nineteen votes in all). The conduct of foreign affairs rested with the States-General, which was no more than an assembly of the deputies of the sovereign provinces, bound by the instructions given them by the respective provincial States. The Stadholder was a minister of the various provincial States, although reminiscences of the royal period, when he was the representative of the common sovereign, continued to cling to the office : he had, for instance, a say in the election of town councillors and magistrates, that is, ultimately, in the appointment of his masters, the delegations composing the States of the province. From 1650 to 1672 and again from 1702 to 1747 Holland managed without a Stadholder, but when there was one, his function was always essentially the same.

This immobility, which to the modern observer seems astonishing, made it possible for a legend to grow up in which the party struggle, the antithesis between regent class and Orange, was reduced to the simplest terms and all the successive conflicts were explained thereby.

I should have said : *two* legends, for each of the parties, the Orangists and the Statists, had its own legend. The political contest was largely waged with the aid of arguments drawn from history. This is one of the characteristics of public life in the seventeenth- and eighteenth-century Dutch Republic, and a phenomenon to which I have devoted a good deal of attention.[3] Each party cultivated a view of the past in which the great men of the rival party cut sorry figures : the Stadholders were maltreated in the history of the Statists ; and so were the great Grand-pensionaries, the States of Holland, Amsterdam, in the history of the Orangists. Each side used these self-constructed bogies in order to cast ignomy on its contemporaries of the other persuasion. In those impassioned controversies cool historical criticism did occasionally make itself heard, but this — not exclusively, yet mainly and more effectively — on the side of the Statists.

Take what was called the 'Wittian War', an eruption, in 1757, of pamphlets attacking and defending 'the character of the Lord Grand-Pensionary Johan de Witt'. The protagonists on the opposing sides were Jan Wagenaar and Elie Luzac, and when I studied their writings I was struck to notice how much stronger was the legendary element in the history presented by the Orangist Luzac than in the expositions of the Statist Wagenaar. The whole of Luzac's method consisted in deducing conclusions from dogmatically advanced constitutional (or one might say, party) premises, while Wagenaar at least attempted to discern the facts and place them in a context of their own.

The Orangist legend, so prevalent in the historic consciousness of the Dutch people, owes its vitality largely to the connection with religious sentiment. The fact comes out very clearly, after the downfall of the Republic and after the miserable episode of the gradually increasing dependence on France, in the opening decade of the kingdom established in 1813 to 1815. The legend was then reanimated and given a new lease of life by that great counter-revolutionary eccentric, the protester against the spirit of the age, Bilderdijk. As far as the period after the sixteenth-century separation of the Netherlands is concerned, Bilderdijk's *Geschiedenis des Vaderlands* is no more than a highly seasoned rehash of the Orangist party stuff dished up by eighteenth-century writers like Blomhert and Arnoldus Rotterdam, Elie Luzac and R. M. van Goens. The twelve volumes of Bilderdijk's work are indeed one protracted pamphlet, and one of unprecedented virulence. The pathological bitterness of that dynamic personality exercised, not a wide, but a profound influence. Soon it was canalized, and purged of its worst excesses, in the work of a younger man, Groen van Prinsterer, who, when a student at Leyden, had followed the master's unauthorized lessons. Groen used to emphasize his independence with respect to 'the acrimonious Bilderdijk', and not without justification ; yet in a way he acted as the apostle of the older man's message.

Groen's *Handboek der Geschiedenis van het Vaderland* appeared in 1846. It is free from the vehemence, from the wild fantasticalities and scurrilous invective, by which Bilderdijk's work is disfigured. There is infinitely more genuine research behind it. But it follows the same party line, while even more exclusively interpreting events from the religious point of view. It is a religious epic of the chosen North Netherlands Republic, chosen in order, under the leadership of the providential House of Orange, to provide a shining example of God's mercy showered on a Reformed people. By his indefatigable resistance to dominant liberal thinking, Groen van Prinsterer, the political free lance, was a potent force in helping his co-religionists, later in the nineteenth century, to constitute once more a strong, coherent political group. The historian's authority with them was enormous. His *Handboek* was reprinted again and again. Even today countless teachers at orthodox Protestant schools [4] will swear by it.

Contemporary liberal historians had protested from the first. Yet they too, and especially Fruin, absorbed more of Groen's leading ideas than they were aware of. The influence of Groen's version of our history went, in any case, far beyond his own circle. The specifically religious motivation can, it is true, have its full value for the like-minded only ; that is, for the orthodox section of the old Netherlands Reformed Church and for those who, dissatisfied with the liberalist watering down of the religious life within its precincts, seceded from that church to set up orthodox churches of their own (there were secessions in 1834 and 1886, resulting in what is now called *Gereformeerde Kerk*).[5] Yet Groen's views found sufficient support in general Protestant (as distinct from specific Calvinist) sentiment, which in the nineteenth century still dominated public opinion.

But the Orangist tendency in the interpretation of Dutch history appealed to entirely different sentiments as well, sentiments that could in part still be connected with the ecclesiastical motif, but partly were completely free from it. Otherwise it could not have shown such tenacious vitality.

There were unreasoning feelings of loyalty toward the reigning family, or more generally, a kind of snobbism, an inclination to assume that the regents, being shortsighted merchants and moved by self-interest, could not but compare unfavourably, on the score of political wisdom, with princely personages like the Stadholders. One reproach levelled at the States was that of blindness to the dangers threatening from France. This, curiously enough, although nobody could deny that Frederick Henry (Stadholder, 1625–1647) and his son William II (1647–1650) had based their entire policy on co-operation with France, and that it was Amsterdam and Holland that had raised the cry 'Gallum amicum non vicinum' against the Franco-Dutch alliance of 1635 aiming at a partition of the Spanish Netherlands.

An important factor, too, was the satisfaction with which the men of the nineteenth century regarded the unitary state that had at last been achieved in the closing years of the century before. The liberals set at least as much store by this acquisition as did the conservatives, and in historic appreciation it was the Stadholders who benefited, for it was taken as an axiom that they had, in the days of the Republic, been the bearers of the idea of unity. Again, however, the current view was not quite in accord with the facts. At times, certainly, the Orange party had made much of the principle of Generality before Provincial Sovereignty, but long before the end of the Republic the Stadholders had become the supporters of things as they were, of the constitution as it had been inherited from the glorious forefathers, and unity had to be realized by the Revolution and against Orange.

Then there was — this, too, a point of great importance — the modern aversion to oligarchy. The Stadholders had indeed been the only power that under the Republic constituted a counterpoise to the regents. In order to represent them on that account as the protectors of the people's interests, historic truth had nevertheless to be drastically simplified, even distorted.

All these elements, without the qualifications, will be found in Groen's history, and the whole system can actually be traced back to writers like Luzac, to the party propaganda of the Stadholders' own days. And however much the liberal writers of history of following generations may have revised the picture, correcting the obvious errors and toning down the more extreme partialities — the grand-pensionaries, for example, they treated on the whole with respect — traces of these old tenets of the Orangist legend will frequently obtrude themselves. This is true of the work of Fruin, of Fruin's contemporary Jorissen, and of Fruin's disciple Colenbrander, of the work of Japikse, of Elias — to mention only a few. A considerable part of my own work, *William IV en Engeland* (1924), some of the essays in *Kernproblemen van onze geschiedenis* (1937), *Oranje en Stuart* (1939), also my studies of seventeenth- and eighteenth-century party literature (1947, 1950, 1953), has been devoted to this problem. By means of an exact investigation of the events and an analysis of the expressed opinions I have attempted to substitute for the legend the much more complicated, sometimes radically different, reality of history.

Let me now consider separately each of the points enumerated. I shall do this in connection with the great crises I mentioned in my opening paragraph — or rather, in order not to take up too much time, I shall confine myself to those of the seventeenth century, that is, those of 1618 and 1650 and the long-drawn-out one under De Witt which was violently resolved in 1672.

Only in the first crisis did the church question stand in the forefront, and I want to emphasize at once the fact that each of those conflicts bore a character of its own. To think that one fixed opinion concerning those two powers, the Stadholders with their adherents and the States of Holland with its dependents and sympathizers, will supply the key to the reading of them all, is to begin with a serious error of historical method. Each conflict should be studied in its own circumstances. But I need hardly say that I am not here propounding a novel principle.

Only in 1618, then, did the dispute turn — in outward appearance at least — on the relationship between church and state. There was not yet at that time any tradition of antagonism between the Holland regents and the House of Orange. Friction with Calvinist ministers had been of frequent occurrence from the beginning, but William the Silent himself had been at loggerheads with zealots as well as had certain Holland town governments. His relations with the regents, on the other hand, had on the whole been harmonious. Young Maurice [6] had originally been entirely the man of the States of Holland. Oldenbarnevelt, the States' powerful 'Advocate', gave Maurice all the support in his power to acquire the stadholderly dignity in other provinces. As late as 1610, Grotius, still a young man at that time, but a typical representative of Holland regent circles, had, in his famous little book *De antiquitate reipublicae Batavae*, praised the constitution of the youthful Republic for being a mixture of the three forms enumerated by Aristotle; democracy, aristocracy, monarchy. His identification of the democratic element is done somewhat perfunctorily, but monarchy he wholeheartedly admitted was represented by the Stadholder's powers and position. Later, when the antithesis had become traditional, Orangist polemicists never missed an opportunity to remind the Statists of these words of Oldenbarnevelt's theoretician, who had become so great a saint in their calendar. When Grotius wrote them down, in 1610, a tiny cloud was already appearing in the political sky. Maurice, who was by now a great figure, an internationally famous army commander, had opposed the conclusion of the truce [7] with all his might, and now that Oldenbarnevelt had succeeded in forcing it through, was still grumbling.

But the occasion for the crisis was the dispute about the powers of the church. The Reformed Church was the only one officially recognized in a country where there was still a great variety of religious convictions. The problem now was whether that church might through its own organs purge itself from ministers inclined (under the influence of the teaching of Arminius) to gloss over some of the severer aspects of the Calvinist doctrine and whether at the same time it might impose that doctrine (as maintained by Gomarus) on public life in its entirety ; or should not the state have a say in the matter to see that comprehension, and tolerance, were enforced? The attempts of the States of Holland to act in the latter sense gave rise to a storm of protest. From having been a mere dispute between theologians, the quarrel took on national dimensions. The passions of the people were roused — of the Reformed people, that is, and it should never be forgotten that, even though these constituted no more than a fraction of the nation, the Catholics, the Baptists and other Protestant dissenters were too timid, or too cowed, to count for much in the great political contests.

What brought Oldenbarnevelt to the block and Grotius, now his most intimate adviser, to imprisonment in the Castle of Loevestein, was not, however, the church question alone. The small provinces championed in the States-General the cause of orthodoxy, but not only because they were orthodox. And likewise, if the Prince of Orange, Maurice, who had for so long followed Oldenbarnevelt's lead in political matters, now declared against him (and Maurice's choice of sides was more than anything else to prove the decisive factor), it was principally the difference of opinion on the great question of war or peace that moved him. Maurice, the Stadholder-Captain-General, and the Calvinists were at one in their irreconcilable hostility to Spain. But the consequence was that from now on the combination of Orange and the Calvinist small middle-class with its ministers in opposition to the regent class, which was inclined to be more opportunist in religious matters and generally speaking more worldly, came to constitute an almost constant feature in the political life of the country. It may at times have been crossed by other contrasts, or have for a while lost some of its distinctness in the public mind. But down to the end of the Republic it could be revived to sudden potency. The after-effects made themselves felt by fits and starts all through the nineteenth century, and even in our day the pale reflection can still be observed.

The cry of the seventeenth-century church was for liberty. The most serious charge against the States of Holland, in the hectic years that led to the decapitation of Oldenbarnevelt and the imprisonment of Grotius, was that by supervision and interference (intended to protect and maintain the minority of Arminian, or Remonstrant, ministers) they were in fact reducing the Church to a position of slavery; that their pretended tolerance amounted in reality to spiritual tyranny. The charge was repeated on many occasions in the succeeding generations, and in the nineteenth century Groen and his school made the most of it, but even in the hearts of many Dutch liberals these bitter complaints of the Calvinists raised an echo. It was the liberals who had, in 1848, in the new constitution, proclaimed the freedom of churches and of schools. 'The claim [of the Contraremonstrants in 1617] was justified,' so Fruin, who was far from being a Calvinist, wrote in 1858 : 'without freedom the church cannot develop.' [8]

Now I, too, find it a repulsive spectacle when the States of Holland in their 'resolutions' lay down (as they did in the years preceding their spectacular defeat in 1618) exactly what may be demanded of a new minister's orthodoxy as being indispensable for salvation ; when they prohibit dealing from the pulpit with the points in dispute, threatening the preacher who transgresses the order with suspension or dismissal and dispelling by main force congregations assembling elsewhere to hear him in their despite. But must not the historian remember that the problem as it presented itself in the seventeenth century was different from what it is in the nineteenth or twentieth? [9] The church for whose freedom the seventeenth-century Calvinists contended was a state church that took it upon itself to supervise the government in the matter of orthodoxy. It claimed freedom to expel whoever deviated from the right doctrine ; but expulsion from the church meant expulsion from the state, from political life. The church wanted to be free in order to dominate the state.

This was an ambition every government was bound to resist. It was out of the question for the States of Holland, even after, in consequence of Maurice's *coup d'état*, they had been purged of Oldenbarneveltians and filled with 'Contraremonstrants', docilely to hand over the reins to the ministers. The Synod of Dort was (in 1619) left free to draw up the *confession of faith*, but in the 'church arrangement', laying down rules for *the relations between church and state*, the gentlemen saw to it that secular authority prevailed. They proved to be regents before they were Contraremonstrants. The zealous Calvinists were far from content. It was seen that the crisis had not really, or at least far from exclusively, been about the church question. What had been uppermost in the minds of Maurice, of Holland, and of the other provinces was the desire to get rid of Oldenbarnevelt.

Maurice's successor, his younger brother Frederick Henry, was not a true Contraremonstrant at all. If, after some years, he in his turn fell out with the States of Holland (which, after the purge effected by Maurice, was for quite a while much more concerned about Calvinist orthodoxy than he was), it was about foreign policy. Frederick Henry obtained Charles I's eldest daughter as wife for his son William, and when this young man had become Stadholder, it was not long before another crisis of the first magnitude broke out. In 1650, some prominent members of the States of Holland were arrested and sent (again!) to Loevestein, while the Stadholder-Captain-General tried with the army of the States-General to surprise Amsterdam. And the real issue of the conflict still was nothing but foreign policy.

At least, that is my view of the case as I have expounded it in my *Oranje en Stuart*.[10] The current interpretation was that young William II, who had indeed procured a vague commission from the States-General, was forced to bring the province of Holland to reason because it had, of its own authority, disbanded certain regiments, for the pay of which the province was responsible, but which none the less resorted under the States-General. The conflict, in other words, was one, on that view, between Holland particularism, resulting in nothing less than a breach of the

Union, and the Captain-General, protecting the Union's rights. Looking a little more closely, however, one will observe that William II, continuing along lines started by his father, had succeeded in making the States-General a tool of his purely personal, or dynastic, policy. The deputies from the smaller provinces were for the most part dependents of his. The States-General had become (as I put it years ago, to the indignation of Dr. Japikse) 'a corrupt body'. To see the Stadholder as the avenger of the Union is to let oneself be misled by the outward appearance. Naturally this was the propaganda reading advanced by his party in 1650, but the reality was that he used the Union slogan to mask his private war schemes : a renewal of the war with Spain (he had been unable to prevent peace from being concluded at Münster in 1648), prepared in secret confabulations with Mazarin, and simultaneously a war on behalf of his relatives by marriage, the Stuarts, directed against the newly established Commonwealth of England. In order to oppose that adventurous policy the Hollanders had no other possible tactics than to fall back on the entrenchment of provincial sovereignty ; the disbanding of the regiments no doubt was irregular, but it was a desperate measure to prevent a war that might well have proved disastrous. 'The constitutional slogans', so I wrote in *Oranje en Stuart*, 'were not the issue of the struggle ; they were the weapons with which it was fought.' [11]

Religion at any rate did not come into the conflict, at least not in the way assumed to be normal in the legend : it was not possible on this occasion to mobilize Calvinist opinion against the Holland regents ; William II had, on the contrary, antagonized it by entering into a connection with the Anglican and Romanist Stuarts. Nor can it be said that the Stadholder had the backing of any strong popular opinion. When he appeared before the walls of Amsterdam with his army (the army of the States-General, rather), the town government had no reason to feel worried over the attitude of the citizenry. The civic guards manned the walls without showing any sign of disaffection to the burgomasters.

The surprise failed, and the undertaking ended in a compromise that left both parties in their old positions. But a few months afterward William II died quite unexpectedly, and now the States of Holland, controlled by his adversaries, the Loevesteiners (after the repeated residence of their leading men in that castle, that is how the thoroughgoing Statists were beginning to be called), decided to manage without a Stadholder. A son was born a few weeks after his father's death, and when he grew up, and especially when in 1660 his uncle Charles II was restored to the English throne, young William III constituted an anxious problem for the States and its new Grand-Pensionary, in effect its leader, De Witt.

De Witt and his political friends, who easily dominated the States of the province down to 1672, were determined to see to it that the new Orange would never combine the high military and civil offices traditional in his family. The danger of the combination of the stadholdership with the captain-generalship had become sufficiently clear under Maurice, Frederick Henry and William II. The attempt on Amsterdam in 1650, especially, was not easily forgotten, and there now sprang into existence what had hardly existed before — a sharply anti-Orangist doctrine, consistently and intolerantly Republican. Fruin admits :

> It was not only love of power and partisanship if after 1650 we notice this ardent opposition to the idea of appointing a Stadholder who would at the same time be Captain-General. An all-too-natural anxiety for the threatened liberty, a well-founded fear for an arbitrary and adventurous policy contributed to this feeling.[12]

It is surprising, however, when he continues :

> I strongly blame the repression of the House of Orange, especially because it was done against the ardent desire of the nation and exclusively in the interest of an egoistical and dishonest aristocracy.

It is surprising, because he had just admitted that the States' suspicions were based on valid reasons of public interest. But it is in itself extraordinary that Fruin in this passage does not seem willing to ascribe to the regent class any qualities except those of self-interest and dishonesty.

The 'ardent desire of the nation', moreover. It is a fact that the lower middle-class, which filled the civic guards and from which were drawn the most devoted followers of the Calvinist ministers, in moments of danger, even during this 'stadholderless' period, were apt to think of Orange.

In 1653 for instance: De Witt had only just taken up his office of grand-pensionary, at a moment when the first war with England was on and was going very badly indeed. De Witt and the States of Holland had looked upon that war as a mistake from the start. As a matter of fact, the Orangists had contributed not a little towards its breaking out. Among the deputies from the land provinces on the States-General the clients of Frederick Henry and William II were still numerous. The public, even in Holland, naïvely included in its affection for Orange the unfortunate Stuarts, who were now wandering in exile on the Continent. When in 1651 special ambassadors had come to The Hague on the part of the Commonwealth of England to discuss the points of friction, the States-General had not been co-operative and The Hague mob had insulted the regicides in the streets. No wonder that the States of Holland were anxious, in 1653, to make an end of this disastrous war. The multitude, too, wanted peace : the effects of the blockade were felt grievously enough. But the measure for which the multitude clamoured, the elevation of the baby prince to the dignities of his ancestors, with his cousin the Stadholder of Friesland as his deputy, could only have the effect of making Cromwell intractable, for to him the connection of Orange with the deposed Stuarts was a sore point. De Witt felt it to be his duty to remain firm against the popular demand, and from his point of view he was perfectly justified.

After 1660, with Charles II reigning in England, the Orange-Stuart problem took on an even more serious aspect. The dangers came to light during the second war with England (1664–1667) in the Buat conspiracy. Colonel Buat, who had been a page to the young prince, entered into a correspondence with the English government and collected a number of Orangist regents with a view to overthrowing the Statist régime and arranging for a peace on English terms. It was an ominous symptom of the direction in which Orangist partisanship had been developing that this man Buat, after his execution, was venerated by many as a martyr of loyalty to Orange and of the Calvinist faith.

The outcome of this war, after the glorious raid on Chatham, placed De Witt and the régime for a short while beyond the reach of criticism. The Triple Alliance (Dutch Republic, England, Sweden) to make a front against French northward expansion seemed an impressive success. When, however, soon afterwards Charles profited from Louis XIV's resentment, which was directed against the Republic alone, to enter into an agreement with him (Dover, 1670), and the concerted attack of the two kings brought the Republic within an inch of its ruin, De Witt and the dominant faction in the States were held responsible. In panic and fury the people gave clear evidence once more of their inability to grasp the realities of the situation.

William III had already been appointed Stadholder by the distracted States of Holland, and De Witt had resigned his office (his murder was to come later), when a little party of English gentlemen on their way to Utrecht, where Louis XIV was now residing, came ashore at Helvoetsluis. The object of their mission was to arrange with Louis the details of the projected partition of the Republic, but first they called at William III's headquarters on the Holland 'Water Line', in order to offer to their King's nephew the sovereignty, under the protectorship of the two kings, over what would be left of the country. The extraordinary point that I want to bring out is that in the small towns through which they passed these ambassadors of the treacherous Charles II were loudly cheered. Crowds raised frantic shouts of 'Long live the King of England and the Prince of Orange!' and 'Death to the States!' If William III had so wished, he might have sold the country. But he was not the man to play the part of a petty client to the Stuarts which his adherents were casting him for. He replied to the tempters that honour and duty bade him observe his engagements with the States. It was the greatest moment, perhaps, in the life of this great Orange, the moment in which he laid the foundation for all his later astonishing achievements.

De Witt's distrust, then, was put to shame. It is the tragic note in his life and in this period of Dutch history that, with what he had experienced so far, and knew, he had to act as he did. The tradition of the Orange party *had* for a generation been lacking in national purpose. How could De Witt have foreseen that the young William would have the strength of mind to break with that tradition? But it is worth noticing that William III chose his direction in close contact with other prominent representatives of that same Holland regent class that at that moment seemed, with De Witt, to have been brought low. Van Beuningen and Van Beverning, at one time intimately associated with De Witt, but who had been seeking *rapprochement* with the Orange court even before the crisis, were now William III's advisers. The young noblemen from the land provinces who surrounded him, like the infatuated Holland multitude, were all for accepting the English conditions and 'hanging a dozen or so' of the States' members. William III was sufficiently realistic to understand that only with the States was a national policy possible.

The 'ardent desire of the nation'. It is a phrase that takes it for granted that the regent class was in a completely isolated position. One frequently comes across passages in our historical literature that seem to have been inspired by that thoroughly false assumption. The regent régime was an oligarchy, and it certainly was not without the vices that almost inevitably go with that system : nepotism, for instance ; pride. But what were the alternatives? The experience of Frederick Henry's last years and of William II's short term of office had not given a high opinion of princely rule ; and indeed under William III, too, great figure that he was, and sincerely living by an idea (an idea primarily concerned with international affairs), practices were used, all through the years from 1672 on, which were far from suited to elevate political life.

As for democracy, it was unthinkable. The people as a rule unquestioningly respected the authority of the gentlemen regents and saw in them their representatives. Only church questions and international crises were capable, occasionally, of rousing them against their lawful rulers, and if the idea of a change of régime was then raised, it meant in practice no more than that the Prince of Orange should be placed in the traditional position of eminence, to be a kind of popular dictator able to bridle the regents. The people might at times chafe at the existing order, but in constructive power they were completely deficient.

Take the year 1660, when the church-state question had once again led to shocking incidents. The town government, and also the provincial States, of Utrecht had exiled two ministers for having delivered offensive sermons; in order to bolster their capacity for maintaining order they had, before undertaking that risky measure, obtained the loan of troops from the States of Holland. After the two ministers had left Utrecht, the consistory of Medemblik (a Holland town) extended a call to one of them, but immediately the States of Holland issued an interdiction and once more dispatched troops to prevent disturbances — at Medemblik this time. 'The citizenry of Medemblik', a burgo-master of the town wrote to De Witt, ironically, 'regard the Reverend Van de Velde as a pattern of all Christian virtues.' The irony becomes intelligible when one reads that 'accursed and godless' were the qualifications applied by this man to the peace of Münster, then twelve years old. 'The Lord God', he had assured his congregation, 'has wept over this peace with a succession of rainy years; visitation after visitation have the provinces suffered since, and God has walked with us in contrariness.'[13] De Witt, for his part, wrote that Van de Velde was 'generally known for a man who seems to set his course to a madhouse rather than a pulpit'. And here he indulged in a somewhat more general reflection:

I could have wished that the circumstances of the affair had permitted us, without risking disturbance of the country's quiet, to defer a little more to the inclination of the consistory and commonalty [of Medemblik]. But it has been judged the course of duty to look after the interests of Their Noble Great Mightinesses' subjects [Their Noble Great Mightinesses refers to the States of Holland, which felt obliged to see to it that what was best for the people, the subjects, be effected], even against their wish or inclination; for they don't know themselves what will serve their peace and preservation; like the father of a family who, if he were to give way to the wish and preference of his children, would very likely do them the greatest harm.[14]

Such paternalism goes against the grain with us moderns. I hold, however, that the historian must see it in relation to the opinions and conditions of the time, and when I have tried to do so I can accept it as the perfectly sincere expression of the profound conviction of a ruler's duty. The States of Holland were a little too fond of mentioning their sovereignty and too eager to call the citizens their subjects. But with the best of the delegates the consciousness of being called to promote the interests of the community, and to do so after the dictates of conscience, without allowing themselves to be confused either by popular fury or by princely frowns, had the quality of an ideal. Human imperfections were not thereby ruled out, but the invigorating effect appears, as I see it, in a heightened style and bearing. The whole of De Witt's correspondence and state papers could be adduced in evidence; and De Witt, for all his individual greatness, was typical of an elite.

Many modern authors, Japikse for instance, will never use the current phrase to designate the system, the System of True Liberty, without an undertone of sarcasm. Up to a point this is understandable, for that liberty was found in the States of Holland's unrestrained fullness of power, unrestrained by a Stadholder, unrestrained by the commonalty. Nevertheless, acceptance of the system was by no means limited to the regent class. There were first of all the non-Reformed, who generally looked to the regents to protect them against the intolerance of the ministers. The cultivated, even among the members of the Reformed Church, often were repelled by the fanaticism of the more extreme among the ministry and in consequence regarded the regent régime with the more sympathy. Vondel had glorified

Oldenbarnevelt as the martyr of Liberty, afterwards Oudaen and Paets did the same for De Witt. Vondel, of course, was, before he was converted to Catholicism, a Baptist. But it would be wrong to conceive of Reformed and Statist as necessarily making a contrast. Most of the regents of the True Liberty brand were as good Reformed as any, and many Reformed ministers accepted them with befitting respect and submission as their lawful governors.[15]

Not long ago a number of *Anti-revolutionaire staatkunde*[16] fell into my hands, in which was printed an article by Dr. De Pater, a well-known Dutch historian, entitled 'The Policy of Johan De Witt', and directed against my *Oranje en Stuart*. The number dates from 1941, but at that time I was abroad,[17] and I had so far missed it. I found it most extraordinary reading and I will not conceal from you that it was this article that suggested to me my present reflections.

The writer takes exception to my remark that the System of Liberty found its firm basis in a healthy nationalism. That remark was the summing up of a lengthy exposition in which it was shown that the Orange party (in the years following upon the marriage of 1641) simply followed the line dictated by England (or by Stuart) and that this was one of the principal reasons why the States kept power so jealously to themselves. But the policy of De Witt and *national*, this is for De Pater a contradiction in terms. Did not Bilderdijk write that the town government of Haarlem (one of the few generally Orangist towns in the States of Holland) proposed in the States assembly, at the time of the popular commotion of 1653, that 'this entirely *national* desire should be satisfied and the young Prince be recommended to the States-General for the post of Captain-General'? (The word *national*, by the way, was not used by Haarlem, but by Bilderdijk.) And does not Groen van Prinsterer, in his *Handboek* exclaim:

> This form of government [of True Liberty] did not agree either with the people's rights and the constitutional make-up of the Commonwealth or with the spirit of the majority of the nation.

It is true that Dr. De Pater does not suggest that the matter is settled by an appeal to the authority of those great names of Bilderdijk and Groen van Prinsterer. He goes on at length to argue the case by an examination of the facts. Nevertheless, both when he dissects my arguments (a large proportion of which indeed he ignores) and when he adduces arguments of his own, I cannot help feeling that he gives but another instance of the method of historical interpretation I have just observed with so much interest, and I must say amusement, in the 'Wittian War' of 1757.[18] Luzac, in his pamphlet, began by asserting that the stadholdership was an essential part of the form of government (in 1757). He first tries to prove the contention, with the aid of old 'resolutions', but when Wagenaar and others pointed out that these were relevant only to the circumstances prevailing at the time they were taken, he tried to prove it by boldly advancing as a general truth : that a unifying authority is salutary and indispensable. This is to him so obvious that the people, when at the time of the foundation of the Republic they implicitly abandoned their rights, could not to his mind but have intended that there was at all times to be a Stadholder. This argumentation really (as I put it in my essay) 'describes a circular course', for 'he uses the very thesis he had set out to prove as a chief argument'. Luzac nevertheless concludes triumphantly that a statesman who wanted to abolish that stadholdership cannot therefore be called a faithful servant of the state, which dispenses him from the obligation to make an exact and unprejudiced study of the achievements and of the circumstances. He knew the conclusions before setting out on his investigation.

Now this is exactly how Dr. De Pater proceeds. He does not speak unkindly about my book, but, judging from what he has to say about it, it has simply not succeeded in piercing through the armour of tradition and convention with which he protects his conception of history. He takes hardly any notice of the facts and arguments with which the book is filled to overflowing.

But now let us analyse the pronouncements of those great anti-revolutionary prophets, Bilderdijk and Groen, which De

Pater accepts and attempts to substantiate. As regards Bilderdijk, I shall only refer to what I said at an earlier stage about the impossible and self-contradictory aim of the burgher movement of 1653. But Groen? With which rights of the people did the stadholderless régime disagree? Groen was probably thinking of the Stadholders' participation in the appointment of councillors and magistrates. It is undeniable that as a result of the office being in abeyance the oligarchic system came to rest even more exclusively upon itself. But had the Stadholder exercised this particular function with any regard for the interests or wishes of the people? No; mainly in order to get docile adherents into the corporations or magistratures. In 1672, William III, when the intimidated States of Holland had given him a free hand to change the personnel of the town governments, took no notice of a list of candidates submitted to him, at Amsterdam, by a group of citizens anxious to have the urban government régime democratized. At his death in 1702, in many towns there occurred outbursts of popular fury against the henchmen with whom, in his single-minded desire to obtain blind support for his anti-French policy, he had filled the councils. I have already discussed Groen's reference to 'the spirit of the majority of the nation'. It is surprising to find this leader of 'antirevolutionary' thinking, who vehemently rejected the principle of popular sovereignty as a product of the Revolution, demanding, if only implicitly, that the legitimate authorities should alter the form of government after the pleasure of the multitude. But Groen would have contested, and so does De Pater, that *altering the form of government* is a fair description of what the enemies of True Liberty wanted. Restoring it, preserving it, is what they were out for. I quoted Groen to the effect that the stadholderless régime was itself a departure from 'the constitutional make-up of the Commonwealth'. And hear De Pater :

> The development in the direction of the centralized state, which had been arrested by the revolt against Spain, had been resumed by the Princes of Orange striving after unity and monarchical authority. But Johan de Witt, in his aversion to Orange, reversed

this trend again. Once more particularism held up the advance toward unity and centralization, of which the Princes of Orange in their offices and persons had been the embodiment. Looked at from this angle, the form of government defended by De Witt and his party clashed with the historic and national principles of the constitutional law growing up in this country.

I pointed out already that this view, particularly as regards the rôle here assigned to the House of Orange, will be frequently found expressed in the historical writings of the liberal school. Fruin held it; so especially did Colenbrander.[19] I can only say that to me it seems to be a construction, a construction derived not from the facts as they present themselves to historical investigation, but from the authors' preoccupation with the outcome they know and value and which they impose upon the past as a postulate.

The Princes of Orange striving after unity? I believe that we should begin by recognizing that nobody in the Republic — among the Orangists any more than among the Statists — had any idea of transforming it into a truly unitary state. Nobody wanted to tamper with the independence of the provinces. The revolt, after all, had been directed against the centralizing tendencies of the monarchy, and the federation resulting from it could not but bear the stamp of that reaction. On a continent where absolutism and centralization went hand in hand, the Republic, down to 1795, stood apart as a medieval survival. At most, attempts were made, repeatedly, to introduce certain improvements in the machinery at the centre, improvements intended to speed up decisions — decisions that even might make possible measures of coercion, however carefully qualified, in the case of a province being remiss in the actual payment of contributions to which it had consented. Already Oldenbarnevelt had mooted such projects — the States of Holland man par excellence. After the sensational victory of 1618, even though it had been won under the Generality cry, Maurice had neglected the opportunity (or do we only imagine that one offered itself?) to reform the constitution. Frederick Henry, it is true, attempted, fifteen years afterwards, to get foreign policy entrusted to a Committee of the States-General (the *Secreet Besogne*), formed round his person, which might no doubt in the long run have meant a considerable progress in that sphere. By abusing the committee for his dynastic aims, unfortunately, he radically spoiled the atmosphere required for its harmonious working, and William II's reckless action in 1650, in the name of (as I put it) 'a corrupt States-General', made matters worse.

But Orange was not the only rallying point for attempts of this nature. I recalled those of Oldenbarnevelt. As a matter of fact the preponderant importance of Holland supplied the potentiality of a cohesive factor and motive force on which a Union policy might be built. Under Frederick Henry and William II the States of Holland had been compelled, in self-defence, to fall back upon the impregnable stronghold of their provincialist principles. During the stadholderless régime, however, De Witt, without losing touch with that safe backing, resumed the attempt to implement a somewhat more vigorous general policy, a policy of what he used to call 'the general dear Fatherland'.

I note that De Pater explains the provincialist reaction after 1650 simply by De Witt's 'aversion to Orange'. That the happenings under Frederick Henry and William II made that reaction inevitable, is a leading thesis of my book. De Pater does not even allude to this. In passing he draws his own picture — and what an idyllic one! — of William II's policy, but without making any reference to my argument. I do not of course claim that my argument, with conclusions and all, should be one hundred per cent accepted. I know that no account can put an end to the endless discussion that is history. But to overlook all the arguments adduced and just to repeat traditional phrases and generalities is not to make a contribution to the discussion — or to history.

After the revolution of 1672, William III like Maurice after 1618, neglected to recommend any constitutional reforms. His position, in which he had to work with irregular means of influence, no doubt had some effect for a little while. During the second stadholderless period, which followed, a grand assembly of all the provinces was held (in 1716) for the revision of the federal constitution. Here the most thoroughgoing proposals (although these, too, aimed at no more than a more expeditious organization at the centre) were put forward by the Hollander Van Slingeland. Again the practical result was nil. The tradition of particular rights, the jealousy of each province, and within each province of each town or group, in guarding its own, the veneration of that impossible system as the only safeguard of liberty — these idiosyncrasies seemed to rule even more completely in the eighteenth century than before.

In 1747 William IV, married to George II's daughter, until then Stadholder of Friesland only, was appointed Stadholder of Holland and of each of the other provinces. Just as in the case of William III in 1672, a popular movement set going by a French invasion brought about that miracle. There being one and the same Stadholder in each of the seven provinces did in itself contribute to the possibility of conducting a more vigorous Generality policy. Before 1747, in the war of the Austrian Succession, William IV had not scrupled to use his position in Friesland to obstruct the policy of Grand-Pensionary Van der Heim with all the traditional particularist methods.[20] This at least had now become unthinkable. But when he was in this unprecedented central position in The Hague, the idea of any drastic reforms occurred to William IV no more than as it had to any of his predecessors. As for William V, he considered it to be his task to 'preserve everyone by his rights' and loved to say that he was 'no friend to novelties'.

The incapacity for taking one step in the direction of centralization came to light most strikingly when in 1787 the Orange régime, practically overthrown by the revolutionary Patriots' movement, had been restored by Prussian intervention. This last episode of the old Republic (1787–1795) shows Orange in alliance with all the forces of conservatism, not only with the Reformed Church, but (*mirable dictu*) with the regent class, which saw no salvation anywhere else in the face of the advancing burgher democracy. From the point of view of centralization these last years were completely sterile, however greatly Grand-Pensionary Van de Spiegel, an unexceptionable Orangist of course, exerted himself. Yet how modest, how merely technical, how careful in leaving the seven provincial sovereignties intact, was Van de Spiegel's programme. Only when the Revolution swept northward, in 1795, did the great transformation from sevenfold confederation to unitary state take place, through new men, backed by the dynamic power of revolutionary France. That is to say — and I said it already — the change came . . . in spite of Orange.

When one surveys this course of events, it becomes apparent how unhistorical it is to denounce De Witt's resistance to an excessive arbitrary power as if it were tantamount to blocking the development towards closer unity, of which only the House of Orange could be the agent. Let every epoch be viewed in its own setting. Do not let us require of the men of the third quarter of the seventeenth century that they should have guessed that at one time, in 1813, a unitary state under an Orange king was to be established. Let us rather try to understand that generation's problems, the memory of 1650, the shocking event of Buat's conspiracy in 1666, and so much more.

It is only fair to Dr. De Pater to assure you that his article, which, as I have noted, served as a starting point for these reflections, contains several shrewd remarks that give one food for thought. Nevertheless, the extremeness of the method is very marked, and I have fastened on that aspect in order to bring out the more clearly certain tendencies that are no doubt less prevalent in Dutch historiography than they once were, but that have by no means lost the significance of actuality.

Finally — I hope that you have not got the impression that I have wanted to sing a hymn of praise to the Holland regents. De Pater suggests that in my view the Dutch nation in Johan de Witt's time was constituted by the regents only.[21] Nothing can be further from my intention. And if I have observed the

Orange party during a certain period to have been characterized by somewhat unattractive tendencies, I do not dream of wanting to extend my observation either to the entire party or to the entire period of its existence. All that I desire is that historians, in judging the men of the seventeenth century, should not use indiscriminately standards borrowed from our own time, as for instance, Democracy ; or Free Church ; or Unitary State.

VIII

The Batavian Revolution, 1795–1798
(1956)

I PROPOSE here to offer an interpretation of the Batavian Revolution as it occurred during the years 1795 to 1798. Let me begin by recalling the main facts.

The Batavian Revolution had had a prologue, before the French Revolution broke out, in the Patriots' movement. In it at first the 'regents' — that is, the governing patricians — especially of the province of Holland, co-operated with the middle class against the Stadholders, but soon it developed into a middle-class democratic movement directed against the regent oligarchy. It was stopped in mid-course in 1787, when a Prussian army, backed by English diplomacy, invaded the country and re-established William V in The Hague. The régime overthrown in January 1795, when the French revolutionary army crossed the frozen rivers, was that of this restored Orangist party, blindly addicted to a policy of no-change and with no roots in broad middle-class opinion anxious for reforms. Thousands of Patriots had emigrated in 1787, most of them to France, where they soon witnessed a Revolution on lines at first simply parallel to those on which their own ideas had run, but before long reaching out to encompass extreme ambitions of which they had never dreamed.

When the French came, in January 1795, the Orangist régime collapsed. The Stadholder fled to England. The French left the revolution-making to the Patriots, who had a widespread secret organization and now set immediately to work. First in Amsterdam, then in one town after another, the oligarchic town governments were dismissed — all in an orderly and almost ceremonious manner — and, to the acclamations of the crowd, new men were installed : all this before the French troops were actually on the spot. Of these new men, a few were ex-regents of Patriotic principles; most were well-to-do burghers immediately below the regent class. There was, however, also a sprinkling of humbler men. A striking departure from the old ways was the appearance of Catholics and Protestant dissenters among the elected : the political monopoly of the Reformed Church was, after two centuries, broken. The revolutionized town councils in each of the seven provinces sent deputies to their respective provincial capitals, and thus the personnel of the provincial States assemblies was everywhere changed ; the revolutionized States assemblies sent deputies to compose a new States-General in The Hague.

A new States-General, but still no more than an assembly of delegates of the provinces. The first task confronting the new men was to reorganize and strengthen the Union. It could be tackled only after relations with the French deliverers (or was it conquerors?) had been regularized. The treaty concluded in May 1795 was onerous and disappointing, but at least the Batavian Republic now had the recognition of the French Republic.

As for the establishment of a real union in the place of the old loose confederation, it was especially the province of Holland, crushed under the load of provincial debt, and radicals all over the provinces, who wanted the provinces to be merged into the Republic. Many of the old Patriots, however, anti-Orangist and enlightened as they might be, did not want to give up the provincial positions. Long disputes and negotiations were needed before, in the spring of 1796, a National Assembly could be elected by the Batavian people as a whole (including even the people of North Brabant, the Catholic region, which under the old Republic had been no more than 'Generality Lands', not represented on the States-General, administered from The Hague); an assembly no longer dependent on the provincial States assemblies, but representing the nation.

Before consenting to this revolutionary innovation, however, the smaller provinces had stood out for restrictive conditions.

The *Règlement,* in which these were embodied, greatly hampered the Assembly in its first task, that of devising a Batavian constitution — for even now the provinces were still completely self-governing, and the independence of the National Assembly with respect to them was more nominal than real. A first constitution was submitted to the primary assemblies (that is, to the electorate) in 1797 and was rejected by a combination of radicals and reactionaries. A second National Assembly was still hotly quarrelling over a new constitution when the radical minority, supported by the French army still stationed in the Republic, carried out, in January 1798, a *coup d'état* after the French pattern. The Assembly was purged of moderates, and a unitary constitution carried through with a high hand. The radicals who thus came into power were driven out five months later, and the moderates now ruled the Batavian Republic, becoming more moderate at every successive crisis in the following years. Only, the unitary constitution introduced by the short-lived radical régime of 1798 was retained. The old system of provincial sovereignty was gone for good.

In 1810 the country was annexed by France. In November 1813 independence was proclaimed by Van Hogendorp and his friends at a moment when a French army was still in the country. The Kingdom of the Netherlands, under the House of Orange, was subsequently founded.

Neither the Patriots' movement of the middle eighties nor the Batavian episode beginning in January 1795 has had a good press with Dutch historians. It is small wonder, really, that the first generation after the restoration could not take an objective view of the passions and ideals of twenty years before. The intervening period had been a series of humiliations and disappointments, culminating in the complete loss of independence. Many ex-Batavians occupied leading positions under the new Orange king, but they were Batavians come to resipiscence; they preferred not to remember their giddy youth in any detail. 'Forgive and forget', the official policy, suited them excellently. There was, too, a group of full-blooded counter-revolutionaries, not politically influential, but vocal, and indeed the inspirers of a revival of orthodox Calvinism; these men propagated a view of history in which the Batavians were no better than traitors to God, to their country and to the divinely appointed House of Orange.

All this is as one might expect it to be. But long before the middle of the nineteenth century there was a vigorous liberal movement intent upon reforms that can be seen as aimed at the resumption and continuation of the work of the Batavians where it had got stuck or been undone by the conservative reaction that had set in soon after 1798. It is at first sight surprising that liberal historians should not have done more for the rehabilitation of the men of 1795. On the whole, these historians, too, were critical of Patriots and Batavians, although indeed they criticized them from a different point of view than did the counter-revolutionaries and the Catholics — for the Catholics, too, forgetting that they owed their emancipation to the men of 1795, were unsympathetic.[1]

The liberal attitude of depreciation reached its zenith in the work of a modern professional historian who began writing just at the opening of the twentieth century, Colenbrander, later Professor of National History at Leyden. Every student of the period is in Colenbrander's debt, for he edited an impressive row of volumes (entitled *Gedenkstukken*) containing documents — not so much official, as correspondence from many sources both Dutch and foreign. (Among the documents there are many in French and in English : let nobody be frightened off by the title!)

But with all respect for the *editor* and his great knowledge and bold conception, the influence of the *historian*, in his introductions and in the monograph he published in 1907, was as unfortunate as it was profound. In examining the events and the men of 1795, Colenbrander could never rid his mind of the dogmatically held conviction that the spirit of the time, or the tide of history, was leading irresistibly to a change from the traditional society of privilege and particularism to the modern one of equal rights in state unity and centralization. But if the historian judges the men of the past by the standard of the actual outcome that environs him and allows *it* to determine and limit his awareness, if he requires of them that they should know it all beforehand as he knows it afterwards, he will not be capable of a fair, of a truly historical, vision.

Now this was exactly Colenbrander's attitude towards the Batavians. And it was not only that he judged them by the outcome, he allowed his mind to be dominated by the grandiose spectacle (or so it seemed to him) of the French Revolution. He was not singular in this. Many Dutch writers took — unconsciously — the French Revolution as their model of how a revolution should be conducted, and poked fun at the Batavians, who prided themselves upon their *calmness* — a word frequently used with some complacency by the men of 1795. This revolution without bloodshed seemed but a poor specimen of the genus to later writers, although, and that is the funny part of it, they themselves were far from being in their own day such fierce revolutionaries — Colenbrander no more so than any of them.

And yet we find him writing that

> the Batavians were ill fitted for the great work of renovation that awaited them. Only a small group among them was animated by a genuine revolutionary faith and had done with the past.

What an extraordinary saying, this, when one comes to think of it. How was it possible for a quiet, liberal, middle-class scholar of the early twentieth century so to identify himself with the Revolution? 'To have done with the past' is indeed the customary illusion of all revolutionaries, but however sincere they may be, they will generally experience painfully enough, or at least the historian may afterward notice, that the past had not done with them.

Colenbrander, moreover, seems to think that all the Batavians had to do was to take their revolutionary wisdom ready-made from France. 'The School of Revolution' is what he calls the exile in France of the refugees of 1787; and when the Batavian Revolution, after its hopeful start, appears to lose impetus and spirit so quickly, he blames it on the Patriots who had stayed at home and had missed that enlightening experience.

After getting to know the period a little more intimately than was possible from textbooks, I began to realize that the Batavian Revolution had its own character and necessarily tended to follow a course of its own. Tenderness towards the past, which one can indeed every now and again observe in many of its leaders, was a national feature distinguishing the Batavian from the French Revolution, and it sprang naturally from the circumstances and conditions in which the Batavian Revolution was set, circumstances and conditions differing markedly from those that made the French Revolution what *it* was.

There were two great problems, or sets of problems. Let me first take the problem of unity, of the merging of the provinces into a unitary state. I mentioned the confused bickerings in which three years were wasted, until the Gordian knot was cut by a *coup d'état* that was assisted by the French. Not a very inspiring story no doubt. But before one pours scorn on the small provinces and the conservatives generally, who resisted, and on Holland and the radicals, who proved unable to overcome that resistance more quickly or more independently — before, especially, one talks as if the French were gifted with more political insight or energy than these half-hearted, fumbling Batavians — it is well to remember one or two things.

The One and Indivisible French Republic, which emerged so impressively from the Revolution — not without murderous party struggles however — had been for centuries prepared by the monarchy. Since Tocqueville's great work, *L'Ancien Régime et la Révolution*, which appeared in 1856, historians are familiar with that view. In France all local independence had been, if not destroyed, left an empty shell. The decisive figures in the administration had become the intendants, as against whom neither the provincial governors, drawn from the high nobility though they were, nor the provincial States assemblies, in so far as the provinces still had any, counted for much, and these intendants were themselves but the executors of the orders of the central government. It was an easy matter for the Revolution to sweep away the remnants of a feudal past that had lost all reality and therefore all power of resistance. Whereupon the *Comité de salut public*, and soon Bonaparte, found in the monarchical tradition of centralization, firmly grounded in usage and habits of thought, the foundation — and more than that — for a rigid unitary system.

But was this system so salutary that we must blame that generation of Dutchmen when they jibbed at having it forced upon them? At any rate, nothing had prepared them for it. Under the old Republic, federalism [2] had very nearly preserved its medieval vigour. In his daily life the Zeelander knew no other than Zeeland authorities and laws, and the same was true for the Frisian, for the Hollander, etc. As for the building up of a system of officials who would meddle from The Hague in the internal affairs of the provinces, undermining, or even touching, the full authority of the provincial States assemblies — in the matter of finance, for instance, or of justice — such a thing had never even been thought of.

There can be no two opinions about the inconvenience of the existing system from the point of view of the Union. Defence and foreign policy, the only departments really with which the Union was supposed to meddle, had suffered only too badly from the need to make seven sovereign provinces agree before any decision could be taken. Yet the fact remains that no radical change had ever been so much as contemplated. *Corrections*, in order to strengthen the central government — even the Patriots had not gone any further than that.

Pieter Paulus, in his four-volume *Comment on the Union of Utrecht*, published in 1777, had written that, if only some small improvements were introduced, he could not imagine a better constitution for the Republic. This same Pieter Paulus in March 1796 became the first President of the National Assembly, an assembly that promptly went against the revered Union of Utrecht and was, under the pressure of Paulus's province of Holland — and this with the full concurrence of Paulus personally —, to devise a new constitution that was to leave exactly nothing of it.

Paulus was not the only one to experience this sudden and drastic change of mind. Another Patriot wrote, a few years before 1795 :

> When I observe the pinnacle of enlightenment and understanding attained by Patriotism here [he means, in France, where he was living as a refugee], and I remember the ideas I used to entertain about Patriotism [before 1787, he means], I blush to think how narrow they were!

Here we can see that exile in France did indeed serve as a 'School of Revolution' — to some men, and especially, in some respects! The spectacle of the National Assembly at Versailles, soon at Paris, and later on, the fanatical detestation of *federalism* as tending to weaken the Revolution — these were the examples by which the French Revolution exercised its most direct influence on the Batavian. Unity! away with provincial independence! — this was indeed something novel. But just because it was, the idea proved hard to realize.

If the change could have been attempted in the first revolutionary onrush, it might have been feasible. But nothing came of the plan that the radicals had once entertained for a revolution carried out by a central revolutionary committee backed by French military power. It has been seen from the bare outline I have given how, on the contrary, the change of régime was carried out locally, in town after town, then in the provinces, and finally in The Hague by these provinces ; the States-General was retained in 1795, only the men were changed. The Revolution, in other words, permeated the federal system, without overthrowing it. The States-General proclaimed all the new slogans, but it was still a conference of sovereign provinces ; of the various provincial *peoples* or *nations*, in fact : could anything more augustly sovereign be imagined than the nation of Zeeland (150,000 souls), or the nation of Friesland (50,000)?

By the time the idea of a national assembly was seriously taken up, in May 1796, the Revolution was firmly settled in the old federal framework. Is it after all surprising, does it show the unfitness, or denseness, or feebleness, of the Batavians, that it proved so arduous an undertaking to break through that framework and to merge the many into one?

Principles or phrases could not alter the fact that round every provincial nucleus not only sentiments, habits, traditions, but *interests* had gathered which were bound to be put on the defensive. One has only to remember the present-day movement for European unity to realize that slogans and projects are not enough. To effect so fundamental a change by negotiation, by a reasonable exchange of thoughts, by common-sense give-and-take, is almost without precedent in history. What is needed, generally speaking, is violence, that is to say, war or revolution. In the Batavian Republic the idea was seriously mooted only when the revolutionary moment had passed. In the end the question was solved somehow, as I told you, by means of a *coup d'état*; if not by violence, by the threat of violence; and a miserable business it was, there is no denying it. But that does not alter the fact that the long-drawn-out debate between Unitarists and Federalists in the National Assembly, a debate within the orbit of the revolution, was an inevitable and natural product of the situation.

Colenbrander (to quote him once more, and for the last time) found the heavy tomes of the *Journal of the National Assembly* merely dull. To read these debates, he says, is exhausting work, to listen to them must have been awful. Indeed, there was a very great deal of talk, and that generation, not of Dutchmen only, was inclined to be long-winded in its eloquence. But to dismiss the speeches, and the whole of that contest between two opposing philosophies of politics and of the state, in so airy a fashion seems to me to be the sign of a curious lack of perception. I, too, have at times felt overcome by weariness while seeking my way through those many thousands of closely printed pages. But I was nevertheless fascinated.

The Federalists, champions of provincial rights and separateness, who are generally pictured as benighted reactionaries whose arguments are too contemptible to note, had a great deal to say for themselves and at times said it very well. They defended provincial independence as the palladium of true liberty, of liberty in the true Netherlands tradition. The radicals might talk as if the Revolution asked its adherents to speak all of a sudden of the Union of Utrecht with nothing but ignominy. 'The Gothic monstrosity', 'the misshapen constitutional abortion' — such were the terms the radicals seemed to look upon as obligatory when referring to it. But there were many who stood up manfully for the honour of the glorious ancestors. Thoroughly unrevolutionary utterances (utterances that Burke would not have disowned) were at times heard from supporters of the Revolution, and not only from citizens of the smaller provinces alarmed about their particular sovereign rights, but from Hollanders.

'This is the question' (I quote now from the pamphlet of a well-known publicist, Swildens) :

> Where can the ultimate guarantee and mainstay of our civic freedom reside most safely, for every town, for every village, for every family, for you and for me, for each and for all? . . . In a national assembly after the French example, that is, in the top of the tree swept by the winds? Or, in accordance with the nature of our provincial representative bodies, at the bottom, in the resisting fundamental roots?

And in the National Assembly itself similar sentiments were expressed. Long before 1798, when the stumbling block of the federalist *Règlement* was at last removed by the *coup d'état* of the radicals, there had been proposals to circumvent or get rid of it. Speaking on one such occasion in opposition to Vreede, the radical leader who later on, after the *coup d'état*, was to become one of the five Directors, De Mist, from Overijsel, warned against the tendency of domination inherent in all government, and against the despotism of an unfettered assembly.

Bicker, an Amsterdam ex-patrician, did not scruple to give point to the allusion by reminding the Assembly of the French Convention under Robespierre three or four years before, which he had witnessed from near by, for he had spent the years after 1787 in exile. Apparently 'the School of Revolution' had taught *him* to be on his guard. Bosveld, too, a Reformed minister at Dort, another Hollander, had nothing but contempt for the arguments of a radical speaker who had denounced, as bordering on sacrilege, all doubts of the wisdom of an assembly directly representing the people. To Bosveld, that was no more than a new fashion in flattery, similar to 'the flattery that used to be showered on the great ones of this earth'.

Must the resistance to a development that we all know has on the whole triumphed be dismissed with a shrug as the futile efforts of men who lagged behind their time? If one approaches these debates in that frame of mind, one will hardly *notice* utterances such as I have quoted, and all the protracted quarrelling and shilly-shallying will appear senseless and indeed arouse no other feelings than those of boredom. But no, the opponents, too, can claim the attention of the historian, and as soon as he listens to them, he will understand that they, too, had a foothold in reality. The reality in this instance being that in the Netherlands — profoundly differing from France! — local autonomy was still untouched, and for all that it may have hampered and paralysed the conduct of Union affairs, in its various particular domains it retained a full measure of self-confidence and of vitality. But indeed, if I spoke a moment ago of a development that has *on the whole* triumphed, this *on the whole* may well be particularly stressed. The moderates sounded a specifically Dutch note, and they did make their contribution to the future.

It should certainly not be overlooked that in France, too, a strong reaction was making itself felt against the dangers, which had been only too patent, inherent in one all-powerful assembly. This reaction had found shape in the constitution of the year III (1795) with its two-Chamber system and five Directors. In the debate about that constitution, Sieyès had roundly denounced the principle of absolute and monolithic public authority, and by implication the doctrine of Rousseau. But why was it, according to him, that the idea of popular sovereignty had taken on such overwhelming importance in the imagination of the French? Because (and I quote from the *Moniteur réimprimé*), their minds being still full of the superstition of royalty, the French had looked upon it as their duty to equip the sovereignty of the people with the entire heritage of imposing attributes and un-limited powers from which the usurped sovereignty (of the kings) had borrowed its splendour. This was the reason why (as Sieyès could not foresee in 1795) the new French constitution was soon to be displaced by one in which authority was again pushed to the farthest limits. Now this tradition was non-existent in the Netherlands, and here we have one of the reasons why the radical-revolutionary solution could not really flourish there.

Moreover, in the Netherlands — and this has, of course, a great deal to do with the fact just mentioned — the social order left behind by the old régime still possessed a good deal of prestige. It had defects, no doubt. The blackest spot in the picture was the disarray of the country's economics caused by the falling off of the old carrying trade and resulting in permanent unemployment and a distressed proletariat, but the defects that had roused articulate political opinion were those that proceeded from the practical monopoly of political offices enjoyed by the burgher regent class and the nobility, and also from the pre-dominant position of the Reformed Church. Most of these defects had been done away with by the Revolution in its first stage. And apart from this, there had never been those crying abuses of the unequal incidence of taxation, of the arbitrary methods of dispensing justice. There was not that deep-seated hatred between the various classes that had in France led to the dissolution of all social ties when once the Revolution began.

There, indeed, dissolution was far advanced even before the crisis. Tocqueville gives an impressive picture of a society broken up into a multitude of particles, all powerless, all separated one from the other by jealousies of rank or privilege ; nowhere were a dozen men to be found who were used to working together independently for a public purpose. And indeed the Frenchmen reporting home on conditions in the country newly liberated (or conquered) remarked on the surprising number of men available in the Dutch provinces who were practised in public business of some kind.

This brings me to the second problem, or set of problems. After the conflict between unitarism and federalism, the conflict between democracy and aristocracy, between — practically speaking — the lower middle-classes and the higher, close to, or connected with, the old ruling group of the regents. Here rises the question of 'the people'.

There was a good deal of unrest among the small middle-classes, focused in the agitation of the clubs, or popular societies. The clubs threw themselves into the forefront of the fight for unity, but what really moved the classes for which they spoke were social grievances and social aspirations. They demanded equality in real earnest. They fulminated against the men who, while professing to be supporters of the Revolution, wanted to preserve all that they could of the old order, who (as a speaker said in the National Assembly) 'swore by Roman law and the Union of Utrecht'.

Roman law, or indeed law, seemed to the radicals nothing but an obstacle in the path towards the rights of nature and towards enlightenment. A revolutionary régime had been set up late in 1795 in Friesland, with the connivance of the Holland moderates and of the French, both of which groups were working for more unity in the government and wanted to break the obstruction of the Friesland Federalists. Friesland now did indeed vote for the National Assembly, but the radical régime in the province pursued social aims that the Holland Unitarists (who were by no means radicals in the social sense) and the French government (which at this moment detested Jacobinism) were soon watching with grave concern. This Frisian government got involved in a violent quarrel with its own provincial Court of Justice, and in the course of it, it passed a decree expressly to abolish the ancient rule that in order to qualify for membership of the Court the degree of doctor of laws was required ; after which it went on to compose a new court out of club agitators — a spirited publicist, a dissenting clergyman and so on.

These were indeed ideas and actions inspired by the true revolutionary spirit. Advocacy of a total renovation, not only political but social ; impatience with all restraints ; and above all, a wholehearted conviction that the radicals' own views and policies were the only true ones, the ones needed for the well-being of *the people*. For — to complete the picture of revolutionary mentality and method — although so obviously representing only a minority and freely admitting the fact, the radicals none the less claimed the exclusive right to speak and act for *the people*.

Listen, for instance, to Vreede, who, even after the miserable failure of the radical dictatorship established by the *coup d'état* of January 1798, not in a single province, but in the Republic as a whole, remained firmly convinced of his having been in the right. After the five months of his directorship, he had gone into hiding and during this time wrote a memorandum to justify himself. What had been the purpose of the *coup d'état*?

> On January 22 it was decided that not all parties should participate in the conduct of the state, but that only one of them, the Republican party [he means the Radicals] should enjoy this privilege, in order that all the other parties, under its energetic lead, might passively enjoy the benefits resulting from the wise constitution *it* was to draw up.

The one-party state, the dictatorship of the proletariat, or at least, the minority dictatorship — offspring of Rousseau's conception of the *Volonté générale*, that is to say, not really the will of the majority, but the people's will toward its own well-being, of which the people, misled or divided, may not be conscious, but which must in that case be realized by an energetic minority — this thoroughly revolutionary programme is here expressed with admirable lucidity.

Unfortunately, however, that short-lived radical régime of 1798 had, in spite of Vreede's self-assured tone, shown little else than its complete incapacity to govern. In the forefront of its propaganda there stood two points, and it was these that roused the clubs to the highest pitch of eloquence and fury, made the surest appeal to the wider circle of their sphere of influence, and indeed formed the issue of all the riots and commotions that occurred, not only in Friesland, but at various times all over the Republic, especially in Amsterdam and Rotterdam. These were the two points : the dismissal of all officials, down to the humblest, in towns and villages, to make room for good Patriots ; and the confiscation of the property of all ex-regents, of all the numerous members of the local oligarchies overthrown in 1795, as a contribution toward the payment of the war tribute to France.

Jobs, and spoliation so as to obtain a relief from taxation. Not an impressive policy!

The small burghers, who had greeted the Revolution with high hopes, experienced in reality nothing but ever-more-depressing economic conditions due to the interruption of trade consequent upon the war with England to which the alliance with revolutionary France condemned the country. Envy of the security of officeholders and resentment at the easy circumstances of the ex-regents, who in their day of power (so the club orators kept on reminding them) had plunged the country into its distress by their wicked subservience to England — such feelings must have come naturally to these men.

So the radical régime of 1798 had become an orgy of the most reckless corruption and persecution. The popular societies now had it all their own way. The dismissal of the officials began at once. In a town like Amsterdam it led to chaos, for the club Patriots had more pretensions than experience or ability. Meanwhile, the voters' lists were revised in the most arbitrary manner by agents of the new directorate, and the names of thousands of citizens were cancelled — not of Orangists, for these had never been admitted, but of Patriots of a more moderate way of thinking, who proudly regarded themselves as no less good Patriots than were the managers of the purge. When the régime was swept away in June of the same year, 1798, the old officials were reinstated and the voters struck from the lists put on again.

What seems to me most noticeable in this course of affairs is the indignation to which opinion in the country had been roused by the spectacle of these wild doings. Notions of law, of decency, of respect for the social order, proved to be powerful, and not only among the Orangists, who had from 1795 on been standing aside, but among those who had taken an active part in the Revolution. Their own leading officials, their generals, Daendels, who had put them in power on January 22, turned against the Directors. The press, too, all Patriot of course, was openly critical. The spirit, the temper, of the Batavian Revolution, it becomes plainly apparent, was not truly revolutionary. Why so much less than was the case in the French Revolution? When one remembers the derelict mass of the unemployed proletariat, one will hardly reply : because the society out of which it sprang was sound. Yet, such as it was, it disposed of powers of resistance that had been lacking in France. Viewed as a whole, the large middle-class, higher and lower, was still bound together by respect for law, for property and by a willingness to co-operate in compromise.

Very characteristic is the tenacity, and the success, with which throughout those years the favourite scheme of the radicals, the confiscation of the goods of the ex-regents, was resisted.

The tone had been set at once when in January 1795 the new municipality of Amsterdam, put in office by popular acclamation, elected a well-known lawyer, Schimmelpenninck, to be its president. Schimmelpenninck promptly told the members of the Town Council that if — perhaps soon — the cheering were to give way to discontent and grumbling, he would still expect them to follow the dictates of 'fairness, justice, and generosity'. And when as a matter of fact the cry for the spoliation of ex-regents was raised, he got the municipality to issue a proclamation — as early as February 1795 — in which the demand was firmly declined.

The order of law would be overturned if punishment were meted out for actions other than those that, throughout all times, apart from political considerations, are considered to be morally reprehensible.

It could not be stated more plainly that the Revolution must not lay hands on the 'order of law'. 'Throughout all times' : no new calendar was introduced in January 1795 (as had been done by the French in September 1792), and no new code of morals.

If these principles are abandoned [the proclamation continued], all stability in human relationships will be undermined. . . . To counsel differently is in effect to preach the law of the strongest, the favourite law of tyrants.

The Amsterdam municipality, then, put its foot down. The radicals on their part never gave up their cherished idea. Now here, then there, the demand was put forward, often supported by violent popular demonstrations. And yet, never was the spoliation carried into effect anywhere. The radical régime set up in Friesland in December 1795 had at once attempted to do this. It had been stopped firmly by the National Assembly when it met in The Hague three months later. After January 22, 1798, the Friesland radicals, exulting at the triumph of their party, believed they would now be allowed to mulct the ex-regents of their province. But on the contrary, the National Assembly, although now purged of some fifty moderates, maintained the veto decreed before the *coup d'état*. Van Langen, one of the Directors, a Catholic, in a letter, expressed his disgust at this proof of the hold that moderate counsels had on the minds even of his party.

Yet another principle besides that of respect for property or for the established rights of individuals was plainly stated in the Amsterdam proclamation of February 1795 : the popular will was to have no absolute force. Quotations could be multiplied to make you realize the force and the clarity with which that fundamentally conservative view was maintained against the impetuous claims of the extremists. The presumption, too, of the popular societies in claiming to speak for the Batavian nation —

for 'the right-minded portion' they said at times, but at all events they claimed that *they* were entitled to lay down the course — that presumption was diagnosed as such and denounced.

It was a logical weakness in the position of the moderates that they had co-operated in enacting regulations intended to exclude Orangists. But the radicals reproached them for being far too ready to fraternize with Orangists at the first sign of a defeated adherent of the old order acquiescing in what had been done.

> It is proper to their principles [so Vreede wrote of the moderates in his memorandum of 1798] to unite with anybody willing to be reconciled, and in consequence they now count among their number men known to be moderate partisans of Orange, of aristocracy, and the rest.

Indeed, after the experience of the radical régime of 1798, the moderates did enter into an ever-closer coalition with the really conservative forces in Dutch life, even with the more pliable portion of the Orangists — as Vreede had foreseen. But it was Vreede's intransigence as well as his inability, while in office, to control his followers which had left the moderates no choice. One can regret this development. But it would be a very speculative and unprofitable regret. The radicals had been shown up in their insufficiency. The atmosphere of Dutch society apparently did not favour this kind of growth. The moderates were a truer expression of the national spirit. And they were far from being reactionaries. Even during the period of turning away from democracy after 1798, they did not break faith with the basic principles of the Revolution. The archmoderate Schimmelpenninck, who was placed in a semi-dictatorial position by Napoleon in 1805 (by 1806 he had to make way for Napoleon's brother Louis, who was to rule over the country as king until 1810) had among his ministers some of the ablest men of 1795 and enabled them to enact some important measures to carry these principles into effect — a system of national education, a system of national taxation. Even under Louis Napoleon useful work was done — and done by Dutchmen. But nothing came of the improvement of the lot of the masses, of which the radicals had talked. The radical movement fizzled out, and the masses had to wait.

But meanwhile, the co-operation between Batavian Patriots and Orangists had an important effect in securing the future of the reforms that *were* introduced, by 'nationalizing the Revolution' — to use a favourite phrase of Schimmelpenninck's, who had worked deliberately to bring this about. It facilitated the change-over in 1813 and 1814, when the elevation of William I to the sovereignty was effected without any internal shocks. No opposition, no blind reaction : William I accepted the new position 'only under the guarantee of a wise constitution', and the constitution drawn up by a commission of men of different shades of opinion in fact meant not so much a restoration as a consolidation of the main achievements of the Revolution, avoiding extremes, or what were then regarded as extremes. One can no doubt think that the result was but meagre, and also, that the slowing down and stiffening of the public spirit that characterizes the period after 1798 was a high price to pay for it. In themselves, nevertheless, the achievements of the Revolution, such as the nineteenth-century Kingdom inherited them, were important enough. Provincial sovereignty, which had made the government of the old Republic practically unworkable, got rid of ; North Brabant and Limburg incorporated in the nation ; the Catholics, over one-third of that nation, in possession of equal rights, at least legally ; the oligarchic system overthrown ; and the principle of popular election maintained, however restricted in practice : the basic conditions for a normal development in the modern West European sense were there.

And one has only to remember France, and the terrible scenes of the White Terror in the south of that country, indeed the permanent feud between supporters and opponents of the Revolution which remained behind and was to trouble the life of the French nation for generations to come — and there will seem to be more virtue in moderation than Colenbrander was willing to admit.

'The virtues of moderation.' It may have seemed that this

has been the leading theme of my rehearsal of the Batavian Revolution. Let me assure you, however, that it has not been my intention to preach a political sermon — on that or on any other theme. It is only that the incorrigible (or shall I say indomitable?) moderation of this Batavian Revolution has struck me as its most remarkable feature and that I have therefore tried to bring it out, and at the same time, to explain it.

To be moderate is not possible for everybody in all circumstances. And we have all of us *that* within us which makes us feel that history would be the duller if moderation were to be universally practised. And yet — is dullness the only alternative to high drama punctuated by shocks and violence? I must say that I have found the history of the Batavian Republic far from dull. I can only hope that I have succeeded in making that clear to you.[3]

IX

The United Kingdom of the Netherlands, 1814–1830, the Flemish Movement

WILLIAM I, although formally still 'Sovereign Prince' of the Northern Netherlands alone and in Belgium only representing the Allies, was already effectively governing Belgium as well as Holland, when Napoleon, escaping from Elba, invaded the country once again. Just before Waterloo, he assumed the royal title, and the defeat of the Emperor formed an auspicious setting for the beginning of his reign.

'The Restoration' is a somewhat misleading description of the period which opened for the Continent of Europe in 1814. Far from attempting to do away with the innovations introduced by the Revolution and confirmed by Napoleon, most of the new governments retained those that had curbed local, class and Church privileges and independence. The centralized and secular state survived the downfall of the Empire practically everywhere. In few countries was there so strong a reaction as in Belgium, where the changes mentioned above had been imposed by the foreign conqueror with hardly any participation by the population. In order to recover their position, the dispossessed groups — the nobility, the old municipal privileged bodies, the clergy — had hoped for a return of Austrian rule; not that in Austria the tradition of enlightened despotism had completely disappeared. William of Orange was in any case too patently a man of the new age, a Liberal, in the current phraseology, though it was obviously good propaganda to remind the Catholic population that he was a heretic — a Calvinist. As a matter of fact, in Holland, where the true Calvinistic tradition was revived not long afterwards (without achieving anything like a dominant position), it clashed with William's conception of government no less than Catholicism did in Belgium.

There the new régime found itself almost at once in bitter conflict with the episcopate. The exclusive recognition of civil marriage, on which the Government insisted, was contested by the Church, which, generally speaking, could count on the support of the masses, especially in Flanders. If the Government was able to carry its point, it was only because the new classes of industrialists, of administrators, of lawyers, had a vested interest in the new state of affairs and stood behind it. Even in Flanders, as I explained in an earlier lecture, these classes had now become accustomed to using French for professional purposes and, more generally, for social and cultural purposes. It was not long before the Government took the language question in hand, and this roused opposition against it on a different front.

William I realized that if his new kingdom was to endure, the community of language between the North and the larger half of the South, now obscured by the gallicization of public life in that southern region, must be made effective. The new Government tried — at first gradually and cautiously — to encourage the use of the national language in Flanders, in the law courts, for notarial acts, in municipal administration, until in 1819 a decree was issued, to take effect in three years' time, by which for all these purposes the use of Flemish (or Dutch) was made obligatory (in Flanders,[1] that is ; not, of course, in Wallonia). This was no more, really, than undoing the measures imposed from Paris in the period just past for the purpose of gallicizing the entire legal and administrative régime of Flanders, measures which had ruthlessly disregarded the interests of the large majority of the population, and had degraded them to the status of aliens in their own country. If the decree needs any further justification, it will be enough to observe that the normalization of Flemish society at which it aimed — and which, as we shall see, it was powerless to achieve — has since in large measure been brought about by the Flemings themselves, in a long-drawn-out struggle culminating in the linguistic laws of 1932. But in William I's day the classes which would have been the first to benefit by it were so accustomed to take their opinions from their betters, and counted for so little in politics, that the entire debate was carried on over their heads.

Feelings in the debate ran high. There were a good many of the professional classes, and of the intellectuals generally, in Flanders who were ready, or even eager, to co-operate, but protests streamed in from Flemish lawyers and officials who, even though the measure amounted to a rehabilitation of what was after all their own language, had come to feel that they could preserve their dignity only by using French. Walloon lawyers and officials also joined in the fray, and so vehement were their protests that they have often led foreign historians into the error of thinking that William was trying to impose the language of Holland on the French-speaking part of Belgium. But no! Their anger was due to the fear that they would lose their profitable engagements in Flanders, where with their native French they had so far had the advantage over their Flemish colleagues, however well versed the latter might be in the language. The struggle continued for some years, but in 1830, just before the outbreak in Brussels of the July revolt, the Government, whose position was already being made uncomfortable by the oppositional attitude of the Belgians, voiced now by the Liberals especially, gave way on the language decree, weakening it so as to make it practically inoperative, to the great regret of a minority of clear-sighted Flemish lawyers and intellectuals. The fact that the question had at least been posed did, no doubt, contribute to the awakening of Flemish opinion in the period following upon 1830. But for the moment the episode serves to show what an uphill task it was for the Dutch régime to right the existing lop-sided state of affairs in the face of prejudice and self-interest and amid the apathy of the sufferers.

The Government was also hampered in its efforts by the lack of interest shown by Dutch opinion. There were some, to be sure, who understood the importance of the prospects offered by the reunion. But, generally speaking, the Dutch public were unable to look beyond the bounds set by over two hundred years of separate existence. The tone of society and of culture was, in the North, still marked by Protestantism. The Catholics, a good third of the population, had, it is true, been emancipated in the first flush of revolutionary enthusiasm in 1795, but it would take several generations for the legal emancipation to develop into a real emancipation. Representative Dutch opinion continued naïvely to identify true Dutch patriotism and the essence of Dutch nationality with Protestantism. The Flemings were regarded as strangers, and that — apart from being Catholics — they were also given to speaking an odd dialect (if not French) was accepted as a fact of nature.

It needed an exceptional mind to perceive the realities of the state of affairs in Flanders. Van Hogendorp, the man of November 1813, in a note made after a tour of the Southern provinces in 1817, wrote as follows :

In society gatherings French is spoken, but ordinarily everybody speaks his Brabant or Flanders dialect, which in course of time will become Dutch. At present they are inclined to feel that the regional language is unfit for anything distinguished or elevated. They have difficulty in following us when we use our standard language, and the style of our best authors requires study on their part. The influence on the national spirit is considerable : all that is great, noble or intellectual immediately presents itself to their minds in the French language and in the French manner, the dominion of the French thus being as it were continued. Only time, education and mutual acquaintance will be able to effect a change.

The insight revealed by this passage was not given to many in Holland, and the few Flemings who were hoping that the reunion might result in a revival of Netherlands culture in the South often felt discouraged by the lack of interest they met with on the part of Hollanders.

On one important point, nevertheless, the régime was able to effect an improvement that was to strengthen the position of the Flemings in the protracted struggle that lay ahead of them. Dutch-medium elementary education, so sadly neglected during the French period, was reformed and equipped with a staff of reasonably efficient teachers. This was largely the doing of a Dutch civil servant, Van den Ende, who had from the start been associated with the practical working of the Dutch Education Act of 1806.* Attempts to introduce Dutch as the medium of education in secondary schools in Flanders not only met with more opposition but were hampered by the lack of competent teachers ; and in any case all that was achieved in that respect was swept away immediately after 1830.

For the Belgian revolution led to a violent recrudescence of the gallicization of Flanders. The initiative from which sprang the revolt had been taken in Brussels ; it was inspired by the July Revolution in France. Wallonia had at once sided with Brussels, but the Flemish provinces for some months kept wavering. If they finally went over to the provisional government in Brussels, it was largely because Dutch public opinion, rallying to the King, and incensed by the spectacle of revolutionary lawlessness offered by Brussels (such was the language used by the Dutch press), lumped Flemings and Walloons together in the same detestation. The passions of the moment blinded the Dutch more completely than ever to the differences between Wallonia and Flanders, and to the possibilities of a closer understanding with the latter.

In the Belgium that issued from the Brussels insurrection, French was placed in a preferential position almost as much as it had been during the twenty years' annexation to France. The new Belgian constitution stipulated that the use of the language was to be free. In practice this meant that judges and counsel were free to conduct a case in a language unknown to the accused or to the claimant and that town councils similarly were free to carry on their discussions and issue their decrees in a foreign language ; that, in other words, the professional and well-to-do classes in Flanders were free to isolate themselves from the people

* See above p. 190.

and keep all information about public affairs confined to their own narrow circle. When, many years ago, I consulted the municipal archives of a number of Flemish towns, I noticed that as a rule the minutes of council meetings switched over from Dutch to French on the very day that the town was brought under the Brussels revolutionary government. In the law courts it was again only French that was heard, except when Flemish witnesses or the accused himself had their say, which was then translated into French for the benefit of those members of the court who were ignorant of Flemish. The secondary schools, again, considered it their first task to gallicize and de-nationalize their pupils. Hardly any Dutch-language news-papers survived the revolution, hardly any books or even pamphlets in Dutch were published.

In my previous lectures I laid particular stress on the inter-national aspect of the separation and consequent estrangement of Holland and Flanders. I have not so far touched upon that in connection with 1830, and I shall not now deal with it at any length. But let me at least remind you that the aspect had lost nothing of its importance in 1830. The break-up of the kingdom that had been intended as a bulwark against French northward expansion was not all. Many of the leaders of the revolt took their cue from Paris, and the danger that Belgium might again be absorbed into France was not lost upon English diplomacy. It was only as a result of intensive Anglo-French negotiations that Belgian independence could be secured under the guarantee of international recognition of the neutrality of the new king-dom ; a sop, this, really, to French suspicions. But the galliciza-tion of Flanders might in itself prove to result in a weakening of Belgium's readiness or capacity to resist French ambitions, which were by no means dead. It might cause 'the dominion of the French' — to use Van Hogendorp's telling phrase — to be even more firmly established in the Flemish provinces. An English diplomatist had summed it up succinctly in 1813 :

> To think that Holland can be free when Belgium is wholly French is preposterous.

It is extraordinary that Dutch public opinion in 1830 could be so blind to this danger, which was clearly implicit in the break-up of the united kingdom. The systematic gallicization of Flanders, now carried on under the auspices of the new Belgian state, met, as time went on, with unexpected powers of resistance. But as far as the Dutch were concerned, they left the Flemings to work out their salvation by themselves.

And indeed in Flanders the situation was not long accepted passively. When the excitement accompanying the revolution began to die down, dissatisfaction and resentment at the linguistic conditions now prevailing made themselves heard. The Flemish movement got going soon after the final settlement of the separation in 1839. It was for a long time powerless to obtain any practical reforms. The suffrage was of so limited a nature that the socially and economically powerful class could ignore all protests. As a matter of fact, it was not so much the mass of the people that protested as a dissident group of intellectuals, who tried to rouse the multitude — the small middle-class rather than the proletariat — out of their apathy. For that purpose the Flamingants (as the conscious and active Flemings were called) indulged freely in romanticism ; processions were held with an abundance of flags, the glories of medieval Flanders were trumpeted forth. At the same time, no doubt, very matter-of-fact programmes of reform were put forward, relating to administration, justice, education. Over the years small points were occasionally conceded, often only to be whittled down when it came to carrying promises into effect.

In 1855 the twenty-fifth anniversary of the Belgian Kingdom was celebrated, and on that occasion a group of Antwerp intellectuals issued a manifesto that in the midst of the festivities struck a violently discordant note :

For twenty-five years, Flemings, you have been misunderstood, oppressed and humiliated. — For twenty-five years you have been addressed, interrogated and sentenced in a foreign language. — For twenty-five years now you have had French money, a French court, French administration, a French judiciary, all that can contribute to the extermination of your race. — For twenty-five years now you have been aliens on your own soil.

This manifesto created quite a stir, and the Government felt obliged to appoint a commission for the examination of Flemish grievances, which in its final report suggested far-reaching reforms. Very little came of them in practice, but within the confines of municipal administration the Flemish movement could in some cases display its growing strength. In Antwerp, where public feeling was deeply stirred, the town hall was brought under Flamingant sway. In 1866 Dutch was declared to be the town's official language. But in the Chamber in Brussels the coalition of Walloons and Fransquillons could still hold up measures of national, or Dutch-language area, scope. Yet all the time Flemish opinion was becoming more and more articulate. Then, in 1870, France's defeat at the hands of Prussia-Germany resulted in a setback to French prestige. The international factor continued to count and in the 1870s the first language laws (as permitted by the constitution) were passed. The use of the Dutch language in the law courts in Flanders was made — not obligatory, but at least possible. The crying scandals to which the existing system gave rise had been denounced in the Chamber. In the administration, too, the use of Dutch was facilitated by another Act. Then, in 1883, came a reform of real importance, even if, as always, incomplete : Dutch was introduced as a medium of secondary education in Flanders, but only for certain subjects ; side by side with it, French was maintained as the medium of other, and in fact the most important, subjects. An Academy was founded at Ghent, not, however, like the Academy at Brussels, which dated back to the days of Maria Theresa, embracing the whole of cultural and scientific pursuits, but confined to Dutch language and literature.

All these concessions were in their essence limited, and in practice they were in many ways obstructed and whittled down. In 1886 a Flemish newspaper — there were a good many by that time — wrote :

Under the Dutch Government the official use of the languages presented certain difficulties to the Walloons, but not one hundredth part of the humiliations that we are today suffering at their hands. The Walloons started a rebellion in 1830 and we, poor fools, fought for them. Our reward was that immediately after the revolution they cast us into the chains from which we had helped to free them.

A fresh impetus was given to the Flemish Movement when in 1894 universal suffrage was introduced. Even under the limited suffrage that had preserved the well-to-do middle-class rule for so long, militant Flamingantism had been able to come to power in some municipalities : I mentioned Antwerp. Now town councils all over the Flemish country were invaded by small middle-class men and even working-men — socialism suddenly became a force to be reckoned with in Belgium — and their presence alone was enough to end the monopoly that French had enjoyed for so long. Not only that, but even in the Chamber, where Flemish had so far been used only on rare occasions, demonstratively, by individual Flemings, the language began to be heard more and more frequently. The Walloons, obstinately ignorant of the language spoken by the majority of their compatriots, often drowned Flemish speeches with exclamations of ridicule or indignation ; the President of the Chamber did not always call them to order with the requisite severity. In fact, of course, the effectiveness of parliamentary discussion was not enhanced by the introduction of the second national language. The artificiality and precariousness of the Belgian unitary system were shown up by scenes of this nature ; it was only too apparent that it could only work smoothly if the Flemings continued in their traditional docility.

Meanwhile, one proposal after another was debated for the framing of laws that would strengthen the position of Dutch in many fields ; but generally these debates ended in unsatisfactory compromises or in utter confusion. Each of the three parties — Catholics, Liberals and Socialists — had its Walloons and its Flemings, and the Flemings were either Fransquillons or Flamingants, of varying degrees of fervour. The Flamingants were often torn between their Flemish aspirations and their loyalty to the party. It was almost impossible to keep the issue between French or Dutch straight; it always got entangled in the party struggle on which depended the fates of Cabinets. By the time the First World War came along to overwhelm Belgium, the language of Flanders was still far from having come to its rightful position, whether in the administration, or in the dispensation of justice, or in education. And there were many other fields where the language question was causing friction. In the army, Flemish soldiers were commanded, reproved or instructed in a language which a large majority of them did not understand. Commerce and industry in Flanders were, in the higher ranges, conducted in French.

But even in the years before 1914 attention had been given to the problem of university education. It is almost unbelievable now that in those days it was impossible for the young Fleming to get higher education in his own language. For generations the secondary schools, as I have said, had been using French as the medium of instruction in order to prepare their pupils for the university, where everything was done in French. I also mentioned that extraordinary half-and-half system which had been introduced in 1883, by which the concession made to the Dutch language had been balanced by the retention of French for other subjects, always with an eye on the university, where Dutch was still taboo. Let me explain that there were in Belgium two state (or national) universities, one in the Walloon country, at Liège, the other in the Dutch-speaking country, at Ghent. French was used exclusively at both. The plan now put forward by the Flamingants was for the 'flemification' of the University of Ghent. A large unofficial commission worked out the details. Heated debates took place in the Chamber on proposals laid before it by private members. For years the question gave direction to the Flemish Movement, and created among the Flamingants a unity, every now and again, it is true, threatened by differences of opinion on tactics, but, such as it was, unprecedented. An enormous impression was made, from 1910 on, by the public meetings held by a triumvirate of members of the Chamber each belonging to one of the three great Belgian parties : Van Cauwelaert, Catholic ; Huysmans, Socialist ; Franck, Liberal.

It was in itself remarkable that mass meetings could be roused to enthusiasm by the demand for university reform. The fact is that the movement had become acutely aware of the material drawbacks caused to the ordinary man by the abnormal situation with which it was battling. In 1906 a book had been published by Lodewijk de Raet, a man well versed in technique and economics, which drove this point home. The neglect of the mother-tongue in all the higher ranges of culture and of life condemned the majority of the Flemings to remain imprisoned in their position of inferiority. Not only in politics, not only in pure culture, but in the very struggle for existence, the Flemings were handicapped. In industry, for instance, the posts requiring any skill were largely filled by Walloons. It was difficult or impossible for Flemish experts who had acquired their knowledge at French-speaking institutions to instruct Flemish working-men. Similarly, such schools of agriculture as existed in Flanders had perforce to use French as the medium of instruction. Flanders, moreover, had become dependent upon the financial system concentrated in Brussels, entirely in the hands of Walloons and Fransquillons, and with regard to which the Flemish people, bereft of leaders who felt intimately connected with their particular interests, were powerless. Only by putting an end to the system of education devised for the privileged class, by which the humbler Flemings who managed to get to a secondary school and university were systematically alienated from their own class and from the proletariat — a system culminating in, and indeed made necessary by, a French-speaking university — could the Flemish masses, so obviously backward, be raised to a higher standard of knowledge and of well-being.

These were the views put forward by the advocates of the 'flemification' of the University of Ghent, and it was this that gave the agitation its wide popular appeal. The Flemish students themselves were clamouring for the flemification — with the exception, of course, of those from well-to-do Fransquillon homes. Among the Fransquillons indeed, even more than among the Walloons, the attempt to dethrone French at the University in Flanders aroused bitter resentment. Arguments were lost upon them. They dismissed the idea as simply ridiculous. 'Was not French the world language? To 'flemify' the University would be tantamount to erecting a Chinese wall round Flanders. It would be a victory for provincialism, it would lower the University to the level of the proletarian or the yokel. Indeed, it would actually be impossible to teach in so uncouth a language, and where were the books?'

Now there had recently been a remarkable revival of Flemish literature, and of Flemish articulateness in general. This must probably be connected with the admission, on however modest a scale, of Flemish as a medium of education in the secondary schools. Even in Holland the newer Flemish poets and novelists were attracting attention — in Holland, where, although the mutual bad feeling over 1830 had long ago subsided, the Flemish Movement was on the whole still regarded with a somewhat supercilious scepticism. In the field of scholarship and science, it is true, the Flamingants could not point to much in rebuttal of the contemptuous allegations made by their Walloon and Fransquillon adversaries. But here this same indifferent Holland provided them with a triumphant answer. Was not their despised language the medium of instruction at the Dutch universities? And did these therefore count for nothing in the world? The Dutch universities had by 1914 produced six Nobel-prize winners, while the Belgian universities, for all their French teaching, were hardly in the running.

So Holland, while remaining so deplorably passive with regard to the Flemish Movement, proved a great asset to it by her mere existence, by the example she offered of a sound society and culture based on the same Dutch language. You will realize the importance of this factor when I remind you of the situation in Wales, where a popular language survives that has no such background and cannot therefore hope to assert itself as the vehicle of a complete national civilization.

It was in these years before the First World War, in the spring of 1911 to be exact, that I first came into personal contact with the Flemish Movement. In my last year at Leyden I went, with four or five others, to attend a Flemish students' Congress at Ghent. The experience made a profound impression on me. After my return I wrote a long article, which was published in the staid professorial monthly *Onze Eeuw*. Reading it now I am struck to see how, as a youngster of twenty-three, I traced a line there which I was to stick to all through my life. When in 1960 I collected in a pocket edition the essays I had over the years devoted to the Flemish question, I opened the book with that essay of 1911.

What had surprised me in that year was the enthusiasm of these Flemish students for a great question of actual politics — so different from university life as I knew it, detached from the struggling life of ordinary men. It was the moral fervour animating them, it was their desire to be trained for the service of the community, it was their clear realization that the university has another task besides that of pursuing study for its own sake and for the cultural enrichment of the individual student. I was amazed at the new light in which I could now see that noisy language quarrel, and I wondered at the indifference of my compatriots. For just imagine Flanders stripped of its French veneer and once more a growing-ground for Netherlands culture; the territory of Dutch culture would be doubled and the very difference of the Flemish contribution would make it the more valuable. These are the views which were revealed to me over fifty years ago. I still hold them, and they have been for me a constant incentive to work and thought in history and in present-day action.

While the demand for a Flemish university was having this heartening effect on the Flemish Movement, the Belgian Chamber presented a sorry spectacle of half-heartedness. At times there seemed to be a clear majority for the measure, but when in 1914

Belgium was overrun by the German army, and King and Government had to retire to Le Havre in France (their exile was to last for the full four years of the war), it had not yet been passed.

Is it surprising that a number of zealous Flamingants, despairing of ever obtaining what they considered was due to Flanders from the Belgian unitary régime, attempted to use its interruption to push their programme through with the assistance of the occupying power? These 'activists', as they were called, were none of them in the front rank of politicians ; they were mostly younger men. I am not contending that their policy was wise, only that it was a natural reaction to the humiliating conditions in which they had grown up. It was a policy of impatience or of despair. It was not inspired by pro-German feelings, although among the leaders of the adventure there were some who dabbled in pan-Germanism. In 1916 the University of Ghent was actually 'flemified', Flemings and Dutchmen forming the new professorial staff. The German Governor von Bissing opened the first session — enough to infuriate 'Belgicist' opinion, and the large majority of Flamingants kept aloof from these doings. The 'activists', or rather the wilder men among them, were meanwhile driven to more extreme courses. Was not the unitary system of Belgium the source of all the ills from which Flanders had been suffering for so long? A Council of Flanders was instituted, under German auspices, inevitably, which undertook to carry through federalism, or self-government for Flanders. The total break-up of the kingdom was even envisaged by some.

There was nothing strange or novel in the recognition of Belgium's essential dualism. Pirenne was by now halfway through his majestic *Histoire de Belgique*, in which, as we know, he attempted to prove the naturalness and reality of Belgian nationality and of the Belgian state. But in 1912 a fellow Walloon, the prominent socialist Destrée, irritated by the spectacle of the growing presumption of the Flemings, and regarding the scanty concessions made to them as so many attempts upon the

French-speakers' rightful supremacy, had addressed an open letter to the King, beginning : 'Sire, il n'y a pas de Belges : il n'y a que des Wallons et des Flamands.'

But the Allies won the war. The Belgian Government returned triumphantly to Brussels. Most of the 'activists' who had shown their hand too openly fled, some to Germany, most of them to Holland. Those that remained were prosecuted and many sentenced to long terms of imprisonment. The 'flemification' of the University of Ghent was unmade as a matter of course. Walloon and Fransquillon opinion was exultant. The King, while still at Le Havre, had made a public promise that in the restored Belgium the Flemings should enjoy 'equality in law and in fact'. On his return he indicated, speaking on behalf of his Government, certain reforms that were to be introduced, and the Flemish University, or at least the possibility of receiving at Ghent instruction through Flemish, was among them. But actually a wave of anti-Flamingant feeling swept the country. An attempt was made to discredit the entire Flemish Movement with the misdeeds committed by the 'activists'. All the old abuses sprang to life again with redoubled vigour. There was no question of any equality in law or in fact for the Flemings, or of any tampering with the supremacy of the French language at Ghent.

It was only after a while that Flemish opinion began to react effectively. The idea of Flemish self-government had not been entirely disposed of with the discomfiture of the 'activists', but it remained confined to groups which were not very powerful, either socially or politically. What survived of the influence of 'activist' thinking was strengthened by the bitterness with which thousands of Flemish soldiers returning from the Belgian front on the river IJser remembered the humiliations and injustices they had suffered at the hands of their officers, ignorant of Flemish and often showing impatience with and contempt for *their* ignorance of French. Now that it was peace, the widespread secret organization that had been formed at the front provided possible leaders. Together 'activism' and 'frontism' gave rise to a new development of the Flemish Movement, a development in a frankly nationalist sense. In 1919, for the first time in Belgian history, a Flemish nationalist party, a party confined to the Flemish part of the country and free from attachments to any of the three great Belgian parties, entered the Chamber. It had not obtained more than a very few seats, but the rise of a politically-conscious Flemish nationalism was in itself an important factor.

The word 'nationalism' is one of ill-repute nowadays. Large books have been written about the phenomenon ; but, as a rule, very little attention is given to Flanders, and when the Flemish question is touched upon, the writers, without exception, appear to be but poorly informed. I mention Macartney, Boyd Shafer, Hans Kohn ; there is also an essay by Namier. I cannot enter into a real discussion with these writers now. They seem to me, all of them, greatly as their contributions are to be valued, to neglect a distinction that I regard as essential. I mean the distinction between state nationalism (which can arouse fervent feelings among the public at large, often by means of a high-flown cultural nationalism for the purposes of a policy of power and expansion) and popular or minority nationalism.

Of this latter category Flemish nationalism is, of course, an example, and the first thing to be noticed is that it is a perfectly natural reaction to the feeling of being denied social rights. I have not concealed from you the sympathy with which I regard the Flemish Movement, and indeed, from the point of view of human values as understood in our common civilization, I claim sympathy for it. At the same time I know, only too well, that even this type of nationalism is exposed to the danger of subjecting all other considerations to its aims and running into excesses. I have, in the particular case with which I have been so intimately associated, always opposed these tendencies. Let me add that on the whole I have been happy to notice that the Movement, as such, has shown a considerable capacity for resistance to wild phrases and wild courses, and so I have always been able to maintain my conviction that fundamentally it is one of justifiable self-defence. And taking into account the circumstances and the historic setting in which it arose and developed, I feel that the first blame for any excesses into which it may occasionally have been led rests with those who were responsible for the abuses to which it was a response.

For a long time after 1918 the new Flemish nationalist party was not taken seriously by the Belgian ruling classes. Now, looking back, we can see that it was important because it could mobilize forces of feeling in a circle much wider than that of its professed supporters. This was shown dramatically in December 1928, when the small party brought off a *coup* which made an enormous impression and changed the face of politics in Belgium.

For a long time the fate of the condemned 'activists', several of whom were still in prison, had been a theme that the new Flemish nationalist party had dwelt upon with great insistence — all the greater because even the Belgicist Flamingants, the Flamingants in the great parties, and indeed Flemish opinion at large, were by now heartily sick of the way in which the dominant group of French-speakers had exploited the activist trans-gressions. Non-nationalist Flamingants, prominent among them Van Cauwelaert and Huysmans, had been working continuously to obtain at long last the flemification of the University of Ghent and other measures, and the result had never been more than unsatisfactory compromises, made even more unsatisfactory than they looked on paper by sabotage in practice. Did it befit the Belgian Government — so even the moderates were beginning to feel — to punish the activists so severely, when by its remiss-ness it had driven them to commit their irregularities?

This, by the way, was the very argument that I had advanced, shortly after the war, in a letter which I wrote as a testimony to the character of Jacob, one of the friends I had made in 1911 and who was then in prison awaiting his trial as an activist. I had been approached in London by his counsel, and this is what I wrote :

> He is guilty, no doubt; but let the Belgian Government, which has allowed the abuses that drove this man of upright character to act as he did, be generous.

This letter, which did not, as one can imagine, help to mitigate the severity of his sentence (it was for ten years, five of which he actually spent in prison), laid the foundations of what I thought was going to be a lasting friendship. I carried on a voluminous correspondence with the prisoner. I visited him a few times in his prison. He was my tutor in Flemish nationalism. I was backward in the doctrine, having missed the extraordinary experience that the war years (which I spent in London) had brought to my friend and to so many others. I began by listening to him respectfully. But it was not long before I detected in his expositions a trait of abstractness, of unrealism and absolutism, which was foreign to my own way of thinking. With all my admiration for the strength of character that enabled him to bear his long imprisonment, I could not help smiling at the self-assurance with which he undertook from his cell to instruct, not only me, but the entire Flemish nationalist movement, as to the only true course it should follow. When a conflict arose shortly after his release between him and the man who during his imprisonment had shouldered the practical task of leading the Antwerp nationalists, and I was invited to arbitrate, I came down on the side of Herman Vos — that was his name. With him I felt a much closer kinship, for he was a man who thought in terms not of doctrine but of the realities of life ; and he indeed became one of the truest and dearest friends it has been my good fortune to find.

In the 1920s a movement for the granting of an amnesty for the activists still in prison or in exile was organized by the nationalists, though it made its appeal far outside their ranks. An international appeal to the Belgian Government was set on foot. Numerous signatures were collected in Holland. I myself collected a good many, and well-sounding ones, in England. The Belgian Government continued to turn a deaf ear. And then, in December 1928, an opportunity occurred to administer a shock to Belgian complacency.

At a by-election at Antwerp the Flemish nationalists put up as a candidate Dr. Borms, who had been the central figure in the war-time activist Council of Flanders and who was now in his eleventh year in prison. According to the electoral law the entire electorate of the big city was to vote. Herman Vos, now the leader of the Flemish nationalists in the Chamber, and himself a deputy for Antwerp, managed the affair with consummate skill, laying stress on the one issue of an amnesty and avoiding saying anything that might frighten off non-nationalist electors. His nationalism was in fact of a different cast from that of either Borms or Jacob. The result was that Borms was elected with a resounding majority over his Liberal and orthodox 'Belgicist', if not Fransquillon, opponent. Of the 83,000 votes cast for Borms the majority undoubtedly came from members of the Catholic and Socialist parties, who could not, of course, be counted upon to support the full nationalist programme, but who were obviously moved by feelings of impatience that the parties in power could not altogether ignore.

The impression made by this result was enormous. Borms was disqualified for the Chamber — naturally —, but he was set free not long afterwards. And when at the general election in the spring of 1929 the Flemish nationalist party made a big jump forwards, the anxiety in Brussels was intensified. There is not the slightest doubt that it was the atmosphere thus created that made it possible for the Flamingants in the Belgian parties, particularly Van Cauwelaert and Huysmans, to carry through in the next few years the language laws that had up to then always been emasculated before reaching the statute book, if they had not been held up entirely. Now not only the University of Ghent was at long last 'flemified', but Dutch was also made the sole medium of instruction in the secondary schools of Flanders. The reforms also extended to the law courts, the administration, even to the army. The principle by which they were governed, and which now received legal sanction, was that of the recognition of the Flemish provinces as unilingual, Dutch-speaking territory. Situated between French-speaking Wallonia and Dutch-speaking Flanders was Brussels, where after generations of progressive gallicization a special régime had to be applied.

The Flemish nationalists were not the authors of this legislation. The Belgian unitary régime was left in being. Though the reforms were to have a profound effect on the future of Flanders, the problem was not really solved. That it was not is clear from the heated debates that have lately flared up again in Belgium and that are still lustily going on. In any case, the modest rôle of pace-makers (in which history is likely to see them) could not satisfy all Flemish nationalists. In fact it was possible to believe — I myself believed it then and I believe it now — that the ills of Flanders cannot be remedied if the Belgian unitary system is left untouched.

A concrete proposal for a federal solution had been put forward by Vos and his supporters in the Chamber in 1931 : the Federal Statute. Vos and I had drawn it up together and neither of us believed for one moment that it would ever be adopted. Even here 'pace-making' was what Vos intended. We hoped that the proposal might lead to a serious discussion on the federal solution. But unfortunately the extremists (did I not say that even the most acceptable brand of nationalism is likely to breed extremists?) were now a long way beyond federalism. They denounced the Federal Statute as an attempt to save Belgium. As if Belgium were on its last legs! 'Death to Belgium! Political Great Netherland!' — that is to say, Belgium was to be broken up and Flanders united in one state with Holland. Completely out of touch with reality were such ideas. But their sham logic made an impression on what I called at the time, scathingly, 'semi- or half-grown intellectuals'. There was an active Dutch-Flemish students' movement now, much to my satisfaction, for had not the indifference of Dutch opinion been one of my constant worries? But when motions were passed at student congresses in the sense I indicated, I felt that the young men were playing right into the hands of the adversaries. The strength of the nationalist movement was indeed sadly undermined by these internal dissensions.

It was worse when in the middle 1930s German National-Socialism began to exert its unholy attraction on Flemish nationalists and even on Dutch Great-Netherlanders. Vos now left the Flemish-Nationalist party and went back to the Socialist party, through which he hoped to have a better chance of realizing his Flemish ambitions. My relations with him were no less cordial. I myself was now waging a war on two fronts, against the inveterate Dutch habit of underestimating the possibilities for our own standing in the world offered by the emancipation of Flanders, and against the reckless fanaticism manifesting itself among the Flemish nationalists, both in the Death-to-Belgium cry and in the virulence with which they attacked the more moderate nationalists. Let me assure you that only a small minority of the Flemish nationalists were taken in by National-Socialist propaganda, and remind you that the Flemish nationalists as a whole were only a minority of the Flamingants. Nevertheless, these aberrations had an unsettling effect on the Movement as a whole and they were eagerly fastened upon by its adversaries. Also they made a deplorable impression in Holland.

The Second World War burst over Europe and Belgium underwent a second German occupation. The German régime this time stood for a singularly detestable ideology, but there was again collaboration, and prominent in it were again a number of leading Flemish nationalists. As a matter of fact, there were also Walloons. There had for years been a considerable Fascist group among them, led by Degrelle, who is now leading a comfortable life in Spain. In France too opinion was for years behind Pétain and his spiritless collaborationist policy. Yet in Belgium, at the time of the liberation in 1944, there was again, as there had been in 1918, an outburst, only more vehement this time, against Flemish collaborationism, as if it were the natural and detestable outcome of Flamingantism, and an attempt was made to make Flamingantism as a whole share in the odium. The repression, as it was called, was used in the most unscrupulous fashion to rid public life of prominent Flemish personalities. For years Flemish opinion seemed cowed. My friend Vos was now a Cabinet Minister, but he proved unable to do much for the cause he still had at heart. Unfortunately he died in 1952, only sixty-two years old. There seemed hardly to be a Flemish Movement any longer. Many Flemings grumbled in private ; others hid behind the excuse that since the reforms of 1932 there were no longer any grievances worth quarrelling over.

In fact, of course, although the effect of these reforms was to make itself felt with cumulative force, there were still dangerous weaknesses. The effects of a century and a half of gallicization could not be nullified in a couple of decades. In the higher ranges of society, in the business world, in the foreign service, in the officers' corps and indeed in the central government, where Walloons and Flemings meet, the spirit of Fransquillonism still sat enthroned, a truly nationalistic spirit no less than that of the Flamingant extremists, and one marked by a virulent arrogance. If for a while the quiet prevailing in the Flemish ranks seemed an ominous phenomenon, of late years the provocations of the traditionally dominant groups have been rousing the old resistance to new life. And behind it there is now, as I have said, the cumulative effect of the reforms of 1932, which are working automatically and silently. One inestimable result which is making itself felt more with every year that passes is that generations of Flemish intellectuals, lawyers, officials, business men, have been growing up who have had a normal education, both secondary and university, in their own language, and these men are now gradually taking their place in public life. A new Flanders has begun to grow up, and it is only natural that it should be even more sensitive to the humiliations inseparable from the old system. The battle is on again. Even the cry of federalism is heard, in Wallonia as well as in Flanders.

I shall not indulge in any speculations about future developments. In my last lecture I shall speak about Holland under the German occupation, about the economic recovery of that heavily-stricken country, about the loss of the Dutch colonies, and finally about Holland and the Common Market, Holland and the absence of England from that association.

X

Holland During the Second World War and After —
The Tie with Indonesia Severed — Benelux —
The Common Market

IN the concluding part of my last lecture I just touched upon
the Second World War when speaking of the collaboration with
the German occupying power of a handful of Flamingant extremists, and the problems this left behind for the Flemish
Movement when Belgium was liberated. I shall now deal a little
more fully with the war, more particularly in connection with
Holland — although it would be easier for me to do justice to
the story of how it affected the people and of their reactions,
and also of the after-effects and the adjustment to radically-
altered circumstances, if I had the full course of six lectures
before me instead of being left with this one hour.

When I went back to Holland at the beginning of 1936 after
my twenty-two years' residence in London, I found a tense
political situation prevailing there. There was the depression,
attended by unemployment, against which the Conservative
Government, thinking of nothing but economizing and balancing
the budget, stood helpless. And there was, just across the
frontier, the frightening spectacle of German National-Socialist
dynamism. The menace seemed to be the more serious in that
a National-Socialist movement had sprung up in Holland itself,
small and contemptible as regards the intellectual capacity or
character of its leaders, but noisy. I was soon drawn into the
counter-movement of 'Unity through Democracy'. I wrote
outspoken articles and addressed meetings — one of 12,000
people in the gigantic R.A.I. building in Amsterdam. The
general election of 1937 made it clear that National Socialism as

an independent force had no future in Holland, but the international scene became more threatening with every year that passed. The belief in appeasement was far from being an exclusively English fallacy. I was disgusted to witness the relief with which Munich was greeted in Holland, people sending flowers and fruit to Chamberlain, the saviour.

When the invasion came, in May 1940, the Dutch defence collapsed in five days. The Inundation Line had been made inoperative by German air landings in the west, the remorseless bombardment of Rotterdam caused dismay. The Dutch army capitulated; the government and the Queen made their escape to England. I well remember the shattering effect this had on public opinion. People felt left in the lurch. Few realized that by settling in the one country that was determined to resist to the bitter end, the Queen and her ministers were safeguarding our future. Had we still a future? When affairs in France went from bad to worse, the prevailing opinion was that Hitler had won the war and that National-Socialist Germany would dominate Europe. 'We must adapt ourselves to the new situation': this seemed to many the obvious conclusion, and in the first weeks or months of the occupation Seyss-Inquart, the Imperial Commissioner at The Hague, and the military commanders were profuse with soft words. Too many people took their promises at face value and indulged in feelings of relief. I knew too much of National Socialism (I had read and written about Rauschning, for example) to let myself be fooled. The acquiescence I noticed around me I found infinitely depressing. But I comforted myself with the reflection that (as I used to say to my wife) things will get better when they get worse. And worse they did get.

I was, of course, far from being an exceptional case in those early days. There were many, in all parties, in all ranks of society, in all professions, who stood firm in their inward rejection of the triumph of brute force. In June, just after the capitulation of France (not of the French *army*, but of the French *state*), at a particularly gloomy moment therefore, the Hague municipal council was debating a purely local matter. What was to be done with the old country house of Cats, the seventeenth-century poet, immensely popular in his own day? One member, Mr. Drees, a leading figure in the socialist party, who was to become a Cabinet Minister after the liberation, and was from 1948 to 1958 Prime Minister, recited the lines in which the poet glorified the carefree life he led in those quiet surroundings. He was not bothering about the war then (in 1655) being waged by France in Flanders — 'nor about what Britain, after so many mishaps, might at the last still risk or undertake'!

The implication was clear enough, and it needed courage to remind the downhearted, even in so indirect a fashion, that there was still England. Before the end of the year the reality of the Battle of Britain showed what a hard nut the Germans had still to crack. By that time Dutch broadcasts from London were beginning to make an impact on opinion in the occupied country, and no voice was listened to more eagerly than that of the Queen, who all through her enforced exile displayed an unshakable determination and confidence that — as she put it (for these radio talks were of her own composition) — 'Holland will rise again'.

Meanwhile, as I said, the occupying power was beginning to show its true face. Very gradually ; the tactics used were still intended to deceive. One group at a time was made to feel the whip, after which all the others could heave a sigh of relief. But *their* turn came, until in the end the entire nation was feeling intolerably oppressed. And along with that development there did indeed go, as I had foreseen, an increasing detestation of the intruders, and a quickening of the forces of resistance.

I missed any close association with this process in its most vital phase, because early in October 1940 I had been arrested, with some hundred others, politicians (Drees was one, and all parties were represented), journalists, university professors, men in all walks of life. No charge was made against us ; we were described as hostages, and at Buchenwald, where we were kept for thirteen months, we were in a privileged position compared with the prisoners. In November 1941 we were transferred to a place of internment in North Brabant, where circumstances were still easier, although of course the confinement, the enforced passivity, were hard to bear. Many of my companions were released at various times on grounds of ill-health. My turn came in February 1944, after nearly three and a half years. In the meantime I had been dismissed from my chair by the Imperial Commissioner, a distinction made even more acceptable by the reason stated in the paper handed to me : 'Since his general mentality does not hold out any warrant for loyal co-operation.' So even when I was home again, I still had no connection with the affairs of the University, where, as a matter of fact, work had practically come to a standstill. In all respects the situation had in those three and a half years become one of extreme tension.

The most horrible thing that had happened was the persecution of the Jews. After having been subjected to one discriminatory measure after another, they were rounded up, sent to a transition camp not far from the German frontier, and from there were gradually transported to Poland, where — but this did not transpire until afterwards — the gas chambers made an end of them, men, women and children. A full 100,000 of the 130,000 Dutch Jews met this fate. Dutch police had had to assist the German S.S.-men in arresting the Jews — a thing painful to remember. But the position, not only of the police, but of all officials, exposed them to immediate danger, and the half-heartedness shown on so many occasions, lamentable as it remains, was only too human. The assistance lent in the arresting of the Jews was an extreme case. Civil servants, burgomasters, and so on, could often soothe their conscience with the reflection that at the price of carrying out some objectionable behest they might still be of some assistance to the Dutch public, who were sure to fare worse if a docile Dutch National Socialist were to take their place. The underground press, which had meanwhile come into existence, often wrote very scathingly about the collaboration to which numerous men in public positions, most of them no doubt reluctantly, resorted. In fact, the problems of collaboration were far from simple.

And, fortunately, there is much that can be placed over

against the reprehensible weaknesses that were undeniably rampant. I might mention, for instance, the speech of protest made by Professor Cleveringa, of Leyden University, when in November 1940, just after I had been interned, the Jewish professors were dismissed, and the enthusiastic approval of his speech manifested by the students. The Germans retaliated by closing the University. There was also the spontaneous and courageous gesture of the labouring population of Amsterdam (where one-half of Dutch Jewry had their homes) when they called a strike of protest in February 1941. One remembers it gratefully, although the only practical result was that sanguinary reprisals were taken upon the defenceless Jews themselves. When month after month the roundings-up continued, the secret Resistance groups that were now becoming active helped thousands of Jews — no more than a fraction, unfortunately, of the entire Jewish population — to find 'diving-under addresses' (this was the term used) ; and one cannot sufficiently admire the families who gave shelter to these unhappy victims at the risk of being sent to concentration camps if they were detected. The danger became more pressing as the food situation deteriorated and the coupons for obtaining food were hardly sufficient for those in legitimate possession of them.

At a later stage the Germans forced labourers in their thousands to go and work in German war industries. Many tried to evade deportation by going into hiding, while of those who had submitted to the decree a considerable proportion managed to return illegally and helped to swell the number of *onderduikers* (people who had 'dived under') in the country. University students who refused to sign a 'declaration of loyalty' were also transported, unless they managed to make themselves untraceable. By 1944 the number of *onderduikers*, originally composed principally of Jews, was estimated at 300,000. The resistance organizations that had sprung up to help these outlaws constitute one of the wonders of the occupation period. To give shelter to men for whom the German military police were constantly on the look-out was a risky undertaking in so densely a populated country as Holland is, and to find addresses was not therefore an easy matter. But that was not all. The most pressing problem that remained was that of the supply of food. Food was severely rationed on the basis of identity cards as well as food coupons. A great deal of technical skill was spent on forging those papers, and in order to get them into the hands of those for whom they were intended thousands of helpers were enlisted (women numerous among them). Often the resister groups entertained relations with officials in all ranks of the administration who seemed to be docilely carrying on their duties. As time went on the methods of forging and of distribution became more elaborate. Special groups were formed for the purpose of carrying out raids on official depots of the genuine papers. To obtain arms — revolvers — police bureaux were raided. The S.D. on its side was active, their methods becoming increasingly ruthless. Many of the resisters were caught, they were lucky when they were sent to the concentration camps, often they had to face the firing squad. Hostages were taken and indiscriminately shot. Several names are still reverently remembered, but the majority died anonymous deaths. It was not only, of course, work for the *onderduikers* that exacted victims. On one occasion, in March 1943, a number of people connected with an underground paper — as writers, printers and distributors — were detected and dozens of them executed. In October 1944 a *razzia* was held in the village of Putten in Gelderland ; many people were killed, and six hundred were carried off to German concentration camps, of whom only sixty survived.

By then the situation had suddenly become much worse. The Allies had liberated the whole of France and Belgium, and of Holland up to the rivers. But Montgomery's attack on Arnhem, in September, failed, and Northern Holland was left under the Germans for another eight months. The rivers proved an impassable barrier, as Parma had found them to be in the late sixteenth century. I saw my thesis about the true explanation of the partition of the Netherlands into a Northern and a Southern half confirmed in the most dramatic fashion. But it was hardly the moment to rejoice, for the period that followed was to prove by far the most terrible of the five years of the occupation. By order of the Dutch Government in London a railway strike had been called to assist Montgomery's attempt by hampering the German defence. When the Germans were left in possession, they did not let the railways get back into full working order again, with frightful results for the provinces west of the river IJsel and the Zuiderzee; these, the most densely populated parts of the country, depended for their food supply on the eastern provinces. A regular famine reigned ; the big towns suffered especially. People searched the countryside for food. Thousands went on foraging expeditions to the trans-IJsel country on bicycles, or pushing hand-carts ; they were all men and women over military age, for younger men ran the risk of being arrested. The relief obtained in this way was far from meeting people's needs. Thousands died of starvation. Meanwhile the Germans ransacked the country, carrying off to Germany railway stock (more than half the rails even), motor-cars and buses, a million bicycles, machinery of all descriptions — a large number of factories were completely dismantled. The financial position was hopelessly undermined by the way in which the Germans juggled with the accounts relating to their dealings with the subject country. The liberation in May 1945 dawned upon a depleted country and an exhausted people.

The exiled government had played a manful part while in London. I need only mention the name of its president, Gerbrandy. But as soon as North Brabant had been liberated, the cabinet was torn by dissensions. When the country had been reunited and the Queen was back in The Hague, she entrusted two new men with the task of forming a Cabinet : Schermerhorn and Drees, of whom the former became Prime Minister. It was not until June 1946 that a general election was held. In the meantime the pre-war Chamber had not been restored to its old authority ; a council representing the Resistance was called in to heighten its prestige. The Resistance had in the last phase of the occupation developed an elaborate organization, embracing the various groups, most of which were composed of men sharing definite political or religious principles. Both Schermerhorn and Drees had been leading figures in the highest council.

'Political or religious principles.' It is a peculiar feature of Dutch public life that the party system is largely based on religion. There is the Catholic party, which commands nearly one-third of the electorate. There are the two orthodox Protestant parties, the Anti-Revolutionary and the Christian-Historical. And there are also the Liberal party, much less powerful than it used to be in the nineteenth century, and the Socialist party, which runs the Catholic party close in numerical strength. Under the impact of the occupation a strong movement had sprung up for unity, under the vague formula of Christianity and progressiveness; it was represented particularly by Schermerhorn. The Queen was passionately devoted to this idea of unity, and imagined that it was what the Resistance had stood for. But the old traditions were not so easily disposed of, and even among the men of the Resistance co-operation had been the most that could be attained, each group watching jealously over its particular principles.

One important change, nevertheless, which had indeed been prepared in the years before the war, did now materialize. The Socialist party, adopting the new name of Labour party, definitely foreswore dogmatic and anti-religious Marxism. It was going to try and effect a 'break-through' — this was the term used; that is to say, it was going to make an effort to enlist the support of Catholic and orthodox-Protestant voters. As a matter of fact the Labour party group in the Second Chamber has, ever since the general election of 1946, numbered among its members some professing Catholics and orthodox Protestants, but a mass movement away from the confessional parties never materialized.

In fact, the cabinets of the post-war period were national cabinets only in so far as they rested on the co-operation of various groups. At first the Labour members and the Catholics formed the solid basis, Drees presiding over these cabinets from 1948 to 1958, first the anti-Revolutionaries, then the Liberals acting as an Opposition, until, in December 1958, the Labour party was forced out and had to play the part of the Opposition party.

It is an extraordinarily complicated story and I shall spare you the details. What I want to point out is only that these cabinets, working under political conditions that must inevitably give rise to frequent differences of opinion in the council room as well as with the Chamber, conditions which imposed compromise and subtle concessions now to this, then to that point of view, did on the whole make an excellent job of their formidable task. The country had suffered greater material damage, its economic system was more thoroughly dislocated, than was the case in France and Belgium, which had been liberated eight months earlier. Not only was the damage repaired and the economic process set going again, but the movement was, compared with the pre-war situation, accelerated, and a remarkable expansion took place. The population, in spite of its already unusual density, kept increasing at a more rapid rate than in any other European country. It now stands at over eleven million.* (In my schooldays I learnt: four and a half million — and that Belgium had one million inhabitants more ; now Belgium is behind by well over a million.) And work is easily found for every new generation, even though it is more numerous than its predecessor. New industries have spread all over the country. Holland used to live by agriculture and trade ; now industry has become a factor of prime importance in its economic life. Of course Marshall aid was of fundamental importance in helping Europe to get over the paralysing effects of wartime destruction and disorganization, but no country put the milliards of dollars to better effect. The conditions for doing so had already been created in 1945 by the Minister of Finance, Lieftinck, with his courageous monetary policy for getting rid of the abundance of worthless paper money. When the Dutch Government declared in January 1953 that Marshall aid was no

---

* Over eleven million when I delivered this lecture. Now that I revise the proof (Oct. 1963) the twelve million mark has been passed.

longer needed, the economic activity of the nation could go on unabated and prosperity continued to increase.

One event, one catastrophic development, was taking place during these same years which makes this economic expansion even more remarkable. I mean the severance of the tie between Holland and Indonesia, and the liquidation of the enormous capital in enterprise and equipment that had been invested in their 'precious colony' by the Dutch.

The 'decolonization' process set in after the war with irresistible force. There were in Holland unrepentant and unteachable colonialists, but in practical politics these hardly counted. That the old colonial relationship was bound to disappear was fairly generally accepted, but it was hoped that a friendly association on a basis of equality, or free choice, would take its place. This hope was now sadly disappointed. When one looks at the situation as it existed before the war, the conditions for such an association seemed present in Indonesia no less than in India. I shall not of course contend that Dutch policy in the pre-war years was sufficiently aware of the need for concessions, but no more was British policy in India at the same time. And yet in the latter case it proved possible after the war to carry through 'decolonization' and at the same time to preserve friendly relations and economic and cultural ties. The Dutch had been far more intimately mixed up in the affairs of Indonesia than were the British in those of India. The corps of Dutch civil servants in Indonesia were animated by the consciousness of having a task to fulfil for the well-being of the population. There were often friendly and even cordial personal relations between the growing number of Indonesian intellectuals and Dutch officials and experts. And yet the new relationship, the recognition of Indonesian sovereignty attended by a somewhat shadowy union with the former ruling power, could only be agreed upon, in 1949, after protracted negotiations, interrupted or accompanied by intermittent fighting. And even then the Republic, now admittedly sovereign, went on to indulge

in a violently anti-Dutch nationalism; all the agreements just
concluded were torn up, Dutch possessions were expropriated,
the Dutch language, which in education and political and intellectual life had served as the medium with Western culture, was
discarded. How is one to explain the difference between the
'decolonization' process as it actually came to pass in the case of
England-India and in the case of Holland-Indonesia?

This is another chapter in the recent history of Holland that
could be done justice to only if one had a full hour, or several
hours, to devote to it. I shall draw your attention to no more
than one single aspect.

The circumstances in which the Dutch Government, in the
summer of 1945, was suddenly confronted with this problem
were altogether different from those in which England was
called upon to act, and for the Dutch they were to the highest
degree unpropitious. Dutch authority had completely collapsed
when in 1942 the Japanese occupied nearly the whole of the
Archipelago. The nationalist leader Sukarno, who is now
President of the Republic, had thrown in his lot with the Japanese
even before that time: he had greeted Hitler as an ally, he had
reviled Churchill and Roosevelt. The Japanese had employed
him and other extreme nationalists to indoctrinate the younger
Indonesians with hatred against the Dutch oppressor. All this
while the Dutch in Indonesia, not only those in official positions,
but *all*, women and children included, tens of thousands of them,
were shut up in concentration camps. When Japan capitulated,
the task of securing order was entrusted to an English military
force. At that moment the Dutch Government had at its disposal neither ships nor money. Until it was ready to take over,
the English did not set the Dutch internees free. Sukarno had
meanwhile established a republican government in central Java,
claiming to represent the whole of Indonesia. In fact, chaos
reigned in large parts of Java and of the other islands. When
Dutch troops arrived and a Dutch East Indian government was
restored, matters had already gone a long way towards irretriev-
able extremism and confusion. Even then, the Dutch had to

reckon with the English and the Americans, and with the United Nations in the background. All these were inclined to accept Sukarno, in spite of his more than suspect past, as the true spokesman of the Indonesian people. The dogmatic and all too one-sided anti-colonialism of the Americans blinded them too easily to the realities of the situation — to the fanaticism of Sukarno and to the widespread opposition to his claims that in fact existed among the Indonesians themselves. Several leading Indonesian politicians were ready to fall in with the more moderate proposals of the Dutch, but in the end Sukarno prevailed.

I am not suggesting that Dutch policy in these extremely difficult conditions was always wise. On no problem of the many with which it was struggling in those years was there more internal dissension, with unsettling effects, more than once, on the line of policy that was followed. But this seems to me clear: that the tragedy — not of the termination of Dutch sovereignty over Indonesia, of course, for this was an inevitable and natural event —, but the tragedy of the triumph of the systematic fostering of hatred against the Dutch resulting in the *sudden* and *complete* severance of the Dutch-Indonesian connection, cannot be explained as the result of any particular wickedness of Dutch colonial rule in the past, or of any stubborn colonialism on their part surviving the war. It can be fairly judged only if one remembers the particularly untoward circumstances that I mentioned.

When we now look at Holland again, it is indeed remarkable — this is what I said a moment ago, and it was this that led me into my digression about the Indonesian crisis — that Holland, while exerting itself so strenuously to recover from the ravages of the war, could take in its stride this further loss of the connection with Indonesia, formerly responsible, it has been estimated, for about one-seventh of the national income. To find housing and employment for the tens of thousands of Dutch citizens who came streaming back in the 1950s — many of them of mixed blood, to whom Holland was really a foreign country — that too was no small problem, but it was mastered. Leading men in Indonesia, oppressed by the spectacle of helplessness and decline in their own country, expressed amazement at what was accomplished in Holland. In Holland itself gloomy prognostications had been heard as to the disastrous consequences likely to result from 'the loss of the colonies'. But listen to the retrospective reflections of an Amsterdam paper of strong conservative leanings, written in 1957:

> The quick recovery of our country and the catching-up with the industrial backwardness which came to characterize our economy at the time of our East Indian delusions offer a striking spectacle. With it goes the conviction that we owe this not least to the fact that we can now devote to our own country our undivided national energy, all our experience, all our material and intellectual capital.

The Dutch colonial empire, that had collapsed so completely, was a relic of the days when Holland played an active part in world politics. Already, in the eighteenth century, she had been relegated to a more modest rank, and in the nineteenth she could have no higher ambition than that of preserving her neutrality. Neutrality was for a long time the keyword of Dutch foreign policy, and even in the 1930s, when the failure of the League of Nations had become apparent, Holland was left with no other principle than neutrality, often called by a more dignified name now — 'the policy of independence'. In fact Dutch policy was one of helplessness, of praying to be left alone.

When the country had been plunged into the common catastrophe and had emerged thanks to the efforts especially of England and the United States, and when soon afterwards the Continent of Europe, to which its fate was now more definitely then confined, was exposed to the overwhelming menace of Russian communism, this isolationist policy lost its in any case deceptive appeal, and a desire for more regular and permanent forms of association came to dominate the thinking about international relations.

As a matter of fact, a step in that direction had been taken, even before the end of the war, when the Benelux treaty was signed in London by the exiled governments of Belgium, the Netherlands and Luxemburg. Implicit in this treaty was the recognition that the splitting-up of the seventeen Netherlands in the closing decades of the sixteenth century had resulted in a weakening of their position with regard to their neighbours. Not that real unity was now restored. The modern states shaped by the vicissitudes of history cling tenaciously to their political traditions and vested interests. This is only too apparent in the larger movement for European unity that was set going immediately after the war, and in which the Benelux countries participated without abandoning their tripartite association.

Within Benelux, indeed, now that Flanders counts for so much more in Belgium — a result, very largely, of the reforms of 1932, — community of language is making for closer relations. Not long ago the Belgian ambassador in the Netherlands, in a speech before a Dutch audience, said in so many words — and it was a statement almost startling in its novelty, coming from that quarter — that 'the renewal of historiography' and the increasing success of 'the process of Flemish emancipation' were exercising a profound influence on the relations between the two peoples. Cultural integration is no longer a fantastic notion.

And shortly afterwards the Belgian Assistant Minister of Foreign Affairs, Fayat — a Fleming in spite of his French name, and one of the strongest Flamingants in the Flemish wing of the Belgian Socialist party —, addressing a Dutch-Flemish literary conference at The Hague, expressed his belief in the European unity movement, but added that it would be treason to our history if this multilingual Europe were to allow its rich variety to fade away into a colourless uniformity. Within that Europe the Dutch-speaking group of seventeen million people (eleven million Dutchmen, six million Flemings) was becoming more and more aware of its essential unity. Fayat, too, alluded in this connection to 'the quiet revolution' that was taking place in Flanders as a result of the linguistic laws passed thirty years ago.

And again, this was language no one had ever before heard coming from the Belgian Foreign Office.

And now, what about Holland's position with regard to the actual attempts which are being made to constitute Europe? When the war came to an end, the idea of close co-operation was very much in the air — co-operation on a narrower and consequently more solid basis than that afforded by the universalism of the United Nations. The movement for European unity, in which Winston Churchill in 1947 assumed a leading position, quickly led to practical results. In 1948 sixteen European countries came together in the O.E.E.C., whose primary function was to ensure a fair distribution of Marshall-aid money ; and in 1949 there followed the setting up of the Council of Europe, a committee of ministers representing the various countries and an assembly of parliamentarians meeting at Strasbourg. All this, achieved with the co-operation of England, was of undeniable importance. For one thing, it facilitated the re-admission of Germany into the community of European nations. But the European unity movement really aimed at more radical forms of federation, which would involve the integration of military, economic and social affairs and in consequence a partial surrender of national sovereignty. And now Winston Churchill's enthusiasm was seen to wane, and British opinion generally appeared reluctant to go so far. When De Gasperi, Schuman and Adenauer inaugurated more ambitious practical plans for European union, England held aloof. A first attempt to bring together six European states — France, Western Germany, Italy and the Benelux countries — failed in 1954 when the projected European Defence Community (E.D.C.) was refused ratification by the French Chamber — ironically enough, for the scheme had originated in France. The advocates of union, soon recovering from the shock, undertook the *relance européenne*, this time putting economic instead of defence arrangements to the fore. In 1957 the Treaty of Rome was signed and the E.E.C., the Common Market of the Six, was set up.

A problem was thus created which was for a long time ignored in Holland. Personally, I was critical from the start. In January 1954 (when the fate of the E.D.C. was still hanging in the balance) I published an article under the title: 'Unorthodox reflections on the Little Europe policy'. A few years later, when the Common Market was in full swing, I returned to the charge on several occasions.[1]

My first criticism throughout was of the absence of England. I knew, of course, that she had not been deliberately excluded, that she was standing aside of her own free will, and when in 1956 I made a short speech on this subject at an Anglo-Dutch occasion in London, I expressed my hope — not without an undertone of bitterness, perhaps — that England, who had not failed us in 1940, would realize that 'a great constructive task' was awaiting her in Europe. In any case I did not feel that the unfortunate revival in England of that spirit of insularity with which William III had had to contend in his time ought to make any difference to my view that an association in which she did not participate had no right to claim that it was representing or promoting European unity. I feared, on the contrary, that the situation created by the Rome treaty might develop into a dangerous division of Europe.

Moreover, from our own Dutch point of view, it seemed to me particularly unfortunate that we had tied ourselves so closely to those particular Continental countries mentioned above, whose internal situation was so very far from stable, and against which we, even in combination with the other Benelux countries, would find it difficult to make our own views prevail. If I objected to the unitarian character of the new 'European' institutions (I never forgot to place the word 'European' between quotes and to add 'Little-European'), it was largely on account of the company in which we found ourselves.

The worst thing seemed to me the 'European' (Little-European) parliament that was provided for in the near future (as a matter of fact it has not yet materialized), and which was to be directly elected by the constituent peoples. The Dutch

Government gave its consent to this provision only reluctantly, but to the more fervent supporters of the union it seemed to be the crowning victory of the new unitary principle. On paper, yes! But would it work in practice? It struck me as not a little naïve to expect so much of a 'European' parliament when the French and the Italians, who were to constitute so considerable a part of it, were at that very moment making a sad mess of their own parliamentary systems. The Communists and neo-Fascists they were likely to contribute — or were they to manipulate the suffrage for the 'European' parliament as the French were soon to do for home purposes? — gave no promise of stability. But even from a more general point of view, does not the parliamentary system depend for its success on a certain homogeneity in the electorate? Even when one is as firmly convinced as I am that Europe *does* constitute a cultural unit, can one overlook the variety based on different languages, different historical memories, different political traditions?

In reply to these and similar observations I was denounced as a reactionary, an old-fashioned nationalist. The appeal to history that I made — history, which shows how futile or how dangerous it can be to proceed by arguing in the abstract — was found particularly irritating. One of my most strident opponents (a member of the Second Chamber) proclaimed that all that stood in the way of our objective, the unity of Europe, must be cast aside. Traditions and customs that might seem hallowed by age-long practice we must abandon. He described me as a man who stood by the principles of nationality and sovereignty. — Now, as regards sovereignty, I never dreamt of wanting it preserved without qualification. But as for nationality, did he really mean that all national variety was to be thrown into the melting-pot? That was a conception of European unity which was, and indeed still is, abhorrent to me. I quoted the Belgian Assistant Minister of Foreign Affairs a moment ago on the necessity of preserving the multilingual variety of Europe's cultural traditions, and on the fact that seventeen million Dutch-speaking people are as much entitled as are the French, the

Germans, the Italians, to have their identity respected. Fortunately a good many earnest supporters of the policy to which we had been committed would, when it came to the point, strenuously deny that the revolutionary aim professed by my critic was what they had in mind.

But it was one of the weaknesses of our position, as I saw it when I started this debate on fundamental principles nine or ten years ago, that the movement seemed to have got into the hands of — as I put it — 'the enthusiasts and the experts', and that public opinion, neither enthusiastic nor expert, let itself be charmed and impressed by them. 'The enthusiasts and the experts' — that is to say, in my own somewhat sarcastic definitions, 'the professional Europeans', 'the Strasbourg travellers' : the men who were fast acquiring a vested interest in the new institutions, and who, dazzled by the opportunities offered them to play a part on the larger scene of Europe, were apt to argue away or minimize objections based on mere national interest. In the political debates at home, debates held in private very often, their expert mastery of the novel institutional lore that was growing up with the Common Market and allied European creations gave them an advantage over the average politician. This latter soon felt out of his depth and hardly dared to come into the open with his doubts. I myself had had to take my courage in both hands (and I said so) in order to publish my 'unorthodox reflections' in 1954.

In the years that have since passed, some of the illusions which accompanied the start of this great venture have already been dispersed. On many occasions, within the new Little Europe, national interests were seen to clash, and arrangements had to be resorted to which involved uneasy compromises and left sore feelings behind. Obviously the Treaty of Rome had not, as if at the touch of a magic wand, turned the various nations into Europeans : the French were still French, the Germans German, the Italians Italian — and with the realization of this went inevitably the awakening of a keener consciousness of ourselves as still being Dutchmen. The enormous success of the E.E.C. in stimulating, in a few short years, the economy of the participating countries certainly made a profound impression; I myself had to admit that in my early criticisms I had not indeed foreseen so spectacular a development. But at the same time public opinion was becoming more realistic in its approach to the problems of European unity.

After de Gaulle had come to power, one particular danger soon became apparent: that of a French, or perhaps a Franco-German, hegemony, confined to the Continent, more or less suspicious of the wider Atlantic alliance. It was in February 1961 that the two potentates, de Gaulle and Adenauer, at a council of the ministers of the Six held in Paris, sprung upon the other partners the plan they had concocted together of exclusive and regular consultations about foreign policy between the six governments. It was only owing to the perspicacity and the courage of the Dutch Minister of Foreign Affairs, Luns, who in the face of cajolery and browbeating persisted in his solitary veto, that the plan could not be rushed through. Time was gained, and soon Belgium, where Spaak returned to the Foreign Office in May 1961, also Italy, and even, despite Adenauer, influential German circles, came over to strengthen Dutch opposition. Luns had immediately suggested that if foreign policy was to be considered, England should be drawn in. And now this aspect of the situation, the absence from the councils of the E.E.C. of England — England, a country more congenial to Dutch ways of thinking than France, more open to the overseas world which meant so much to the Dutch economy as well, and an indispensable counterweight to France — this aspect came to occupy a prominent place in the discussions carried on in the Dutch press and in the Dutch Chamber about the situation into which the Treaty of Rome had landed us.

I wonder if you can picture to yourselves this wistful looking across the North Sea? 'Can't the English see that their own interests are involved? Are not "the liberties of Europe" at stake as they were three hundred, a hundred and fifty, thirty years ago? Do they really think that they can live apart on

Q 233

their island? — De Gaulle asks for nothing better, but a Continental block would mean not only servitude for us, but a very real danger to them.'

In talks I had with Dutch politicians closely connected with the E.E.C. policy they always laid the blame on England — not without good reason, of course, although the fact that England had neglected both her duty and her own interests by standing aside did not, to my mind, justify the risk taken by our Government in entering in 1957 into an association confined to the Continent, and this on terms which so severely curtailed its future liberty of action. But, so my friends used to point out, something had had to be done even if England persisted in her negative attitude. The E.E.C. was set up as an open association ; it should really be regarded as an invitation, an exhortation, to England to join, and we might expect, sooner or later, that she would come round to the view that she *must* join.

When Mr. Macmillan did indeed, on July 31, 1961, announce the English Government's decision to apply for membership, the satisfaction and relief were general in Holland. I continued to follow the protracted negotiations in Brussels with misgivings. They had their ups and downs, until de Gaulle slammed the door against England on January 14, 1963. His pronouncement caused consternation and indignation in all the five member states of the E.E.C. The Dutch press, radio and television were unanimous in denouncing the arrogance and the narrowly nationalist ambition it revealed. Was it not clear that what was behind his unwillingness to have England admitted was his desire to bring the Continent under his own direction and so to enable France to follow a policy of her own, independently from, if need be in opposition to, the Anglo-Saxon powers? The names of Louis XIV and of Napoleon came irresistibly to mind. Only two or three days earlier the Dutch Chamber had voted a motion, signed by members of each of the five major parties and adopted unanimously, to urge upon the Government (which needed no urging really, but was grateful for the moral support) to bring the negotiations with England to a positive conclusion.

But what now? Consternation and indignation are not enough. What can we do? If de Gaulle stands fast — and can anything else be expected of him? — the association will prove not to be so open as my friends had told me it would be. I had promised them that if England did in the end join, I would apologize for my criticisms and for my contention that, in spite of all the economic success, an unjustifiable risk had been taken when our Government signed the Treaty of Rome. I told them more than once that I was looking forward to the moment when my apologies would become due. When de Gaulle said *no* in that brutal fashion, however, it did not look as if I should be called upon to offer them very soon. Much to my regret, I assure you.

I may seem in these last remarks to have been straying from history into present-day politics. But the problems I have just been discussing are indissolubly connected with the past, so much so that, as I have already hinted, they can hardly be discussed without evoking memories of phenomena and figures and phrases that dominated the history of earlier centuries. Indeed, that history now proves to be far from having become irrelevant as Professor Barraclough in his *History in a Changing World* wants us to believe it has become. Louis XIV and Napoleon, and their ambitions for a universal monarchy confined to the Continent, William III and his stand for the liberties of Europe, the essential function incumbent upon England in that connection, and the insularity of English popular feeling which sometimes withholds or delays her — the recent happenings of which our minds are full simply form a further chapter of an old story. Let us, after the somewhat gloomy conclusion to which developments up to today have led me, comfort ourselves with the reflection that the story is not really ended, and that in chapters still to come solutions may be found which have so far escaped us.

NOTES

I

1. See my *Revolt of the Netherlands* (last edition 1962); and also an essay 'The National State and the Writers of Netherlands History' in my *Debates with Historians* (M.B., N.Y., 1961, Collins, 1963).
2. On the map reproduced on p. 4 the linguistic boundary is indicated by a line of crosses.
3. The current term in English is, of course, Dutch. I shall use it myself from now on. Netherlandish is the literal translation of 'Nederlands'. There is a widespread misapprehension that Dutch, spoken in Holland, and Flemish, spoken in Belgium, are two closely-related but distinct languages. It is promoted by the fact that in everyday speech the Dutchman will generally call his language 'Hollands' (Hollandish or Dutch), while the Fleming will say that he speaks 'Vlaams' (Flemish). In fact, however, although over the entire linguistic area dialect forms of the language survive in varying degrees of vigour, there is but one standard language, for which officially, and in somewhat more cultivated speech, 'Nederlands' is the word used both in Holland and in Belgium.

II

1. I allude here to W. Nuyens (1823–1894), a native of the province of North-Holland, whose work on 'The sixteenth-century Troubles' was to some extent a reaction to Motley's *Rise of the Dutch Republic*.
2. 'Fransquillons' is the term by which the Flamingants denoted the members of the gallicized leading class in Flanders who actively opposed measures to raise the popular language from its debased position.
3. Julius Vuylsteke, of Ghent, lawyer, publicist, Flamingant, active in the 1870s and 1880s.
4. Professor Romein died last year at the age of sixty-nine.
5. Mr. Carr does not use that expression without an ironical apology for committing that 'cardinal sin'; see *What is History?* p. 122.
6. *My* intention also was 'to search the past to find out why things have come about so' (Huizinga) or 'simply to explain what happened and why' (Carr). I suggested that a decisive part had been played by factors other than those commonly advanced, factors difficult to fit into the pattern of 'natural development' that was so much in vogue.
7. So it was put by Tawney in the statement quoted by Carr and with which, apart from that, I agree.

8. In the periodical *Leiding*, reprinted in my volume *Kernproblemen von onze geschiedenis* (1937) ; and later, in 1960, in a pocket book containing a selection of my essays on the problems connected with the relationship between North and South : *Noord en Zuid*.

III

1. *Brieven van N. van Reigersberch aan Hugo de Groot* (Utrecht : Hist. Gen., 1901), p. 51.
2. Vreede, *Geschiedenis der Nederl. Diplomatie* (1858–61), I, 58.
3. In August 1634, for instance, the Groningen member of the Secret Committee, on being told that he must not give any information about the negotiations then proceeding to the States of his province, replied that he would abstain from taking any part in further proceedings except in so far as directed by those States (L. Aitzema, *Saken van staet en oorlogh* (1658), III, 267). Opposition of Groningen did not need to be taken too seriously, but we shall see that this was the very point on which Holland, in 1643, was to aim a deadly blow to the Secret Committee. Under William III the Secret Committee was revived (*Recueil des instructions données aux ambassadeurs de France, Hollande*, II, 168) and again this point at times caused friction ; see Sylvius, *Historiën onzes tijds* (1684), p. 41. The history of the Secret Committee would repay systematic examination. Brief and vague remarks are all that is to be found in Vreede, *op. cit.*, Van Riemsdijk, *Griffie van H. H. M.*, p. 21, Fruin-Colenbrander, *Staatsinstellingen*, p. 187.
4. Arend, *Algemeene Geschiedenis* (1868), III, v, 261.
5. Vreede, *op. cit.* I, 212, n. 2.
6. See the evidence from the *Archives de la maison d'Orange-Nassau* and Van der Capellen cited by Ising in *Bijdragen*, New Series, IV, 255. Fruin has shown, by a reference to the *Clarendon State Papers*, that the suspicion was unfounded. In May Sir William Boswell was already reporting similar rumours from Holland (*State Papers, For., Holland*, CLV).
7. Ranke, *Französische Geschichte*, II, 506 ff. ; Lavisse, *Histoire de France*, VI, ii, 350.
8. I do not think that Marie de Médicis can have been quite honestly in favour of the idea. Sommelsdijk declares that in January she as well as her daughter were enthusiastic about the Spanish marriage (*Archives*, II, iii, 161).
9. Arend, *op. cit.* III, v, 248 ; cf. Aitzema, *op. cit.* IV, b, 75. The instructions, December 6, 1639, are given as an appendix in T. J. Geest, *Amalia van Solms en de Nederl. politiek van 1625 tot 1648* (1909).

10. February 6, 1640 (*Archives*, II, iii, 197).
11. All that we know about this incident is to be gathered from a letter from Sommelsdijk to Frederick Henry of February 2 (*ibid.* p. 198). Brill, in Arend's *Algemeene Geschiedenis*, III, v, 259, n., drew attention to this. The emphatic tone of Sommelsdijk's words leads one to suspect that he thought the Prince needed persuasion.
12. *Venetian Calendar* (1640–1642), p. 110.
13. Cf. *Archives*, II, iii, 161, 206.
14. The inequality of the marriage may be illustrated by contrasting the forms used by Frederick Henry in his letters to Charles II with those of the King's letters to him. The Prince of Orange writes : 'Sire, la gracieuse lettre dont il a plu à V. M. m'onorer. . . . Je lui témoigneray tousjours par mes devoirs et très-humbles services que je suis avec passion, Sire, de V. M. très-humble et très-obéissant serviteur. . . .' The King writes : 'Mon cousin, Vous verrez . . . Je suis, mon cousin, votre très-affectionné cousin. . . .'
15. *Archives*, II, iii, 161.
16. Geest, *op. cit.* p. 91.
17. *Archives*, II, iii, 217.
18. *Ibid.* p. 220.
19. With Mademoiselle, known later as 'la grande Mademoiselle' (*ibid.* p. 218).
20. See *Venetian Calendar*, p. 124.
21. L. Aitzema, *Saken van staet en oorlogh*, V, 336 (I quote from the quarto edition), in relating the visit of the Queen to Holland, remarks in his caustic way that she 'seemed to have been informed of the Prince's great authority and power' and that 'he did as he willed with this state'. Indeed, that is how the position was regarded at the English court : early in 1639 Secretary Coke had written in a letter to Boswell, the resident at The Hague : 'The building of the fort at Breda, as it secureth that place, so it showeth what great power the Prince of Aurenge hath among them' (*State Papers, For., Holland*, CLV).
22. *Venetian Calendar*, p. 119.
23. It stipulated, among other things, that the bride should remain in England until she had reached her twelfth year ; that the marriage portion should be £40,000, payable in four half-yearly sums of £10,000.
24. *Archives*, II, iii, 430.
25. The suspicions of the Parliament had so increased by March that the King's commissioners insisted at the last moment that the envoys of the Prince of Orange should be content with an informal and secret ratification of the contract (*ibid.* p. 400 ; see also p. 460). This is what Baillie, the Scottish Covenanter, must have had in his mind when on

May 7, 1641, O.S. (May 17, N.S.) he wrote from London: 'The precipitation of this marriage is feared by manie' (*Letters and Journals*, I, 351; cf. also *Venetian Calendar*, p. 115).

26. 'De bruid niet in de schuit' (*Brieven*, p. 649). What especially made R. suspicious was 'the care with which the Princess had been kept *intactam*, in fact and in the opinion of the world, which will know what happened for half an hour in the presence of the King, Queen, Ambassadors and some Bishops, the Princess being put to bed in a double shirt, sown fast below and above, between two sheets, over which two more were spread in which the Prince was lying'.

27. *Ibid* p. 674: 'Die praem wat langer zullen willen gebruycken'.

28. May, *Life of Duke of Gloucester and Princess Mary* (1661); quoted in Green, *Lives of the Princesses of England*, VI, 128.

29. Agnes Strickland, *Lives of the Last Four Princesses of the Royal House of Stuart*, p. 28. Miss Strickland's historical appreciations are if possible even more amusing than Miss Green's, but she, too, has done some archival research. Cf. also Clarendon, *Rebellion*, p. 819, and P. C. Hooft, *Brieven*, IV, 344.

30. By an act of February 10/20, 1641/2, *Rawlinson Letters* (Bodleian Library), A, cxv. This volume contains letters written by the Orange family and the Stuarts to Heenvliet and his wife, together with a few official documents of personal interest to them both.

31. Reigersberch, *Brieven*, p. 605.

32. *Ibid.* p. 719.

33. '. . . Hen die van Godt tot Godheid zijn gewijt Ten dienst van 't algemeen.'

34. *Venetian Calendar*, p. 158.

35. For 1642 alone Knuttel, *Catalogus*, mentions some seventy pamphlets connected with the differences between the King of England and Parliament, mostly translations of declarations, proclamations and justifications of the two parties.

36. 'We have met at length sometimes with Dr. Rivett: he is one fullie in our minds and against the Bishops' (Baillie, *Letters and Journals*, I, 181).

37. Although Baillie later on encouraged him to do so (*ibid.* pp. 169, 181).

38. William Spang, cousin of Robert Baillie and one of his most regular correspondents (see Baillie, *op. cit.* II, 75, 115, 180). From the last passage it appears that Spang was sometimes responsible for the printing of the writings that the other man inspired. Apparently the reference is here to the pamphlet numbered 4990 in Knuttel, *Catalogus*.

39. Knuttel, *Acta der . . . Synod en van Zuid-Holland*, II, 505.

40. *Ibid.* pp. 466-504.

41. *Ernstig gesprek . . . tusschen drie personen* (1652 [Knuttel, *Catalogus*, no. 7256]), p. 35. In *De Nederlandsche Nijptang* (1652 [*ibid.* no. 7251]), p. 13, the same accusation occurs.

42. It is true that they were often offended at the worldliness of Frederick Henry and his protégée the refugee Queen of Bohemia (another Stuart!) — I find, for example, in *State Papers, For., Holland*, CLV, a letter from Samson Johnson, 'from Her My's Court at The Hague' (*i.e.* from the court of the Queen of Bohemia), to Archbishop Laud, dated December 5, 1639, in which he says : 'The consistorye in this towne have done all they could for suppressing of the French players licenced by the magistrate and protected by the P[rince] of Orange as his servants, but their invectives for condemning of all stage-players or the like shews have bin soe intemperate in theyr pulpitts, that they ar gone backward rather than forward ; all the preachers were with the P[rince] of Orange to represent the unlawfullness, but it seemes used noe argument that could worke on him, his counsell was that they should preach better and the playes would be less frequented. They came also to her Matye and desired shee would forbeare going ; her Matye told them that shee conceaved 'twas a pastime that might be lawfully used and shee would use her discretion ; and wondred at their incivilitye. I had nothing to doe in the business, they came not to me but formerly they desired me to preach against bare-necks, by reason her Matie uses to goe toe, which I refusing as being not sent to tell her Matie how to dress herself, they let me pass in this business. Beside there has been a proposition made to the consistorye here by the persons of best qualitye that they might have organs for to play with the psalms as in some townes of these countryes, but they plainly denyed it.' The festivals in honour of Henrietta Maria gave offence in the same way (see Knuttel, *Catalogus*, no. 4869). Down to the time of his deepest humiliation Charles never ceased to demand that the stipulations of the marriage contract, guaranteeing the observance of the Episcopalian form of worship at his daughter's court, should be adhered to. On August 6, 1647, O.S. (August 16, N.S.) in connection with the report that there were differences of opinion at the court itself on this point, he wrote to Heenvliet from Stoke with strict injunctions to the same effect (*Rawlinson Letters*, A, cxv).

43. Knuttel, *Catalogus*, no. 4870 ; *Lettres inédites de Henriette-Marie*, ed. Baillon, p. 66.

44. According to Reigersberch, *op. cit.* p. 707, the ambassadors in England 'had been generous in promising as much as 50,000 guilders a year, but this without the knowledge or authority of those who would have to pay. . . . The States of Holland, seeing many provinces anxious to play the generous at their expense, resolved to give what they wished

to give apart and of themselves, leaving the others to carry out their own liberality.' See also Aitzema, *op. cit.* V, 343 ; *Venetian Calendar* (1642–1643), pp. 21, 28.

45. Aitzema, *op. cit.* V, 335.

46. 'Many are only just seeing the results of this alliance' writes Reigersberch, March 24, 1642 (*op. cit.* p. 708), and he adds 'and all do not see it yet'.

47. Green, *op. cit.* VI, 129. The statement of source is not satisfactory : 'Letter of La Fin, page of the Prince of Orange, to his brother, 10th March, 1641'. The date obviously stands for March 20, 1642, N.S. Some of the details, too, are apocryphal. For instance, mention is made of a tribunal of the States-General at The Hague. The letter is to be found in *Somers Tracts*, IV.

48. Aitzema, *op. cit.* V, 467 ; *Archives*, II, iv. 166.

49. Reigersberch writes (*op. cit.* p. 740) on November 1643 to Grotius that 'the present vigour of many has its origin more in umbrage on account of English affairs and religious ideas than in steadfast principles of state policy and freedom'. Reigersberch, a Remonstrant republican, objects to the English policy of the Stadholder but he regrets that the new vigour against the Prince's supremacy had no more steadfast principle as a basis. By 'religious ideas' he means, of course, the Calvinist sympathies with the Presbyterian Parliament.

50. See the dispatch of the States-General to Joachimi, July 26, 1642, in Muller, *Mare Clausum*, p. 318, n. 3.

51. 'Il ne faut pas que le Prince laisse périr le Roy' ; this is what Henrietta Maria said to Heenvliet in January 1642 (*Archives*).

52. Joachimi (correspondence in 19th century copies at Br. Mus.) constantly reported bitter complaints. He could in reply only point to the resolution laying down a policy of neutrality. That gave no satisfaction because at that time the States-General still held that allowing the export of arms was consistent with neutrality.

53. See the letters of his treasurer, Vosbergen, in Worp, *Briefwisseling van Constantijn Huygens* (Rijks Geschiedkundige Publicatiën), III, *passim*. Vosbergen had a great deal of trouble in raising the 300,000 guilders in Amsterdam. They had to submit to an interest of 7 per cent.

54. How entirely dependent on his favour everyone was in such cases appears very clearly in my article 'Troepenlichten en schepenhuren in de dagen van Frederik Hendrik', in *Bijdragen*, 1918.

55. Eva Scott, *Rupert, Prince Palatine*, p. 59, gives 'Coulster' as the name of the captain of the ship placed at their disposal by the Prince. Reigersberch (*op. cit.* p. 728) writes on June 30, 1642, that Rupert and Maurice, 'with a following of some hundred officers', left for England 'yesterday'. That must have been the first, unsuccessful, attempt to cross,

which Miss Scott, however, places in August.

56. *Archives*, II, iv, 40.
57. *Ibid.* p. 42.
58. *Ibid.* p. 39.
59. Reigersberch (*op. cit.* p. 701) wrote immediately : 'The state will profit to this extent : the bride being brought home, they will not have to court England's favour so much [*men minder schoon op sal hebben te dienen*]'. The Queen herself wrote to the King (March 17, 1642) : 'Je travaille avec le Prince d'Orange et espère en avoir contentement, quoyque ce soit une personne malaysée à engager ; mais les intérests ont de grands pouvoirs' (*Lettres inédites de Henriette-Marie*, p. 25).
60. 'Dearest Daughter, I desyre you to assist me to procure from your Father in Law the loane of a good ship to be sent higher to attend my commands. It is that I may safely send and receave Expresses to and from your Mother' (Charles to Mary, Newcastle, September 16, 1646, O.S. [September 26, N.S.], *Rawlinson Letters*, A, cxv). The date 1646 is obviously wrong ; it must be 1642.
61. See, for instance, *Archives*, II, iv, 43.
62. *Ibid.* p. 49.
63. In April 1645 Charles I gave him a barony with the title of Baron de Kerckhove. Whereupon Jermyn wrote to Digby that this was not enough, in view of the fact that the Queen in Holland 'upon the important services she received from Heenvliet' had promised a title for his son by Lady Stanhope. On June 7, 1649, Charles II fulfilled this promise by creating the son himself Baron Wotton of Marley (*Rawlinson Letters*, A, cxv).
64. *Archives*, II, iv, 43.
65. *Lettres inédites de Henriette-Marie*, p. 402.
66. Arend, *op. cit.* III, v, 383.
67. *Archives*, II, iv, 71. The Hollanders were particularly moved by the report that there were 'canons d'état' on board these ships. They found none, but this does not mean that the report had no foundation in fact.
68. *Ibid.* p. 69.
69. Letter to Heenvliet, *ibid.* p. 75.
70. Reigersberch, *op. cit.* p. 727, writes : 'Actually the alliance is made with the King, so that it cannot rightly be proved that arms may be denied to him'. He says also that Amsterdam and Rotterdam in the States of Holland were against a prohibition of export (in June 1642), 'under the pretext that trade must be free'.
71. A year later Boswell still writes about this resolution with the greatest indignation, in a letter to his government which happens to have been

preserved because it was intercepted by the parliamentary party (*State Papers, For., Holland,* CLVII).

72. *Archives,* II, iv, 73. 'Notorious' for his corruption.

73. On November 11, 1642, Strickland writes to Pym that he has given information about a munitions ship to the States-General, 'but there is so much form in their resolutions as to make the work fruitless. When I sought to hasten it the Greffier, who is to despatch the order, told me that he cared not whether she were gone or not. I find him harsh in all that concerns the Parliament' (*Hist. MSS. Comm., Xth Report,* vi, 91). See also *Archives,* II, iv, 43. The Council of State allowed itself to be used by Frederick Henry, and so, up to a certain point, did the Admiralty College of Amsterdam. Concerning Musch, as late as April 16, 1645, Dr. Goffe writes to Jermyn (*Digby's Cabinet* [see below, n. 100]) : 'He is a very serious servant of her Majesties, and ought to be gratified, whatsoever becomes of other businesse.' And, as a matter of fact, at the end of May 1645 he received a gift of 3,000 guilders (*ibid.* p. 39).

74. *Hist. MSS. Comm., Xth Report,* vi, 93. Renswoude, like Musch, was one of the confidants of the Prince of Orange (*Archives,* II, iv, 97).

75. Reigersberch, *op. cit.* pp. 730 ff.

76. *Lettres inédites de Henriette-Marie.*

77. *Archives,* II, iv, 9.

78. *Ibid.* p. 17.

79. *Ibid.* p. 18.

80. Reigersberch, *op. cit.* p. 707.

81. Arend, *op. cit.* II, iv, 371.

82. Willem Boreel (Elias, *Vroedschap van Amsterdam,* I, 540), a member of a well-known Zeeland family, had settled in Amsterdam and had become pensionary of the town in 1627. He was none the less an Orangist. Heenvliet took him into his confidence over the question of the crown jewels (*Archives,* II, iv, 43). One of Heenvliet's sons became a gentleman at the court of Frederick Henry and Boreel took a warm interest in the career of this young man (see Worp, *op. cit.* V, 55). He himself owed his appointment as ambassador at Paris to William II. According to a note, the source of which I cannot trace, he received in that capacity 1,000 livres a year from the Prince over and above his salary.

Renswoude, the well-known Orangist deputy for Utrecht in the States-General, was a brother of Reede van Nederhorst, who belonged to His Highness's council (Waddington, *La République des Provinces-Unies,* II, 257, 260). In December 1642 Strickland wrote, with great annoyance, concerning Renswoude as a strong anti-parliamentarian (*Hist. MSS. Comm., Xth Report,* v, 93). Henrietta Maria received a visit from one of the two which very much pleased her (*Lettres*, p. 31).

83. *Archives*, II, iv, 39. See also Reigersberch, *op. cit.* p. 726.

84. The French ambassador, Harcourt, too, writes in the same spirit (*Archives*, II, iv, 97).

85. *State Papers, For., Holland*, CLVII.

86. Reigersberch, *op. cit.* p. 699.

87. Observations on the wrecking of the Secret Committee by means of this new instruction are to be found in Van der Capellen's *Gedenkschriften*, II, 173; Waddington, *La République des Provinces-Unies*, II, 35 (d'Estrades to Mazarin); and in a French memorandum of 1647 published in *Bijdragen en Mededelingen* (Hist. Gen.), XV, 134. The instruction: Aitzema, *op. cit.* V, 552 ff.

88. Aitzema, *op. cit.* V, 619.

89. *Ibid.* p. 563. See also Duanne Lon in *Venetian Calendar* (*1642–1643*), p. 220: 'The Prince knows how much his authority has suffered since the alliance of his son with the Princess Mary of England, because of what he has had to do in the interests of that Crown' (December 31, 1642).

90. Reigersberch, *op. cit.* p. 734.

91. Baillie, *op. cit.* II, 113.

92. See his letters to Huygens, the Prince's secretary, in Worp, *op. cit.* IV, *passim*; Worp calls Renswoude by his family name, Reede. In these letters Renswoude makes no secret of his anti-parliamentary leanings, *e.g.* 'the government of the Parliament means ruin to our state' (November 4, 1644, p. 95) and 'I understand that Joachimi is working secretly in Holland that he may come with us, which will be to the disadvantage of His Highness and the King; must therefore be prevented' (March 10, 1645, p. 131).

93. Baillie, *op. cit.* II, 143. Shortly after this, he says simply that they were 'sent by the Prince of Orange to serve the King's ends'.

94. Arend gives a detailed résumé of the report handed to the States-General by the ambassadors on their return.

95. Baillie, *op. cit.* II, 155, 167.

96. Arend, *op. cit.* II, v, 501.

97. See Huygens to Joachimi, February 6, 1645 (*Archives*, II, iv, 128): 'Il a esté procuré que nos ambassadeurs n'auront à bouger d'Angleterre pour quelque temps, vers où donc, si la France se résoult d'en envoyer de son costé durant leur séjour par delà, ils pourront entrer dans les communications que vous sçavez et veoir à quelle sorte de concert les affaires se pourront conduire entre leurs mains.'

98. More particularly of the Independents.

99. Arend, *op. cit.* II, v, 518. See also the bellicose tone of a letter from Renswoude to Huygens of August 14, 1645 (Worp, *op. cit.* IV, 192).

100. On March 6, 1646, O.S. (March 16, N.S.), the House of Commons issued an order for the publication of the papers of Digby, which had fallen into its hands in the previous year in a battle at Sherburn in Yorkshire. They were published under the title *The Lord George Digby's Cabinet.* . . . . A Dutch translation of the parts of most interest to Dutch readers appeared under the title, *Eenighe extracten uyt verscheyde missiven, gevonden in de Lord Digby's Cabinet.* . . . Tot Londen, ghedruct by Robert Wood ; Knuttel, *Catalogus,* no. 5252 ; 'Holl. druk' according to Knuttel.

101. *Digby's Cabinet,* Goffe to Jermyn, April 17, 1645, O.S. (April 27, N.S.), 'When the ambassadors are returned, all endeavours shall be used to induce the States to a League defensive and offensive.'

102. *Ibid.* Goffe to Jermyn, 8/18 May 1645.

103. *Ibid.* Goffe to Jermyn, 15/25 May 1645.

104. *Ibid.* Goffe to Jermyn, 1/11 May 1645.

105. *Ibid.* Goffe to Jermyn, 29 May/8 June 1645.

106. Aitzema, *op. cit.* VI, 75.

107. Gelderland and Friesland voted with Holland for the reception of Strickland. The Frisian delegates, it is true, conformed at the express bidding of their Stadholder, although their States had made the opposite decision (Aitzema, *op. cit.* VI, 77).

108. See Kernkamp, *De Sleutels van de Sond,* p. 44.

109. The suspicion that it probably was not that, but 'also an account of the marriage alliance between himself, the King of England, and Denmark', is expressed in Van der Capellen, *Gedenkschriften,* II, 98, and Van der Capellen was by no means inimical to the Prince.

110. *Ibid.* p. 98 : 'om deze coorde niet te stijf te trecken, opdat daeruyt niet erger kome te ontstaan'. The candid man's name is not given.

111. By the revelations contained in *Lord Digby's Cabinet;* see below, p. 77.

112. *Archives,* II, iv, 97.

113. Worp, *op. cit.* IV, 473.

114. See Gardiner, *History of the Civil War,* I, 328-9.

115. *Archives,* II, iv, 98.

116. Arend, *op. cit.* II, v, 493.

117. *Archives,* II, v, 103.

118. *Ibid.* II, iv, 97.

119. The attitude of France towards the English differences was no more honest than that of the Orangist majority in the States-General, but it was certainly more cautious. In the British Museum there is a bulky volume comprising 'Négociations de M. de Sabran en Angleterre en 1644' (Add. MS. 5460). The Instructions, dated April 19, 1644, say that the attempts of Grécy to mediate between King and Parliament were not acceptable to the Parliament because he showed himself too

much an adherent of the King. Sabran is now to 'appuyer les justes prétentions du Roy et le favoriser en tout et par tout', but 'avec tant d'adresse qu'on ne puysse luy imputer qu'il soit son partisan'. 'La raison d'état' requires this, because he is to appear as a mediator and also because 'la raison d'état exige qu'en une chose incertaine on ne se déclare pas si ouvertement que, s'il arrivoit un changement qu'on n'eust peu prévoir, l'on ne se trouve pas hors termes de s'accorder avec celluy qui sera resté le Maistre.'

120. *Archives*, II, iv, 134.
121. *Digby's Cabinet*, Goffe to Jermyn, 29 May /8 June 1645.
122. See Gardiner, *op. cit.* II, 258.
123. In February 1645 Huygens had frankly put the case to Lord Jermyn : there were two tendencies to be distinguished there, the one dependent on the will of His Highness, the other on the States ; as for the first, there would never be cause for complaint ; as for the second, His Highness could only do his best (*Archives*, II, iv, 128).
124. Arend, *op. cit.* III, v, 560 ; *Archives*, II, iv, 128 ; *Digby's Cabinet*, *passim*, particularly pp. 37 ff. These ships were used for the export of tin from the west of England, the only source of income for the Queen ; also to keep up communication between the royalists on the Continent and the King. Captain Colster, or Coulster, who is mentioned in nearly all these reports, took Prince Rupert and his company over to England on the instructions of the Prince of Orange. See n. 55, above.
125. Charles IV of Lorraine, who, after having been driven out of his country by France, as a leader of irregular bands generally fought with the Spaniards.
126. *Archives*, II, iv, 142, 144 ; Worp, *op. cit.* IV, 226. Negotiations had been entered into with Dorp, Huygens's brother-in-law, to act as admiral.
127. Le Clerc, *Négociations secrètes touchant la paix de Münster et d'Osnabrug* (1724), III, 52, 107, 112.
128. *Ibid.* pp. 56, 57.
129. I have described this incident more fully in 'De Oranjes en Antwerpen, 1646–50', *Tijdschrift voor Geschiedenis*, 1925 ; reprinted in *Kernproblemen van onze geschiedenis*, 1936.
130. *Archives*, II, iv, 152.
131. *Ibid.* p. 151.
132. *Ibid.* p. 166.
133. *Ibid.* p. 152.
134. *Ibid.* p. 162.

IV

1. *Archives*, II, iv, 180.
2. The treaty, as noted above, provided that neither of the contracting parties was to conclude a separate peace.
3. *Archives*, II, iv, 235, August 5, 1647.
4. *Ibid.* p. 262.
5. *Hamilton Papers* (Gardiner, 1880), p. 228, letter of Sir W. Bellenden from Amsterdam, July 9, 1648 (presumably O.S.) : 'At all time of my acces to the P. of Orange I did moue him what was to be doin be ws for the conjunction with the Staits, but the trewth is that he is not so ripe and painfull in and for business as his condition doeth requier.'
6. Memorandum from William II to the Prince of Wales, September (?), 1648, *Archives*, II, iv, 267.
7. This matter is known from the letters of De Wilhem to Huygens in *Archives*, II, iv, 263 ff.; published more fully by Worp, *op. cit.* IV, 491 ff. Further, a letter of Sir Edward Hyde in *Clarendon State Papers*, II, 455 ff. He gives the number of men as 900; De Wilhem 500.
8. De Wilhem received a receipt from Bellenden for these munitions.
9. At a later date the Prince of Wales expressed this gratitude most emphatically (letter from St. Johnston, January 21, 1651, *Rawlinson Letters*). From the moment that they had first met in Helvoetsluis. says the King (as he then was), Heenvliet's services had been inestimable.
10. 'Pleust à Dieu que nostre maistre ne s'engageast plus avant avec ces gens sine luce, sine cruce, sine deo; jamais de ma vie je vis un tel désordre et confusion'; September 18; this is to be found only in Worp, *op. cit.*
11. According to Eva Scott (*The King in Exile*, p. 51) it was again the generosity of the Prince of Orange which enabled this fleet to set sail; he had equipped it with three months' provisions. The writer, however, gives no source.
12. The Prince of Wales was received at The Hague in accordance with his rank, and entertained for the customary ten days at the expense of the States-General; the States of Holland refused to allow this term to be prolonged at the pleasure of the Prince of Orange (De Wilhem to Huygens). The young Duke of York, too, was still living at the expense of his brother-in-law. In order to relieve him, the Duke of York went to France in December, while the Prince of Wales's court was curtailed as much as possible (Aitzema, *op. cit.* VI, p. 575). According to Aitzema (*op. cit.* VI, 782), William II gave pensions to the lords of Charles II's court in 1649 of 2,000 guilders each. Cf. also Carte's *Ormonde Papers*, I, 199, 209.
13. William was at the time of these decisions in Groningen. Thence, on

September 15, he wrote to Heenvliet that he had sent a letter to the Princess Royal for the Admiralty of Rotterdam in case the Prince of Wales might like to have a ship to go to Scotland. On September 20 — apparently Heenvliet had in the meantime enlightened him as to Preston — he wrote the following characteristic words : 'J'ay receu vos lettres. Je voy que les affaires sont bien incertaines et qu'ils ne savent de quel bois faire flèce. Me semble qu'il vaut toujours mieux un Royaume [understand : *one* kingdom — Scotland] que rien, mais le temps perdu est beaucoup' (*Rawlinson Letters*).

14. For at that time most people's sympathies were still with the Parliament, says Aitzema.
15. Aitzema, *op. cit.* VI, 682.
16. Eva Scott, *op. cit.* p. 73.
17. Aitzema, *op. cit.* VI, 694.
18. See above, Chapter III, note 119.
19. Aitzema, *op. cit.* VI, 685.
20. The Latin dissertations, both translated into Dutch, were followed by two more pamphlets. See Knuttel, *Catalogus*, nos. 6377-83. The name of the Utrecht writer is not known to me.
21. Graswinckel, *Korte onderrechtinge raeckende de fundamentale Regeeringhe van Engelandt* (Knuttel, *Catalogus*, no. 6375). *Beduncken op de onderrechtinghe*, etc. (Knuttel, no. 6376). In this latter pamphlet no mention is made of either printer or author.
22. Aitzema, *op. cit.* VI, p. 688.
23. See above, Chapter III, note 38.
24. Baillie, *op. cit.* IV, 73 ff. Spang wanted to speak English or Latin, but William II preferred Dutch. Lord Byron, the envoy or Ormonde, says : 'He understands English very well, though he speak it not, so that your Exc. shall not need trouble to write in French' (Carte, *Ormonde Papers*, I, 269).
25. Spang is, as one might imagine, very well disposed toward William II : 'Ye will find our young Prince of Orange one of the hopefullest youths that ever Europe brought forth, and willing to doe all good offices for the cause' (Carte, *op. cit.* I, 83).
26. *Ibid.* pp. 88, 90.
27. *Ibid.* 239.
28. Sophia of Bohemia wrote this to her brother Rupert on April 13, 1649 (*Cal. St. P. Dom.* [1649–1650], p. 85). Baillie, himself one of the Scottish envoys, wrote home to the same effect.
29. The Queen of Bohemia hoped to win Charles for Sophia. The Bohemian family was Calvinist, but most of its members were far from faultless in doctrine. The accusation against Sophia was that she accompanied Charles to common prayer. Cf. Sophia's *Mémoires*.

30. Carte, *op. cit.* I, 264.
31. Byron, for instance, after giving the conditions of the Scottish envoys, writes : 'But the King being now unfortunately in a Presbyterian country cannot resent these indignities so as otherwise he would' (Carte, *op. cit.* I, p. 268).
32. *Thurloe State Papers*, I, 115 ; September 19, 1649.
33. *Clarendon State Papers*, II, 482.
34. *Archives*, II, iv, 309. The assertion in the *Nicholas Papers*, I, 127, that the moneys were procured for the King by William II, 'underhand provided by the States', is most improbable. A similar account is found in 1650 (Gardiner, *Letters and Papers Illustrating the Relations Between Charles II and Scotland in 1650* [1894], p. 77). Strickland wrote in September 1649 : 'Pray, sir, doe but gratifie the States of Holland, and my life for it, P.C., who hopes only to retrieve his game from hence, shall doe nothing, notwithstanding the greatness of the greatest heere' (*Thurloe State Papers*, I, 119).
35. Aitzema.
36. *Archives*, II, iv, 315 ; October 19, 1649.
37. Gardiner, *op. cit.* The Princes of Orange had a special connection with Breda and owned a place of residence there.
38. *Ibid.* p. 60.
39. His reports appeared in *A Briefe Relation*, the organ of the English Council of State, and are reprinted in Gardiner's book.
40. *Ibid.* p. 30.
41. *Ibid.* p. 51. About Voetius, see above, p. 85.
42. Gardiner, *op. cit.* p. 76, *et passim.*
43. About this time the Prince managed to borrow two million from the town of Amsterdam. See below, n. 50.
44. Wynne, *Geschillen over de afdanking van het krijgsvolk*, p. 93. Reprinted in Gardiner. Unfortunately these documents are not dated.
45. Gardiner, *op. cit.* pp. 81, 85.
46. Not far from Delft. He had spent another month in Breda after the conclusion of the treaty, according to the English spy, because he did not want to face the displeasure of the States of Holland at The Hague (Gardiner, *op. cit.* p. 119). In the *Rawlinson Letters* there is a letter from the Princess Royal to Heenvliet, from Breda, undated but apparently of May 1650. She asks him to show this letter to her husband, and continues : 'afin que nous puissions vennir à La Haye. Le Roy est en grande impassiance et ne fait que demander quand vous viendrés icy.'
47. Even William II wrote (June 13) from Schoonhoven to Heenvliet : 'Je croy qu'il sera bien périllieux après avoir attendu cy longtemps de s'embarquer, et il vaudroit mieux remettre l'affaire à une autre fois' (*Rawlinson Letters*). The King was then already on board.

48. Gardiner, *op. cit.* p. 90.

49. Cf. above, p. 943 ; also note 50, below.

50. Cf. *Br. Rel.*, September 9, 1650 (Br. Mus. ; not in Gardiner, *op. cit.* ; published by me in *Bijdr. en Meded.*, 1924) : 'They [the Hollanders] wish verie well to your affaires in Scotland'. I don't quite know what is to be made of the fact that in April 1650 Amsterdam advanced two millions to William II on the security of estates — a capital sum that the Prince certainly did not need merely to wipe out old debts, but that at the same time enabled him to come once more to the assistance of Charles II, who just at that time was preparing to go to Scotland (Wagenaar, *Amsterdam*, I, 550). It looks like a sort of reassurance, an attempt, just when Schaep had been sent to England, to pave the way for friendly relations in the other camp as well. However, in the absence of any certain data as to how the Prince spent the money, it is impossible to decide the exact significance of this fact. This much of course is certain that he, who two or three months later carried out his attack on Amsterdam, did not allow his gratitude for this loan to exercise any influence on his line of policy.

51. *Thurloe State Papers*, I, 113 ff.

52. *Ibid.* p. 118.

53. Aitzema, *op. cit.* VI, 831.

54. One instance of the way in which William II used to get a hold over the deputies. In 1649 he gave a lieutenancy to the six-year-old son of Jonkheer Boldewijn Jacob Mulert, deputy in the States-General for Overijsel. The towns of that province (each province was responsible for the pay of particular regiments of the Union army assigned to it) were so indignant that they decided to refuse payment (Bussemaker, *Geschiedenis van Overijsel, 1650–72*, I, 25). This same Mulert was after William II's death criticized in the States of Overijsel for having voted, unauthorized, in the States-General for the resolution of June 5, 1650, on which the Prince had based himself in undertaking his *coup d'état* (*Brieven aan De Witt, W.H.G.*, I, 33).

55. *Archives*, II, iv, 317.

56. Aitzema, *op. cit.* VII, 23.

57. Article X, of the Union merely prohibited the members from entering into separate 'alliances or treaties' with other states.

58. *Archives*, II, iv, 317.

59. August 16, 1659 : P. L. Muller, 'Spanje en de partijen in Nederland in 1650', in *Nijhoff's Bijdragen* (Nieuwe Reeks), VII (1899), 149. In my opinion Muller is quite wrong in calling this 'a certainly somewhat curious utterance'. His incredulity merely proves how completely neglected have been the aspects of the foreign policy of Frederick Henry and William II which I am putting forward in this study.

60. As it is expressed in the very bitter pamphlet, *Openhertig Discours . . . rakende de subite dood van Z.H.* (Knuttel, *Catalogus*, no. 1651), William II would have liked to subdue all the provinces ; he wanted to dismiss the independent magistrates everywhere and replace them with 'servile' officers, 'and then we should have been plunged into two wars at the same time ; to wit, against the Parliament of England in order to help the King of Scotland, and against Spain to please the frivolous French, in whom he placed all his faith.'

61. *Archives*, II, iv, 298. The document is not dated. Groen puts it down to the end of February 1649.

62. See *Archives*, II, iv, 318. Brasset promises William that France will not insist on French troops being sent back, while Holland would like to see the foreign regiments removed.

63. *Archives*, II, iv, 317.

64. *Gedenkschriften*, II, 281.

65. See, *e.g.*, a pamphlet of 1652, *Ernstig gesprek tusschen drie personen* (Knuttel, *Catalogus*, no. 7256). The author is a States party man. Of his three characters he makes the one he has cast for the part of victim of Orangist propaganda say : 'Our country has before been sold to the English, when our last Prince of Orange [William II, who died in November 1650] was still living. He, knowing this, for that reason went to lay siege before Amsterdam in order to stop them delivering it'. In *State Papers, For., Holland*, CLIX, there is a letter of August 11, 1650, from Utrecht, signed Cha. Ledison (one of the pseudonyms of Sir E. Nicholas), about the attack on Amsterdam ; in it credence is given to these stories : 'Its reported that in order to render themselves soveraigns and to curbe the rest of the provinces a factious party in that city hath by their Agent Monsr Scape now in England, and other underhand instruments, treated with the Rebells there to send them to Amsterdam by the Tassell [Texel] 10,000 men, whereof 5000 were to have come very speedily being (some say) alreddy levyed and reddy to be shipped under pretence of being sent for Irland, and the other 5000 were to be sent a monthe or 6 weeks after. By their complices in England its easy to make a judgment of their designe and intentions ; but I believe untill the English rebells see the success of their forces now marched into the Northe, they will be wary how they sent many men into any foreigne partes.' But Nicholas uttered more radical doubts very soon afterward. On August 15 he wrote : 'Methinkes those who are of the Prince of Orange's counsell should use all possible industry to get proofe of the truth of what is printed concerning the agreement between Scape and the Rebells of England, which is a business of very great importance for these States to knowe.'

66. See above, n. 96.

67. See Wicquefort, I, 522, and 'Briefe Relation' in Gardiner, *Charles II and Scotland in 1650.*
68. Who had left the court of Charles II and had betaken himself to Leyden (Gardiner, *op. cit.* p. 115).
69. *Ibid.* p. 114.
70. 'Be pliant, friend, whoe'er thou be, A virtue 'tis will profit thee.' From 'The Reed and the Oaktree'. Cats is remembered as a poet more than as a statesman. His didactic and rather trite poetry enjoyed immense popularity in his own day and much later.
71. Pelnits to Nanning Keyser; *Bijdragen en Mededeelingen Historisch Genootschap*, XVIII, 356.
72. Aitzema, *op. cit.* VII, 53; *Briefe Relation*, September 9, 1650.
73. The quotations are to be found in a pamphlet of 1668, *Zeeuwsche vreugde* . . . (Knuttel, *Catalogus*, no. 9675). It was against this dedication that Vondel wrote his impassioned little poem; 'On the Rebelliousness of the Godless Zeelander Max. Teellinck'.
74. Aitzema, *op. cit.* VII, 11.
75. See, *e.g.*, Fabio Chigi to the Cardinal-Secretary of State, *Bijdragen en Mededeelingen Historisch Genootschap*, XXXV, 121.
76. *Gedenkschriften*, II, 281.
77. Elias, *Vroedschap van Amsterdam*, I, p. XCIX.
78. The strength of these appears from a letter to the Van der Capellen of the *Gedenkschriften* from his son, published in Wicquefort, *op. cit.* I, 448. Here the dissatisfaction of the 'common man' is spoken of, and it is said that 'most people thought His Highness was in the wrong'.
79. Aitzema, *op. cit.* VII, 155.
80. *Briefe Relation*, September 9, 1650.
81. Wynne, *op. cit.* p. 156 (Duyst van Voorhout), 166 (Nanning Keyser); Ruyl's performance was even worse.
82. *Ibid.* p. 179.
83. Fruin, *Verspreide Geschriften*, IV, 166 ff.
84. Brun writes (August 28, Muller, *op. cit.* p. 166): 'My confidants in the province of Holland say . . . that despite all this their province is not overthrown, as people think, but that she is still as powerful as before and watches her interests and safety more closely than she formerly used to do'. It is true he did not place much faith in these professions.
85. *Briefe Relation*, September 9, 1650.
86. A republican correspondent in London wrote on November 18, 1650, to the Netherlands: 'La mort de Son Altesse d'Orange fauche les espérances de nos ennemis et nous fera sans doute voir quelque grand changement aux affaires d'Escosse.' *Bijdragen en Mededeelingen Historisch Genootschap*, IV (1880), p. 239.
87. Aitzema, *op. cit.* VII, 155.

88. 'The party in these parts increases every day in faction against the Prince of Orange' (*Nicholas Papers*, I, 198).

V

1. As has been done too often by Dutch historians. See essay VII, 'Historical Appreciations of the Holland Regent Class', in which I dealt, in 1954, with this problem specifically.
2. About the marriage of 1641 between Frederick Henry's son William and Charles I's eldest daughter Mary and its political consequences see the preceding essays III and IV.
3. Colenbrander, *Zeeoorlogen*, II, 155; a large collection of documents, many of them in English or French.

VI

1. The remark made to Witsen : in Gebhard, *Leven van Witsen*. I (1881), 358; to Huygens : in *Journalen van C. Huygens* (Jr), *Werken H.G.U.*; 1876–1888, 1915; five volumes.
2. Not without conditions — a heavy financial tribute, annexation of some southern districts — which caused great resentment. An essay on this 'Batavian Revolution' written in 1956, follows under VIII.
3. IX in this volume.

VII

1. 'Regents' refers to the numerous class of men who in the Dutch Republic held office — generally for life — in the corporations of 'voting towns' or were members of the provincial nobilities. Together the towns and the nobility constituted the States of a province, the assembly that represented the province's sovereignty. I mention the nobility with the town gentlemen, although commonly the word 'regent' will suggest only the latter.
2. The title of advocate was later replaced by that of grand-pensionary.
3. 'Het Stadhouderschap in de Partij-literatuur onder de Witt' (1947); 'Democratische tendenties in 1672' (1950); 'De Wittenoorlog, een Pennestrijd in 1757' (1953). (All three in *Mededelingen* d. Kon. Akad. van Wetenschappen for the years indicated.) I have studied essentially the same problem as presented in the sermons, pamphlets and poems with which the fiftieth anniversary of the Kingdom was celebrated in 1863, in an essay, '1813 herdacht in 1863', *De Gids*, July 1954, pp. 14–51.
4. The so-called private schools, which, under the legislation of 1921, are

Notes

fully subsidized by the state. Together, the private Protestant and the private Catholic schools accommodate a considerably larger number of pupils than do the neutral public schools.

5. *Gereformeerd* is the bastard Latin form of the Dutch word *Hervormd*. The old State Church, which in the seventeenth century called itself *Gereformeerd*, now goes by the name of *Hervormd*, while the secessionists have revived the word *Gereformeerd* and laid hold of it for themselves. In English the distinction cannot be rendered.

6. Maurice was seventeen years old when his father was assassinated in 1584. Maurice was appointed Stadholder of Holland in that year. The office was not hereditary.

7. The Twelve Years' Truce, 1609–1621, interrupting the Eighty Years' War with Spain, 1568–1648.

8. *Verspreide Geschriften*, IV, 16.

9. Fruin does not entirely overlook this, although his statement to that effect seems to me somewhat perfunctory. A striking instance is the following remark made by J. C. Naber (no more a Calvinist than was Fruin) in his well-known book *Calvinist of Libertijnsch* (Utrecht, 1884), p. 57: 'There are not many instances in history where a government that counted supremacy over the church among its prerogatives extended its authority so far as did the States of Holland on this occasion.' To which one can only reply: the history of the Reformation, both in Germany and in England, is full of such instances.

10. See the preceding essay.

11. The statement occurs in *Oranje en Stuart, 1641–1672* (Utrecht, 1939), p. 97, in the chapter that follows the two published in 1923 already and reprinted in this volume. In the second of these will be found the remark (see below, p. 102) on the corrupt character of the States-General that drew Dr. Japikse's ire. (Paperback edition of *Oranje en Stuart*, 1963).

12. *Verspreide Geschriften*, VIII, 76.

13. L. Aitzema, *Saken van staet en oorlogh*, IX (1664), 1054.

14. *Brieven van De Witt* (Utrecht: Hist. Gen., 1906–1913), II, 311, 313.

15. M. Th. Uit den Bogaard, *De Gereformeerden en Oranje* (Utrecht: *Historische Studies*, 1954).

16. The Anti-revolutionary party, that is, the party opposed to the principles of the French Revolution, is the party of which Groen may be considered to be the spiritual father. Its voting strength is drawn largely from the members of the *Gereformeerde Kerk*. The other orthodox Protestant party, which also claims Groen as its patron, is called the Christian Historical party; it is supported mainly by orthodox members of the *Hervormde Kerk*. Together the two parties muster some 20 per cent of the seats in the Chamber, as against the Catholics over 30 per cent.

17. Abroad : at Buchenwald.
18. See *De Wittenoorlog, een pennestrijd in 1757*, Kon. Nederl. Ak., 1953.
19. As regards the latter, I pointed this out in detail in an essay of 1950, reprinted in *Studies en Strijdschriften* (Groningen, 1958).
20. See my *William IV en England tot 1748* (The Hague, 1924) ; reviewed by Sir R. Lodge in *English Historical Review*, October 1925, pp. 616-621).
21. It is possible that he misread one sentence in *Oranje en Stuart*. This at any rate is what Dr. Japikse did in *Bijdr. Vad. Gesch.* (1940), and also G. N. Clark in *English Historical Review* (January 1942, pp. 139-43) in reviewing the book. On p. 389 I referred to 'groups of the population politically so little schooled or so much isolated from national life as the commonalty with their ministers and the court nobility'. Both my reviewers understood this to mean that I regarded as well 'the commonalty and their ministers' as 'the court nobility' as groups outside national life. I may have committed a stylistic error, but at any rate, this much is certain : what I meant was that 'politically so little schooled' should be connected with 'the commonalty and their ministers', and 'isolated from national life' with 'the court nobility'.

VIII

1. There *were* descendants who wrote laudatory Lives of their Patriot fathers or grandfathers. One, very uncritical, work was devoted to R. Schimmelpenninck by his son. It was subjected to masterly as well as merciless criticism by the great Thorbecke, the inspiring figure in the liberal revision of the constitution carried through in 1848. Thorbecke's *Historische Schetsen* contain several essays (all written before 1848) showing remarkable gifts of historical capacity and insight. What he wanted to bring out in dealing with Schimmelpenninck, about whom I shall speak in this essay in a more positive sense, was that he had left the great reforming work to which the men of 1795 were called stuck halfway in the conservative reaction that set in after 1798.
2. Let me warn the reader that I use the word 'federalism' in a sense exactly opposite to that which was current in the early days of American independence. In the Batavian Republic the Federalist party wanted to preserve as much as possible of provincial sovereignty. The party out for strong central government was called the Unitarist party.
3. Since I wrote this lecture, the new volume of my *Nederlandse Stam* has appeared ; in it I deal with the episode in considerable detail.

Notes

IX

1. By Flanders is meant here, not the ancient county or province only, but the entire Flemish- or Dutch-speaking area, covering the old duchies of Brabant and Limburg as well as the old county of Flanders.

X

1. See, for instance, two lectures given in the Studium Generale course at Leyden in October 1959 in my volume *Encounters in History*, Meridian Books, N.Y. (1961), of which an English edition has been published by Collins in Fontana Books (1963).

INDEX

259

Index

PRINTED BY R. & R. CLARK, LTD., EDINBURGH